IMAGES
of America

SAN FRANCISCO'S
NORTH BEACH AND
TELEGRAPH HILL

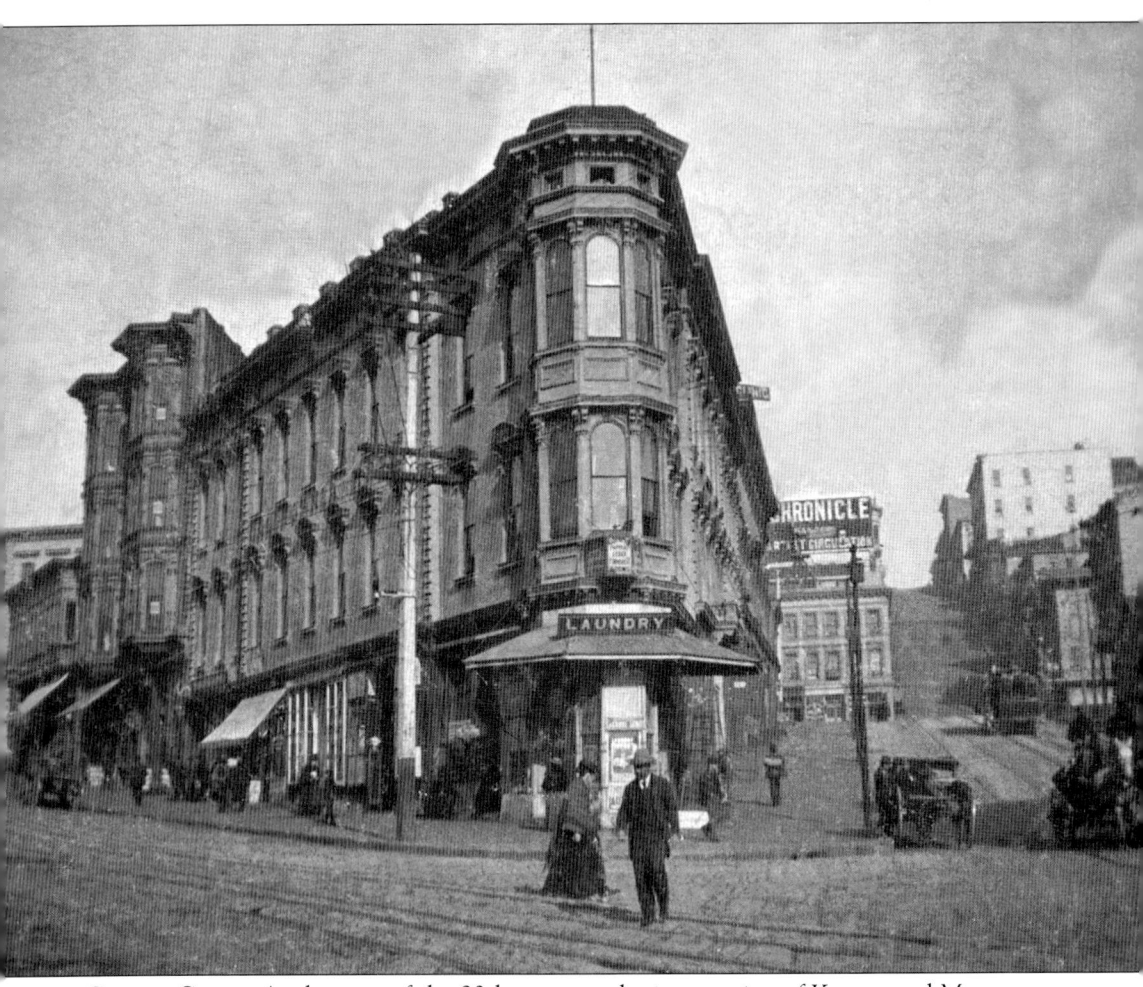

ON THE COVER: At the start of the 20th century, the intersection of Kearny and Montgomery Streets was called "The Gateway to North Beach." A left turn at this location would take one up into the heart of North Beach. Hotels and rooming houses occupied the top floors of these buildings, while businesses occupied the street level. (J. B. Monaco Collection, courtesy of Richard Monaco, San Francisco Public Library.)

IMAGES
of America

SAN FRANCISCO'S NORTH BEACH AND TELEGRAPH HILL

Catherine Accardi

Catherine A. Accardi

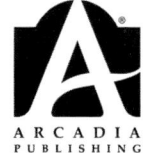

ARCADIA
PUBLISHING

Copyright © 2010 by Catherine A. Accardi
ISBN 978-0-7385-8158-3

Published by Arcadia Publishing
Charleston, South Carolina

Printed in the United States of America

Library of Congress Control Number: 2010928645

For all general information, please contact Arcadia Publishing:
Telephone 843-853-2070
Fax 843-853-0044
E-mail sales@arcadiapublishing.com
For customer service and orders:
Toll-Free 1-888-313-2665

Visit us on the Internet at www.arcadiapublishing.com

To my aunt Desolina, I remember your kindness.

CONTENTS

Acknowledgments		6
Introduction		7
1.	In the Beginning	11
2.	From the Beach to the Hill	41
3.	Neighborhood Culture	63
4.	People and Places	91

Acknowledgments

The images in this volume are from the San Francisco History Center, San Francisco Public Library (SFHC); the Library of Congress (LOC); the J. B. Monaco Collection, courtesy of Richard Monaco, San Francisco Public Library (JBM); and courtesy of the author, Catherine A. Accardi (CAA).

INTRODUCTION

In the beginning, the area now known as North Beach was home to Native Americans. The Yelamu tribal group of Ohlone Indians are said to have been the primary inhabitants prior to the mid-1700s. Historical records indicate an Ohlone village was located in the North Beach area, in the northeastern section of San Francisco. The Ohlone traveled down to the bay from the Sacramento and San Joaquin River areas, arriving in the North Beach area as far back as the sixth century AD.

One of the first Europeans to make note of Telegraph Hill is said to have been Capt. Juan Manuel de Ayala on August 5, 1775. The second was Capt. George Vancouver in 1792. During the Spanish and Mexican periods, Telegraph Hill was called Loma Alta, meaning "high land" or "hill." It was home to Native Americans, and later on, the location of Juana Briones's dairy ranch on the west side near the intersection of Powell and Filbert Streets. In 1839, Jean Jacques Vioget completed a survey of Yerba Buena, laying out the first streets, which consisted of 12 blocks bounded by California, Montgomery, and Pacific Streets and Grant Avenue. Early accounts describe the eastern slope of Telegraph Hill as "swarmed with goats." Nowadays, historical pre-1906 buildings, several scenic garden stairways, and art deco–style structures replace livestock. The district has the greatest number of pre-1870 structures, several dating back to the 1850s.

Telegraph Hill is of such importance that it is California Landmark No. 91 and a San Francisco Historic District bounded by Greenwich, Sansome, Montgomery, and Green Streets. The following statement of significance, dated November 19, 1987, is from Section 10 of the San Francisco Planning Code, *Preservation of Historical, Architectural, and Aesthetic Landmarks*: "Telegraph Hill is one of the most famous hills in the world, as well-known as Sugar Loaf in Rio de Janeiro, and a visual landmark to sailors entering the Bay since its European discovery by Capt. Juan Manuel de Ayala in the San Carlos on August 5, 1775 . . . The difficulty of access on hillside and cliffs, and the proximity to the City's most active waterfront area first produced a community of waterfront workers housed in 'cloth lined' shacks and modest vernacular Gothic Revival houses. Intact groupings of these buildings remain within the District, and comprise the City's largest concentration of pre-1870 structures . . . Due to the cliff side location, steps, wooden walkways and a hidden network of footpaths developed throughout the area . . . The abrupt changes in grade produce dramatic and unique vistas at points throughout the District."

The 1849 Gold Rush in California's foothills seduced many of those arriving aboard ships into San Francisco Bay. By the summer of 1949, over 500 vessels were recorded as being in and about Yerba Buena Cove. Crews and passengers abandoned many of their ships in their fervor to reach gold fields. Hubert Howe Bancroft is quoted as saying: "As late as January 1857, old hulks still obstructed the harbor while others had been overtaken by the bayward march of the city. Even now (1888) remains of the vessels are found under the filled foundations of houses." Dwellings certainly sit atop Telegraph Hill, but they also sit on top of buried sailing vessels from the 1800s. In the 1800s, the northeast shoreline curved along what are now Front, Battery, and Sansome

Streets. Ships clung to the shore and to each other. Five wharves jutted out into this jumble at the following streets: Broadway, Vallejo, Green, Battery, and Lombard. According to historians, no less than seven ships are buried along the original waterfront. The names and locations of the seven ships are: *Envoy* at Battery and Union Streets (used for planking of Battery Street); *Fortuna* at Front and Vallejo Streets (used as a hotel on the block now bounded by Battery, Front, Vallejo, and Green Streets); *Phillip Hone* at Battery and Union Streets (used as a storeship or warehouse); *Japan* at Union and Front Streets (used as a storeship); *Le Baron* at Sansome and Lombard Streets (use unknown); an unknown ship at Battery near Filbert Streets (used as support under Griffing's/ Griffin's Wharf at Battery Street); and *Palmyra* at Battery near Filbert Streets (used as a storeship and currently under Levi Plaza).

A noteworthy discovery was made in April 1978 when the remains of a ship's hull were discovered during excavation for Levi Plaza at Battery Street. The vessel, believed to be the ship *Palmyra*, was estimated to be about 100 feet in length and 30 feet wide. The *William Gray*, *Dalmatia*, and *Dryade* are said to lie underground near Battery Street and at the eastern side of Levi Plaza.

The ship *Arkansas* was uncovered on the north side of Pacific Street between Battery and Front Streets. The *Arkansas* had arrived to the hamlet in December 1849. By 1851, a door was cut into the ship's hull, and it was converted into the old Ship Ale House. The ship remains to this day under the newer establishment, the Old Ship Saloon. The three-story red brick building looks nothing like a ship. At some point, the top of the *Arkansas* was dismantled to make a hotel over the saloon. All that is left of the *Arkansas* is an original black sign, shaped like a ship, hanging from a mast extending over the sidewalk. It is reported that one can still hear the ebb and flow of bay waters when standing in the lowest level. Whether they can be seen or not, buried ships are below, along the old shoreline at the waterfront. The beach was covered with tons of fill, and now it is only a memory.

Loma Alta began to take a different direction after Capt. John B. Montgomery sailed into San Francisco Bay on the USS *Portsmouth* July 9, 1846. It was there that he raised the U.S. flag. The captain ordered a fort to be constructed of adobe bricks. The resulting Fort Montgomery is considered the first officially recorded permanent structure on Loma Alta, the military presence giving its name to Battery Street.

September 22, 1853, celebrated the introduction of the first telegraph in California. Earlier, in 1849, a station house was erected on the hill that commanded a view of the entrance to the Golden Gate. Around the 1850s, a signal pole was erected on the hill so that a sentry could signal the arrival of approaching ships into the bay, and, thus, the site was named Telegraph Hill. North Beach and "The Hill" were dotted with tents, rustic buildings, and dirt paths. By the end of June 1849, over 15,000 immigrants from South America, Europe, and beyond arrived after the discovery of gold in the Sierra foothills. During the four-year period between 1848 and 1852, the pueblo, consisting then of around 1,000 people, grew into a city of almost 25,000. In the beginning, tents and shacks sat in the flat lands west of Yerba Buena Cove.

The land of North Beach afforded relatively low-cost homesites during the 1850s and 1860s, and so the northeast waterfront attracted working-class people. Several of these early buildings will be highlighted in the following chapters. The area continued to be a working-class neighborhood into the 1930s, housing immigrants from countries around the world. By 1853, as the city grew by leaps and bounds, engineers decided to remove portions of the hill to fill in the cove. Land values were still low, a fact that did not escape the notice of real estate speculators. In 1876, a group of businessmen purchased four lots at the crest of the hill for $12,000. In the following chapters, the outcome of these early days in San Francisco history is seen.

On April 18, 1906, a tremendous earthquake would change North Beach forever. By April 20, fires that had burned for several days all over San Francisco reached Telegraph Hill. On Saturday, April 21, most of these fires had been extinguished but not before the disaster devastated a beloved neighborhood. It was quite fitting that the seal of the City of San Francisco adopted in the 1850s should include a depiction of a phoenix rising. North Beach definitely did rise out of the ashes. The seal of San Francisco depicts two working men: on one side a miner and on the other side a sailor with a sextant. Above is a rising phoenix, and behind it are sailing ships on San Francisco Bay. The phoenix symbolizes the city's emergence from the ashes of several devastating fires in the early 1850s. The motto reads, "*Oro en paz, fierro en guerra,*" which is Spanish for "Gold in peace, iron in war."

Images in chapter one illustrate the dire situation for residents after the great fire. The community marched on into the 1920s, when artists and writers discovered the picturesque neighborhood. They created their own historical landmarks, as seen in chapter three. Time also served to define the boundaries of North Beach as Fisherman's Wharf and the Embarcadero to the north, Columbus Avenue to the west, Battery Street to the east, and Broadway to the south.

An article in the April 25, 1925, edition of the *Bulletin* newspaper describes how a campaign to change the name of North Beach to Columbus Valley was discussed by a Dr. V. C. Quartararo at an April 24 meeting of the North Beach Merchants Association. He stated that the area had outgrown its name since the beach was no longer. Apparently, that name change campaign was abandoned.

As depicted in chapter two, North Beach is arguably the most interesting and unique of San Francisco's neighborhoods. The area attracts thousands of victors each year and has been considered a treasure by its residents for hundreds of years. The area offers world-class landmarks, such as Coit Tower, restaurants like Fior d' Italia, unsurpassed vistas, and cable cars. The list is endless.

Telegraph Hill Boulevard, constructed in 1923, changed the hill. Pioneer Park, established in 1876, had existed quietly until Coit Tower became its tenant, thanks to Lillie Hitchcock Coit. She was a well-known supporter of the San Francisco Fire Department and so bequeathed the sum of $118,731 for "an artistic monument" to the memory of the original volunteer fire department. Architect Arthur Brown Jr. prepared the plans for a monumental observation tower to be dedicated on October 8, 1933. A landmark was created.

After World War II, during the 1950s and 1960s, rents and real estate values spiked. Many longtime residents moved to other areas. Residents formed Telegraph Hill Dwellers in 1953, an organization that has been instrumental in preserving the character of North Beach. Chapter three highlights neighborhood culture. Around 1920, artists and writers made the hill home. The opening of Telegraph Hill Boulevard in 1923 brought people up the hill. Roads and trails were paved, and the growing trend hit a fever pitch after the erection of Coit Tower in 1933. Originally, the Greenwich Street cable car line provided transportation, but it ceased in the 1880s. Streetcars did operate around North Beach on Sansome Street, Broadway, and Columbus Avenue. The city municipal railway bus route No. 11 began running from Union and Powell Streets to Coit Tower in 1939. The 1950s brought new concerns to old-time residents of the area. There was much money to be made with redevelopment of charming, scenic-view lots. Development groups sought to replace historical cottages with modern apartment buildings. Some of the newer buildings showcase innovative architecture, while some of the quaint cottages remain, and parks have been revived, reminding everyone who wants to stop and look about that there is no place like Telegraph Hill.

The fictional novel *Laughter on the Hill, A San Francisco Interlude* conveys a young woman's delightful story of her move to Telegraph Hill. She finds a charming apartment on the hill, makes many good friends, and finds her dream job. The book captures the whimsical and romantic essence of life in North Beach. A number of books, poems, essays, and films are set in North Beach environs. Films include *House on Telegraph Hill*, a 1951 mystery movie starring Richard Basehart and Valentina Cortese. The 1947 noir classic *Dark Passage*, staring Humphrey Bogart and Lauren Bacall, was filmed in part just below Coit Tower. The book *The Wild Parrots of Telegraph Hill* was also made into a film.

Architects represented in the area include Bernard Maybeck, 1736 Stockton Street; the Reid Brothers, 1–21 Columbus Avenue, known as the Columbo Building; San Francisco native John A. Porporato (1877–1965), who did many works on Washington Square and area flats; Charles Fantoni (1870–1933), the architect of SS. Peter and Paul Church; and Italo Zanolini, who designed Casa Fugazi and the Cavalli building.

Chapter four focuses on people and places as icons of North Beach and Telegraph Hill. Though the neighborhood was modernized, North Beach retained its original dignity. Although the beaches are now covered with modern structures, one can stand at the corner of Water Street and quietly sense the past.

One

IN THE BEGINNING

In chapter one, the history of North Beach and Telegraph Hill will begin with images and text describing early Native American and Spanish settlers, moving on to early European immigrants and their contributions. This chapter will carry the reader through the 1906 earthquake and fire. In the beginning, there really was a beach in North Beach, in the area now located at Bay and Powell Streets. It loomed up from the area that is now Sansome Street on the east and Broadway on the south. The beach was eventually covered with tons of fill. Native Americans inhabited the region for hundreds of years prior to the arrival of Spanish explorers. Some historical accounts point to Spanish explorers Portola in 1769 and Anza in 1776 as the first non–Native Americans to cast their sights on the now famous Telegraph Hill.

Dairy ranches and the potato patches of Señora Juana Briones occupied the area of what is now Washington Square. The area was under Mexican rule until Capt. John B. Montgomery sailed the *Portsmouth* into the harbor and raised the U.S. flag, on the hill now known as Portsmouth Plaza, on July 9, 1846. Warehouses, docks, piers, hotels, restaurants, and other necessary structures sprang up quickly.

In 1850, the city of San Francisco was incorporated, and in the same year, the state of California was incorporated into the Union. Mexicans and Italians made up a large part of the residents of the hill and surrounding hamlet. New construction began in earnest as the city by the bay flourished around one of its original settlements. A cable car line ran up Greenwich Street in 1880. The top of the hill was decorated with a German castle, while substantial buildings lined Broadway and Columbus Avenue.

Then came April 18, 1906. The earthquake and fire of that day would change North Beach forever. Indeed North Beach took shape back in the 1800s near the beach. The community has marched on through the decades, through earthquakes and modernization. Although the beach is now covered by modern structures, one can still stand on a corner of Water Street and experience the past.

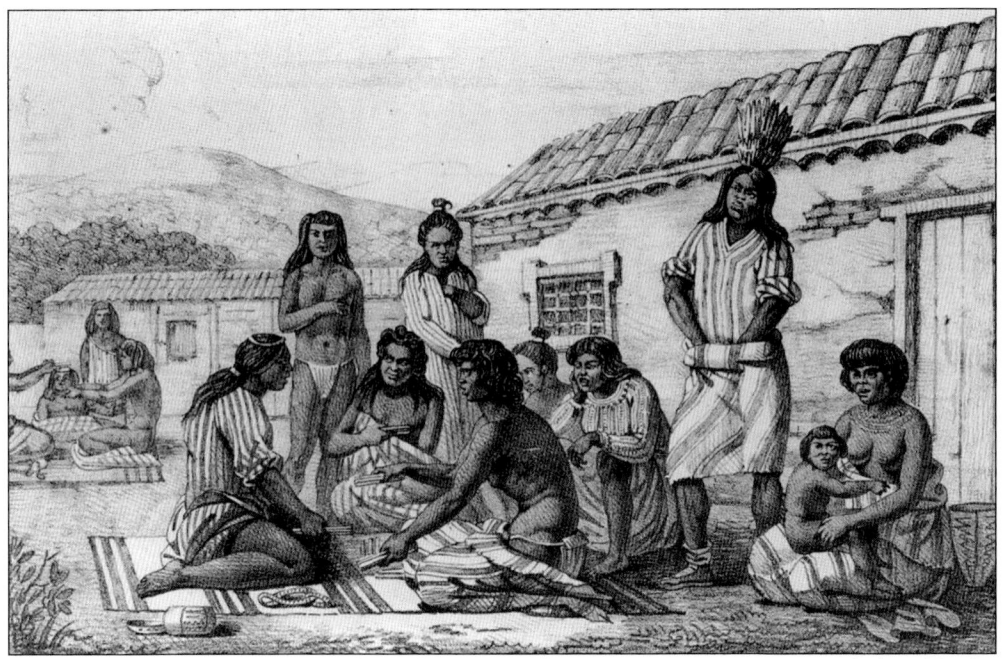

Before the arrival of the Spaniards in the 1700 and 1800s, Native Americans inhabited Yerba Buena, the area now called San Francisco. Native Americans gather here, around 1800, as women watch men playing a game. The Spanish referred to these peoples as Costeos, or people of the coast, and later as Costanos and Costanoans. Native Americans refer to them as Ohlone Indians. Several villages were located around a lagoon in the vicinity of what is now Montgomery Street, and some were possibly even closer to Telegraph Hill. (LOC.)

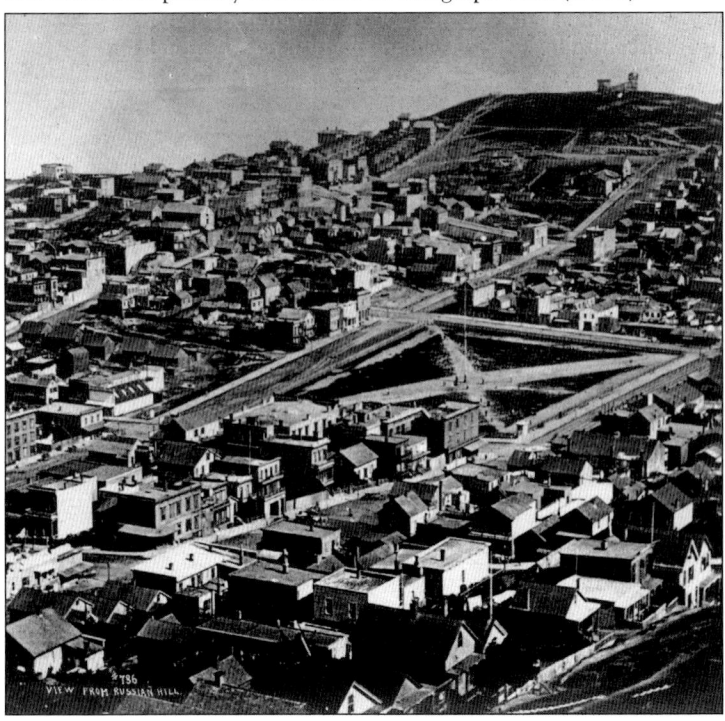

Juana Briones y Tapia De Miranda was a North Beach pioneer. In the 1830s and 1840s, she transformed an isolated cove in the then Mexican hamlet of Yerba Buena into her rancho. Briones often supplied ships' crews with much needed staples, while raising cattle and growing vegetables at the site of what is now Washington Square. This view of Washington Square is from the mid-1800s. A commemorative beach and plaque now occupy the northeast corner. (SFHC.)

This is a stunning representation of Yerba Buena in 1847. The artist included a legend describing structures and ships. North Beach would be to the far right. Visible are the water's edge at Montgomery Street and the home of Francisco Caceres. Caceres was a cavalry sergeant who obtained a 100-vara lot in the block bounded by DuPont, Kearney, Jackson, and Pacific Streets. A vara is a Spanish unit of distance used in Spanish and Mexican surveys and land grants. (LOC.)

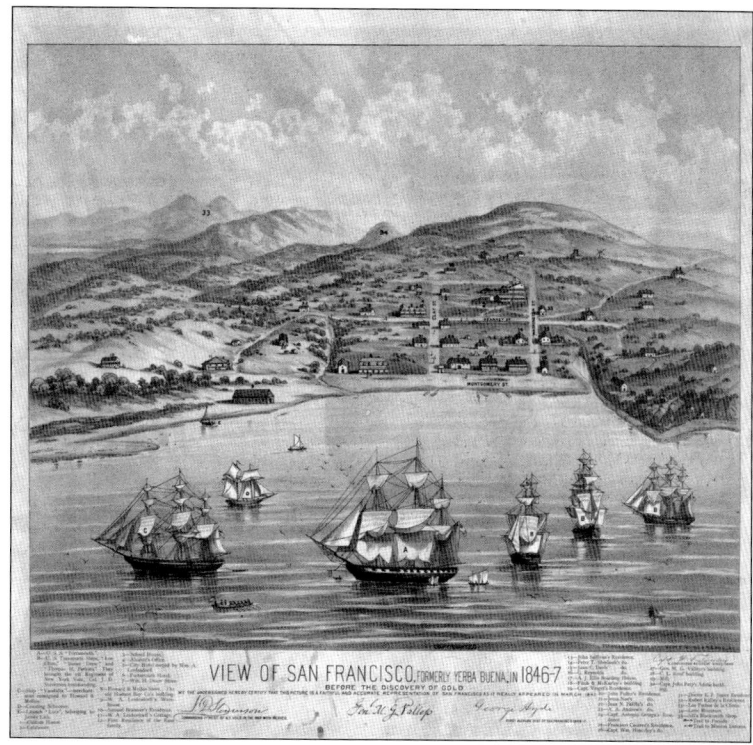

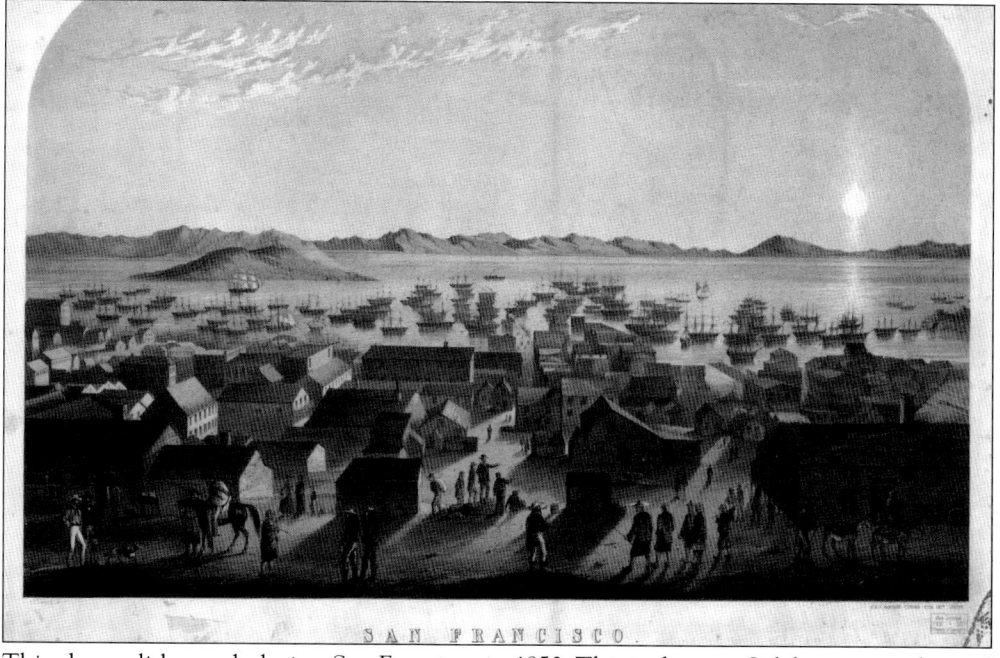

This chromolithograph depicts San Francisco in 1850. This is the year California was admitted into the Union. Until then, Portsmouth Square was the center of business. Loma Alta (high hill), as Telegraph Hill was once called, took on a different character after Capt. John B. Montgomery arrived in 1846. He ordered a fort be built on the hill. It would be called Fort Montgomery and sit at the northwest corner of Green and Battery Streets, giving Battery Street its name. (LOC.)

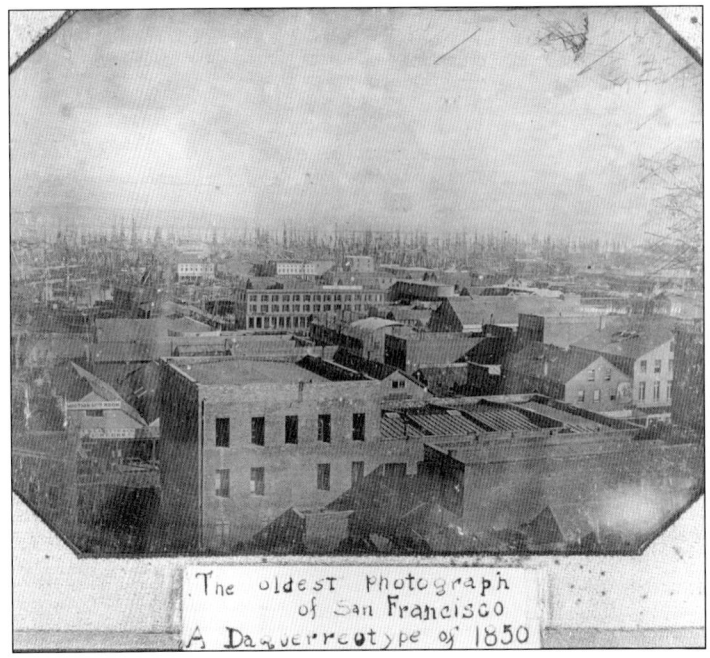

Historical accounts indicate that this 1850 daguerreotype of the San Francisco shoreline is the oldest photograph of San Francisco. At that time, the city existed between Telegraph Hill and Rincon Hill. During the period of 1849 to 1850, the Gold Rush in the California foothills drew more ships around Cape Horn, through the Golden Gate, and into San Francisco Bay than all previous years combined. By the summer of 1850, over 500 vessels were in and about Yerba Buena Cove. (SFHC.)

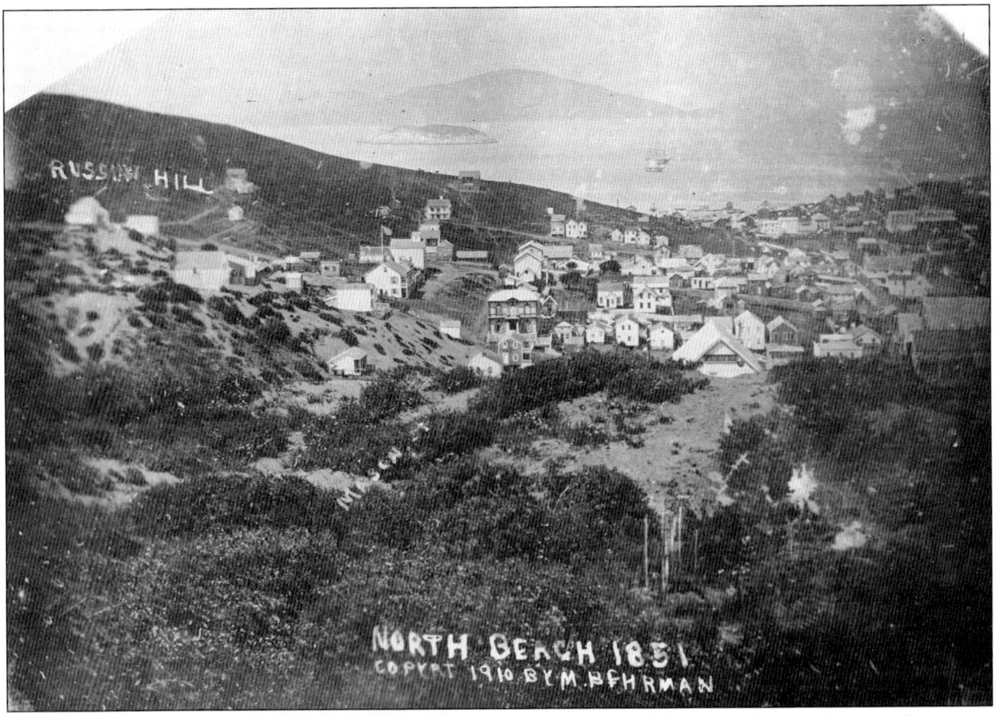

This 1851 photograph is another one of the earliest images of the North Beach area. Between 1849 and 1851, San Francisco experienced a series of six major fires. Afterward, the North Beach area changed in appearance. Here this early settlement is nestled in a gentle valley between the slopes of Telegraph and Russian Hills. (SFHC.)

At right is the official 1852 plat map of San Francisco, created by city surveyor W. M. Eddy on January 1, 1852. The North Beach area at the top right has been well laid out by this time. In 1851, the California Legislature enacted "An Act to Provide for the Disposition of Certain Property of the State of California." The area encompassed by this act included parts of North Beach, shown here. (LOC.)

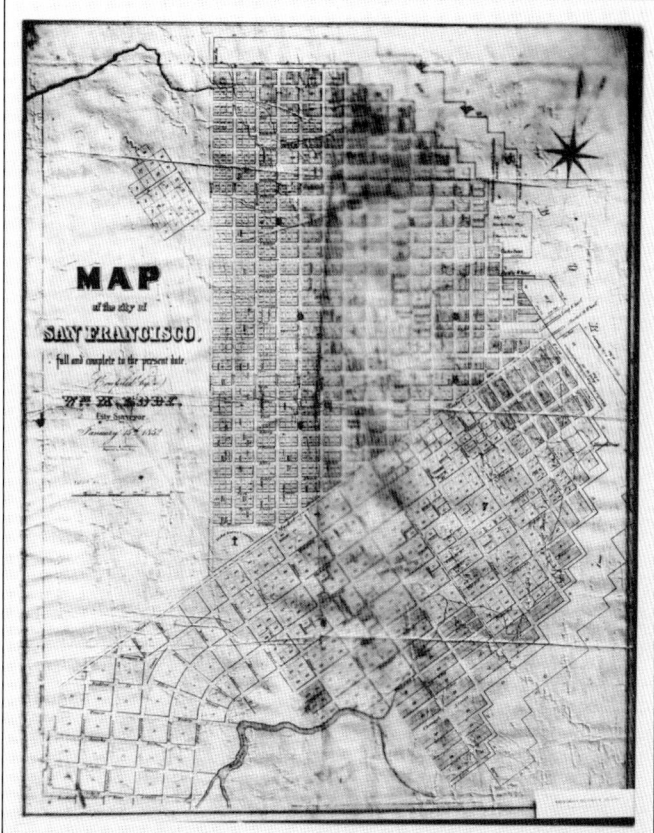

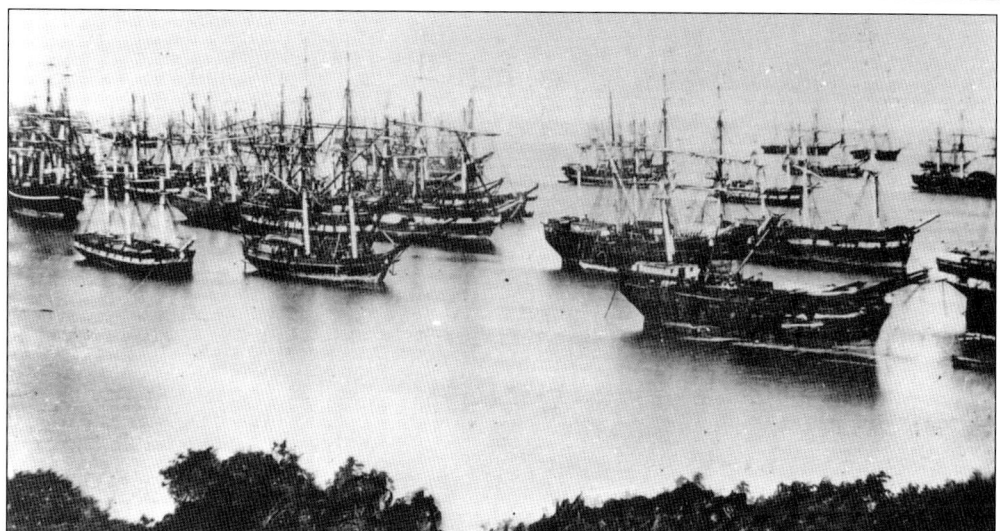

Abandoned ships are the subject of this San Francisco harbor photograph taken around 1851. Crews and passengers abandoned many of their ships in their frenzy to reach the gold fields. Some vessels were left to rot, and some were used for storeships, saloons, hotels, and jails. No less than seven ships are buried along the original waterfront in the area between Broadway and Lombard Streets. The names and locations of the seven ships are listed in the introduction. (SFHC.)

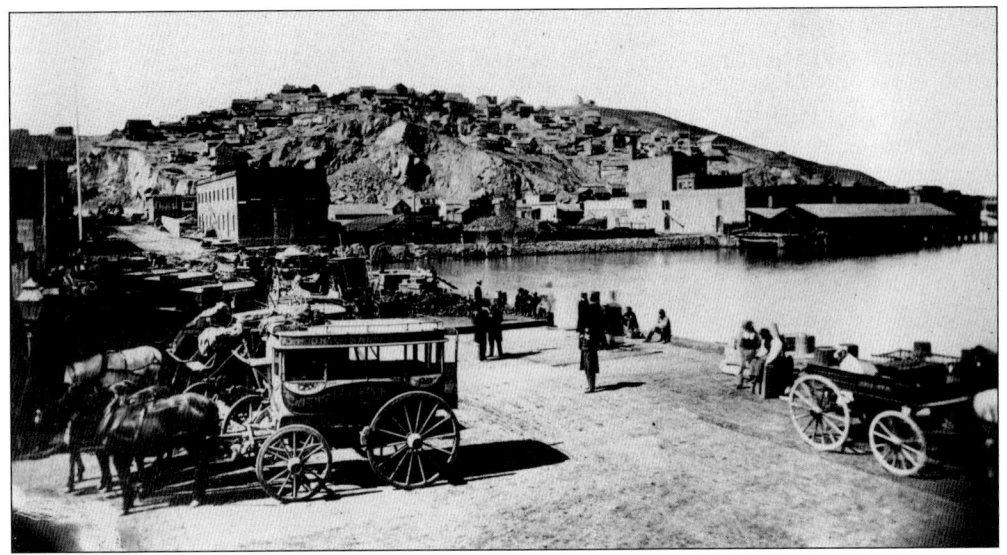

This is the Vallejo Street wharf around 1856. It was in use as early as 1853. Gold was discovered in the California foothills in 1848. Crews deserted most of the ships that docked in San Francisco Bay at that time as the men made their mad dash to find their fortune. In October 1853, the city granted a Mr. O'Brien a 10-year lease authorizing construction of the Vallejo Street wharf. One Richard Chandler secured three old hulks of ships for use as a coal depot. (SFHC.)

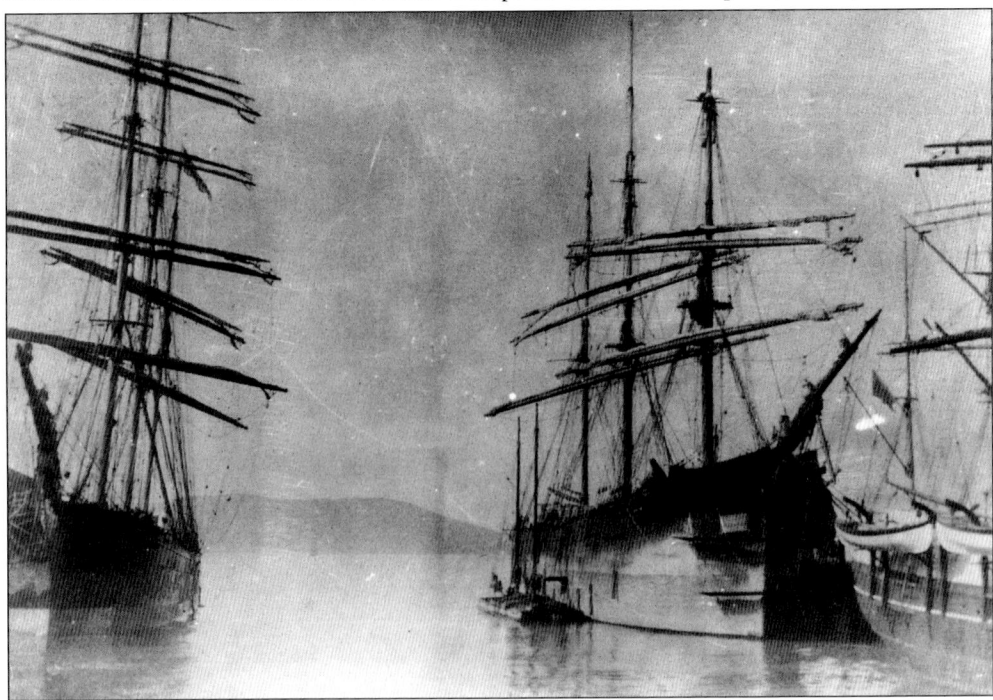

These vessels are anchored near the Vallejo Street wharf in 1867. This particular wharf began to serve San Francisco in 1853, adjacent to the area known then as Clark's Point. Clark's Point was an area at the old shoreline near Broadway and Battery Street. William Squire Clark arrived in Yerba Buena in 1846 and proceeded to acquire land around Telegraph Hill and build warehouses and wharves. (SFHC.)

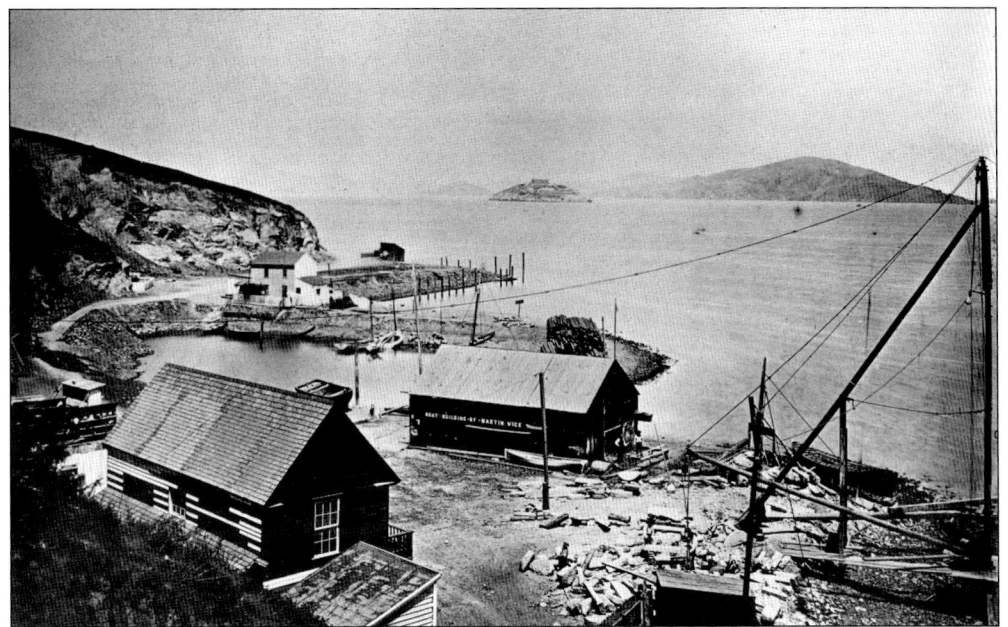

Down at the water's edge were a number of businesses dealing with shipping and building trades. One of these was that of Marin Vice, a master boatbuilder who arrived in California in 1850 from Pennsylvania. Here at the old water line, he provided the maritime community with much sought after equipment. A portion of the road built around the base of the hill to connect the southeast portion of the waterfront with the northern portion is visible. (SFHC.)

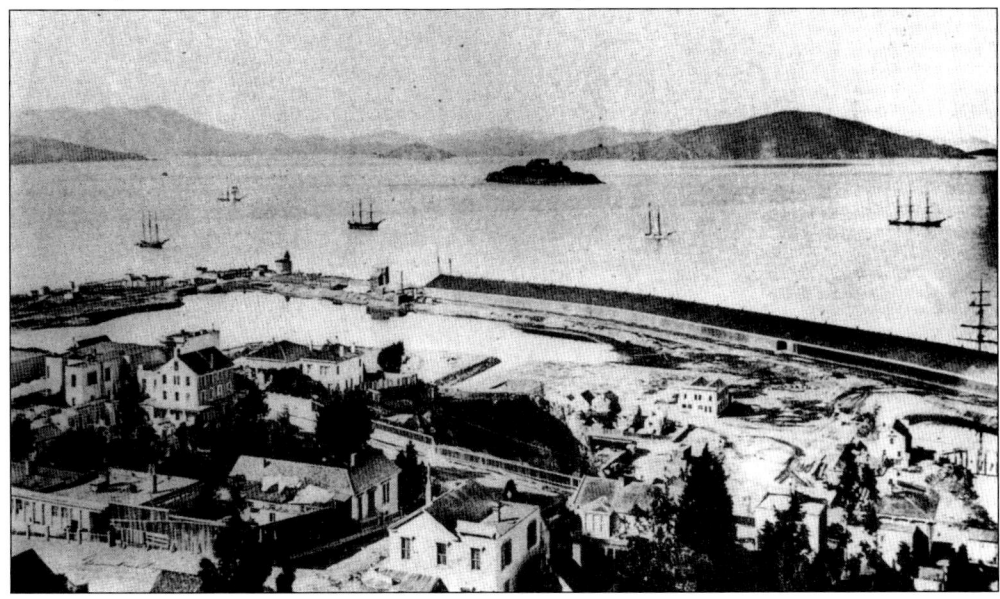

Meiggs' Wharf and the seawall are seen from Telegraph Hill on a foggy day. Today's Fisherman's Wharf can be traced back to this location and to the man who built and named this wooden landing, Henry Meiggs. Originally it served the lumber trade at this cove at the north beach. In the late 1800s, California government constructed a seawall around it. The area became a favorite resort spot. At that time, the northeast shoreline meandered along what are now Front, Battery, and Sansome Streets. (SFHC.)

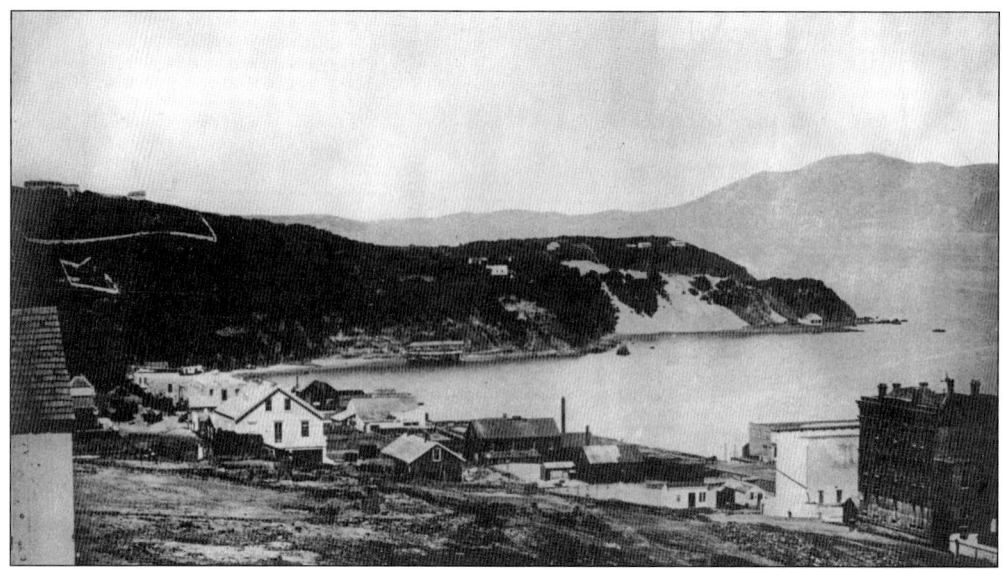

In the past, Telegraph Hill had several names, including Prospect Hill, Signal Hill, Goat Hill, and Loma Alta. The *San Francisco News Letter* report of 1856 states: "San Francisco's population was about 30,000 in 1856. A pinch of gold dust paid for a pie at a bakery. The extension of Commercial Street into the bay was called Long Wharf, where passengers were landed in boats from incoming vessels." (SFHC.)

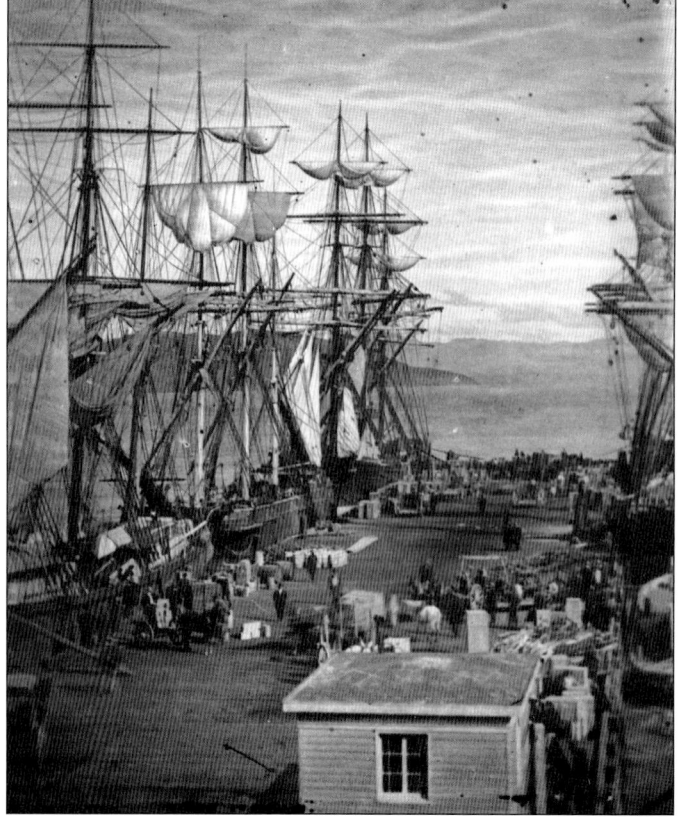

This image was taken at the foot of Vallejo Street before the Civil War, around 1860. Among the six square-rigged vessels in the harbor in March 1849, some 11 years prior to this image, was the brig *Euphemia*. Two years later, this vessel was transformed into a prison, the first in San Francisco. The *Euphemia* then lay in the cove off Clay Street. (SFHC.)

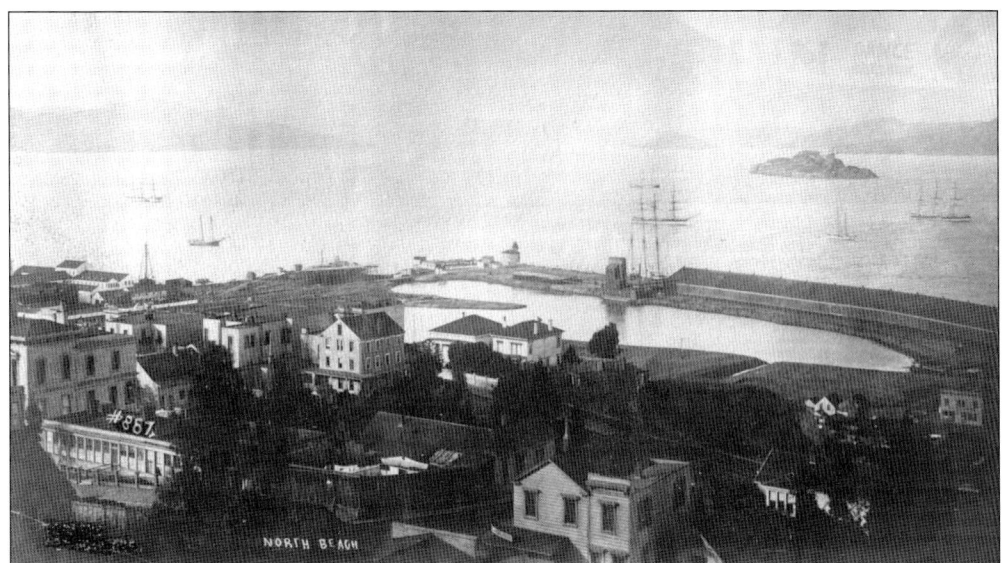

The view down Telegraph Hill looked like this around 1891. Wharves were hastily constructed to accommodate fleets of ships carrying immigrants from around the world. There was no transcontinental railway at that time—whatever came into California and whatever was exported had to be carried over the seas. San Francisco was the only harbor that could be expected to keep pace with the tremendous development of California. (SFHC.)

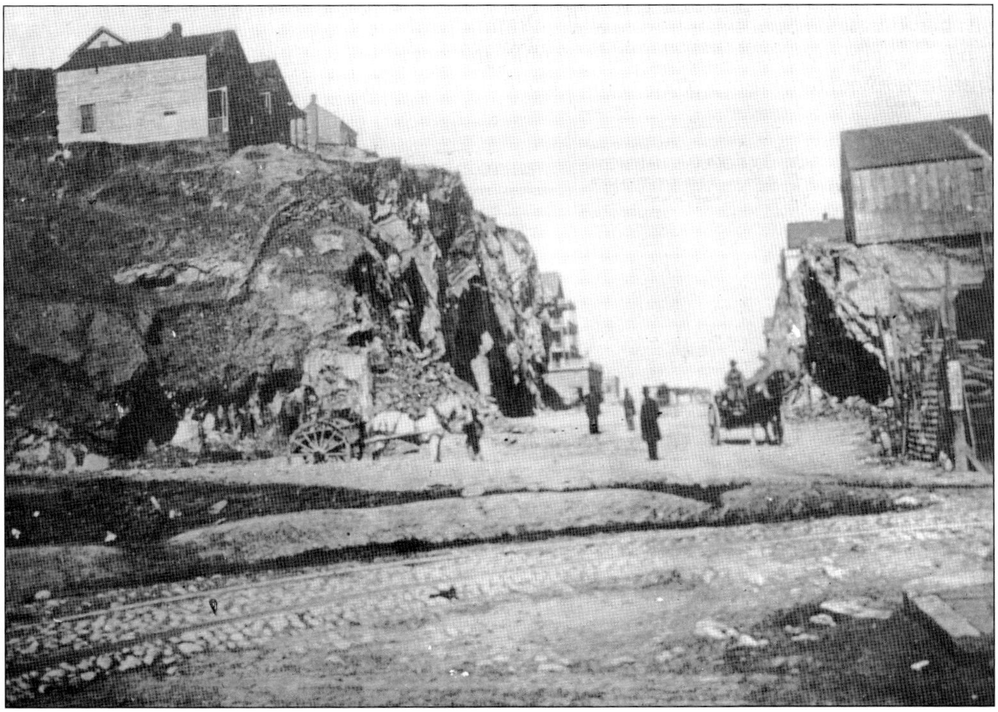

Written on this image is the following: "The deep cut, Broadway & Montgomery. Graded 1864. Cost $30,000." Telegraph Hill originally extended beyond the area seen nowadays. It crossed Broadway and was cut several times between 1850 and 1864. Parts of the hill were quarried for various purposes, including seawalls that required tons of rock. (SFHC.)

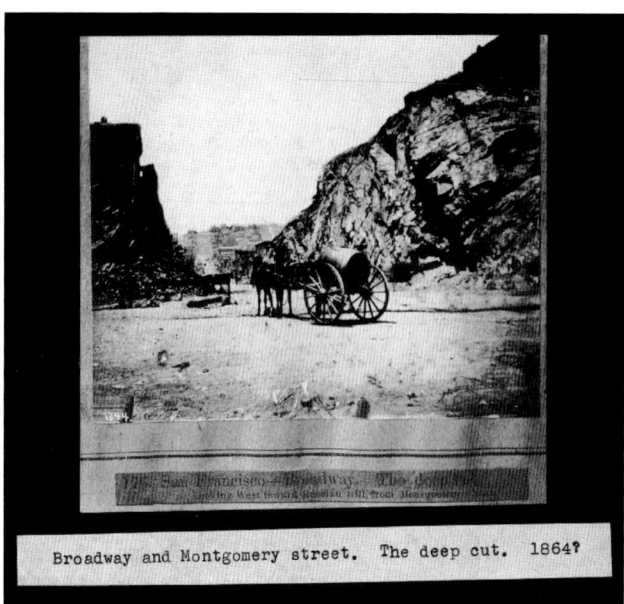

Written on the front of this image is "The deep cut-looking west towards Russian Hill from Montgomery Street." This work continued for a number of years, mostly on the eastern side of Telegraph Hill. The topography today was the result of what is pictured here around 1864. (SFHC.)

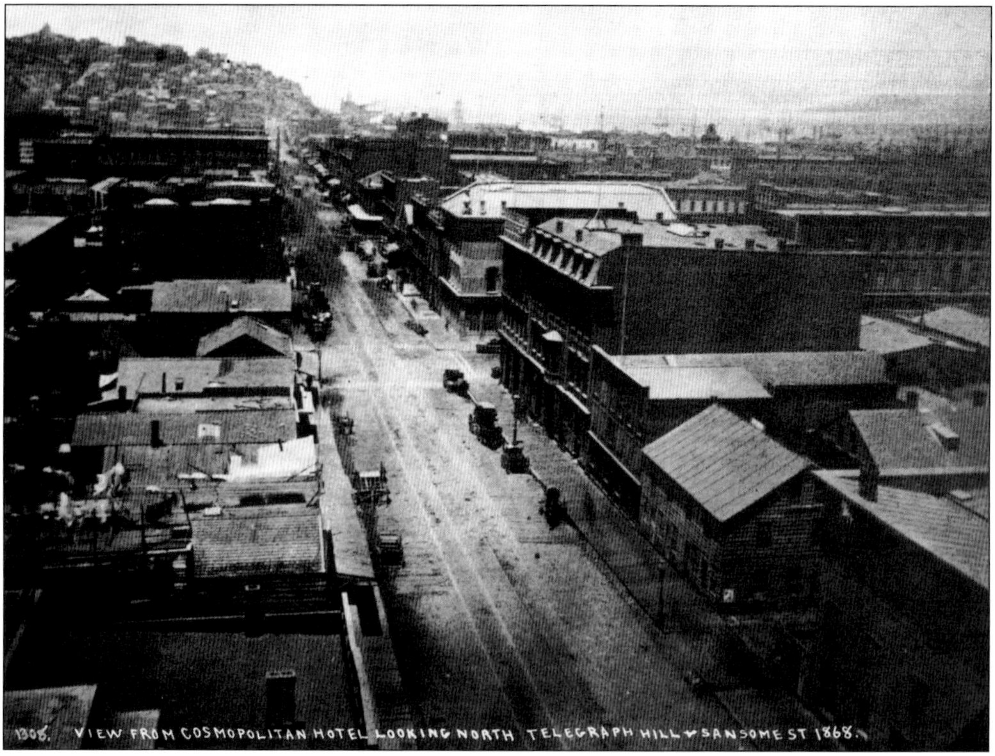

Historical accounts indicate this image was taken in 1868, looking north towards Telegraph Hill from the Cosmopolitan Hotel. The main thoroughfare is Sansome Street. On October 22, 1868, the *San Francisco Morning Call* reported the following: "Yesterday morning San Francisco was visited by the most severe earthquake the city ever experienced. The great shock commenced at 7:53 a.m. and continued nearly one minute, being the longest ever known in this region. Sansome Street suffered very severely." (SFHC.)

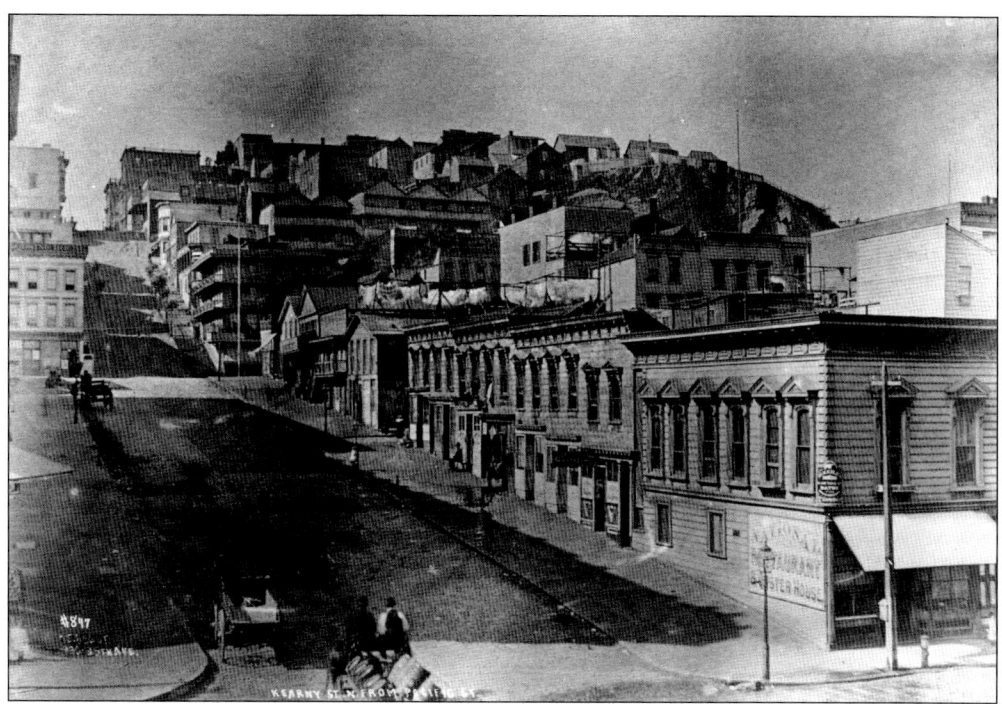

This view looks up Kearny Street from north of Pacific Street around 1892. On Broadway, just out of view, was the first official jail in San Francisco, built in 1850. In 1856, James King, editor of the *San Francisco Evening Bulletin*, was killed by James Casey, rival editor of the *San Francisco Sunday Times*. Casey was housed in the jail until a mob of people, some from the San Francisco Committee of Vigilance, marched up this street along Kearny to the Broadway jail to hang him for shooting James King. (SFHC.)

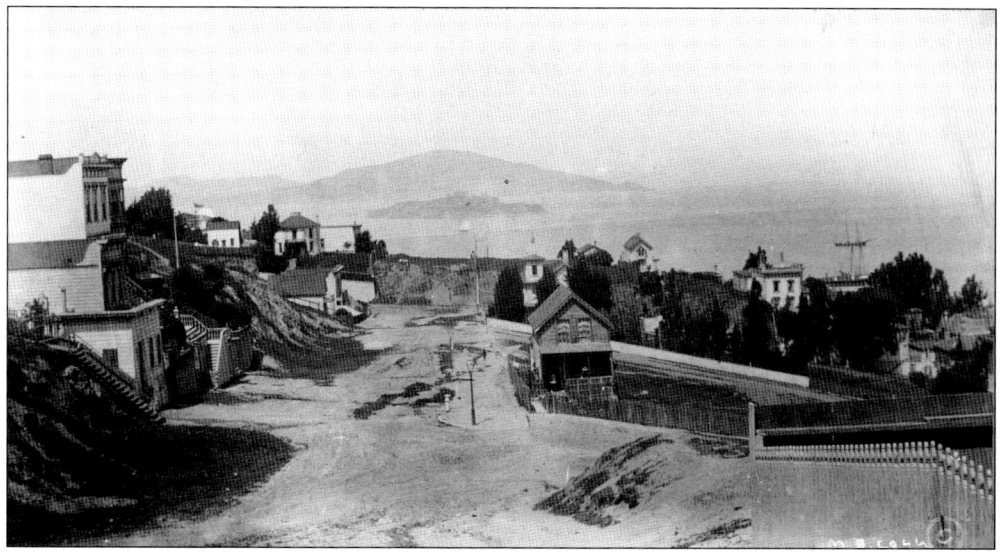

This is a view of Leavenworth Street, north of Filbert Street, around 1867. White picket fences, rustic surroundings, and charming homes can be seen all in one image. There is a woman in the doorway of the cottage at the right and several people glancing about the garden. Down the sidewalk are a child and several dogs. (SFHC.)

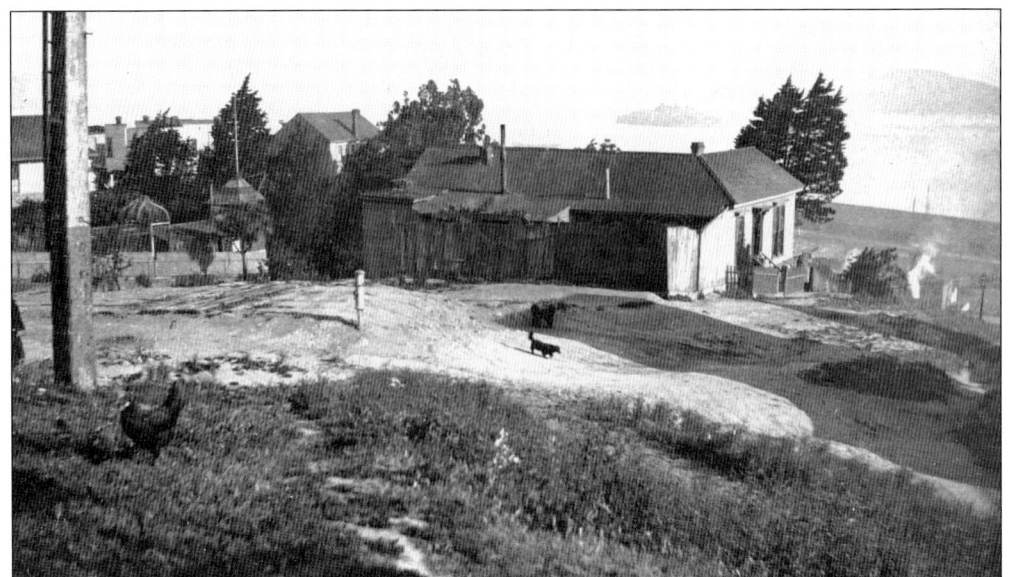

The image above is of an early settlement on the east side of Telegraph Hill in the 1890s, looking north towards the Marin headlands. There is a chicken in the foreground and several dogs. Alcatraz Island is at the top center. The structures on the island were part of the Civil War fortress and military buildings (1850–1934), the federal prison (1934–1963), and the first lighthouse on the West Coast. (JBM.)

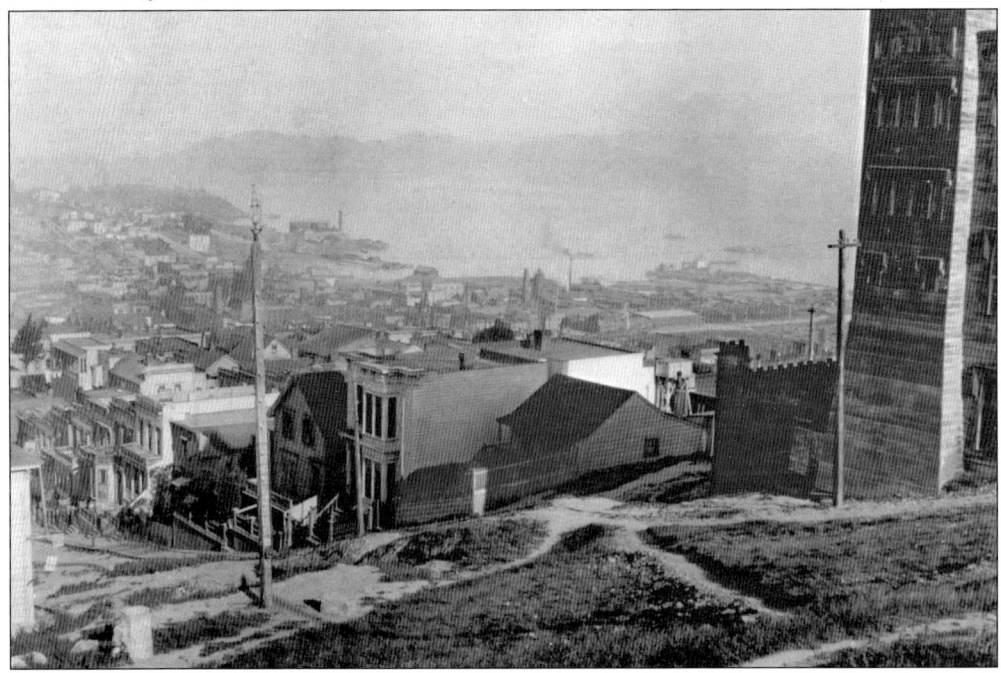

This view from the western side of Telegraph Hill in the 1890s shows how steep it was and still is. Just visible on the far right side is the corner of Layman's folly, seen in its entirety in chapter four. This was Little Italy. B. E. Lloyd wrote of Telegraph Hill in the late 1800s: "It is now climbed daily by scores of busy Italian artisans who, with their families, occupy the houses that are perched along is side, extending almost to the summit." (JBM.)

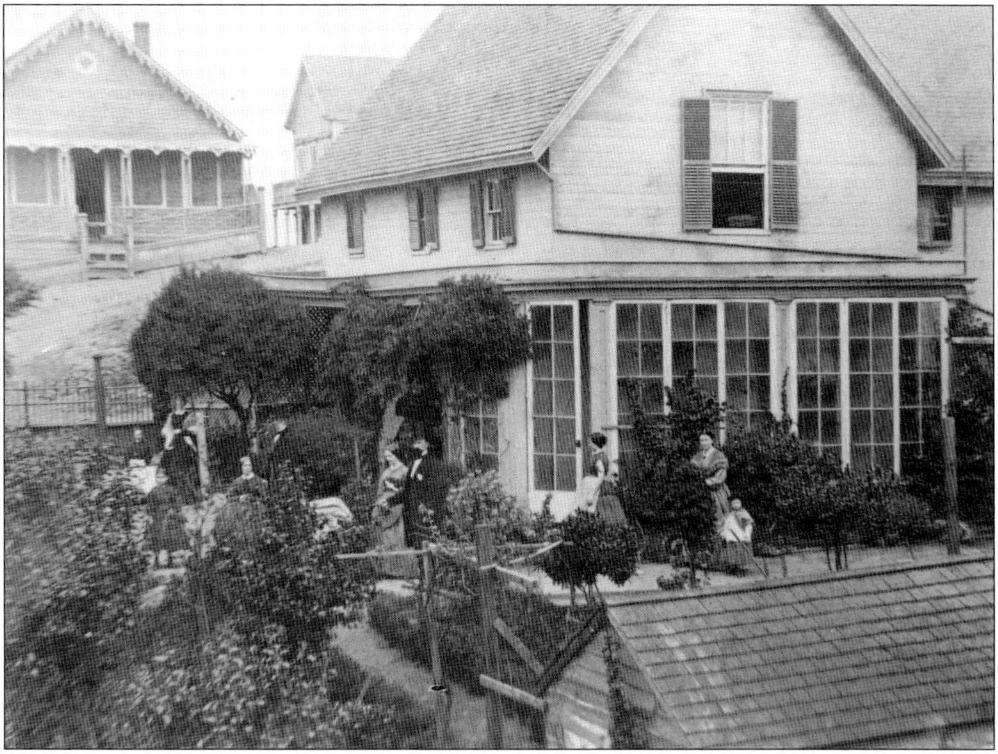

Here is a closer look at a residence and garden on Telegraph Hill on July 4, 1862. It looks like a gathering is taking place on Independence Day. Historical reports describe this day in this way: "The National ensign floated from all the public and private buildings and from the shipping in the harbor. National salutes were fired at morning, noon, and night." (SFHC.)

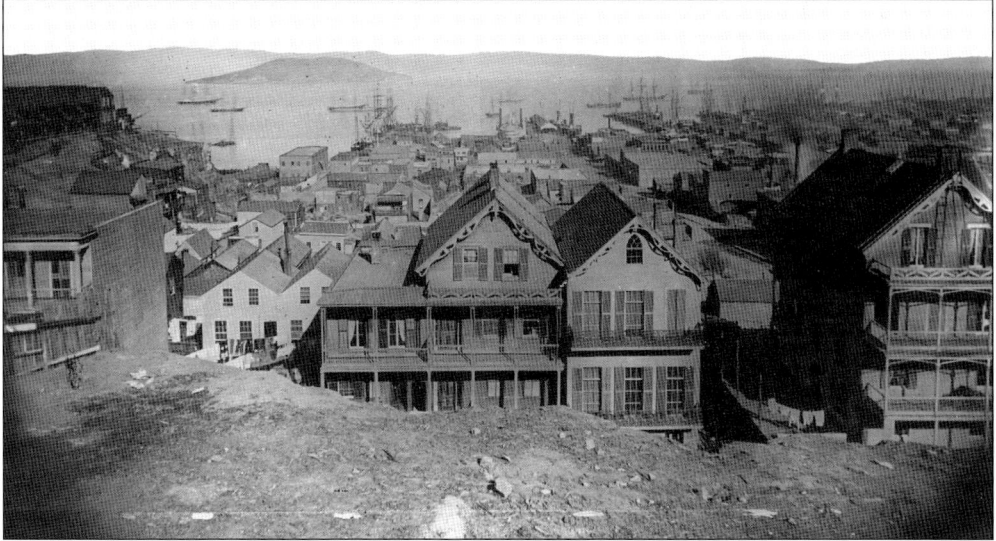

This is a view of the San Francisco waterfront from Montgomery Street between Vallejo Street and Broadway in 1867. What are called Carpenter Gothic houses can be seen in the center. Plots of land all over the hill are filling in with dwellings. City records indicate paving of Montgomery Street was scheduled to take place in September 1867 and May 1868. (SFHC.)

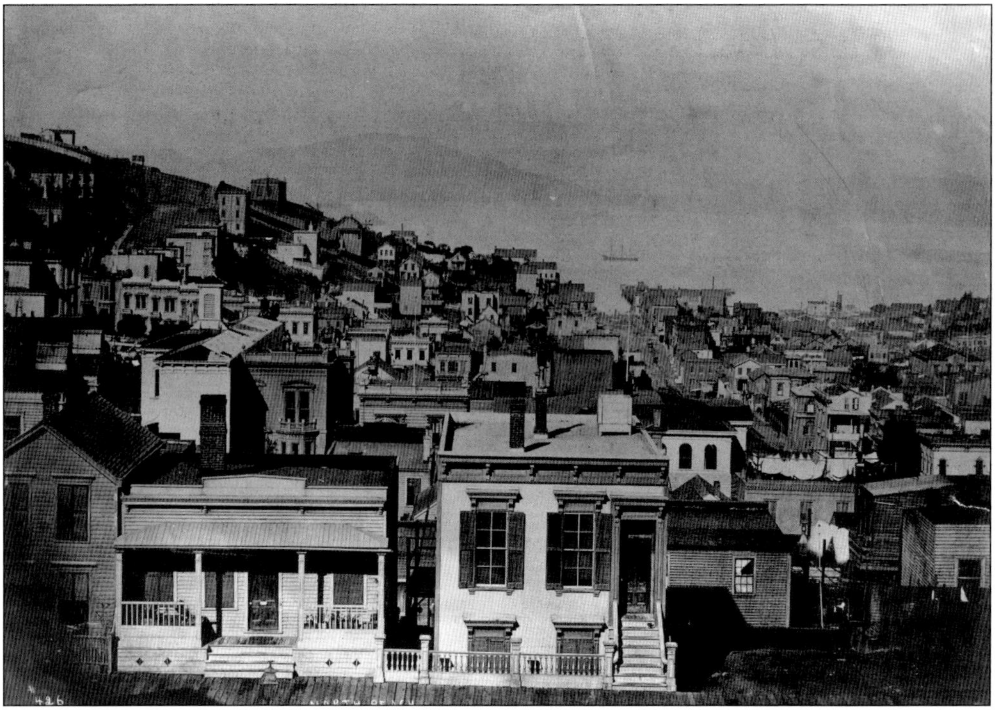

This image was taken in 1875, looking north from Sacramento Street with Mason Street in the center. It shows wooden sidewalks in the foreground and a three-masted ship in the bay. This scene is charming to modern readers, but was just a typical day on Telegraph Hill back in 1875. (SFHC.)

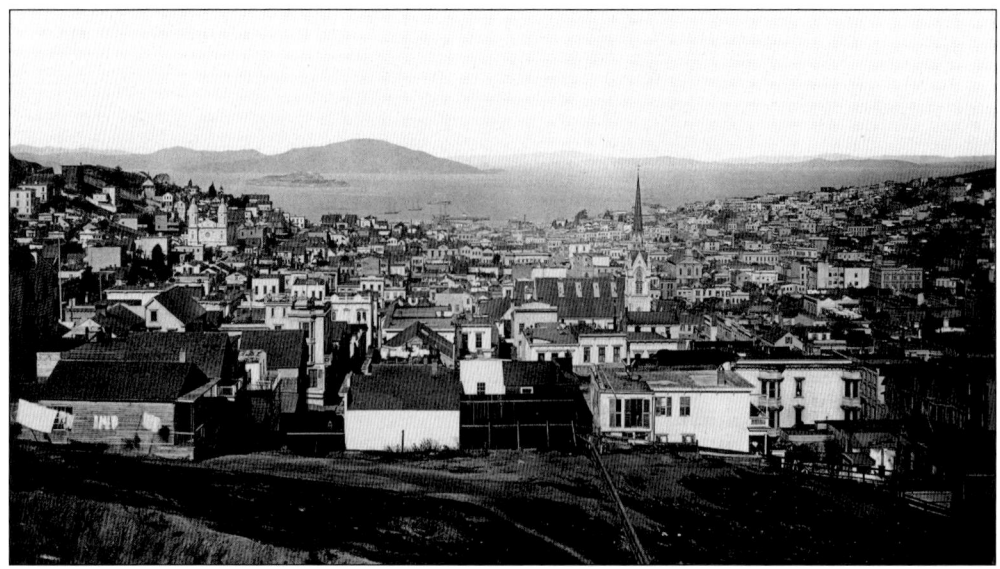

Here is the view of North Beach from California and Powell Streets around 1885. Written on the back of this photograph is: "At left, Catholic Spanish Church dedicated March 1880; centre New First Methodist Episcopal Church erected in 1871." The Catholic church could very well be Our Lady of Guadalupe at 908 Broadway. The other could be the Episcopal Chinese Mission at 966 Clay Street. (SFHC.)

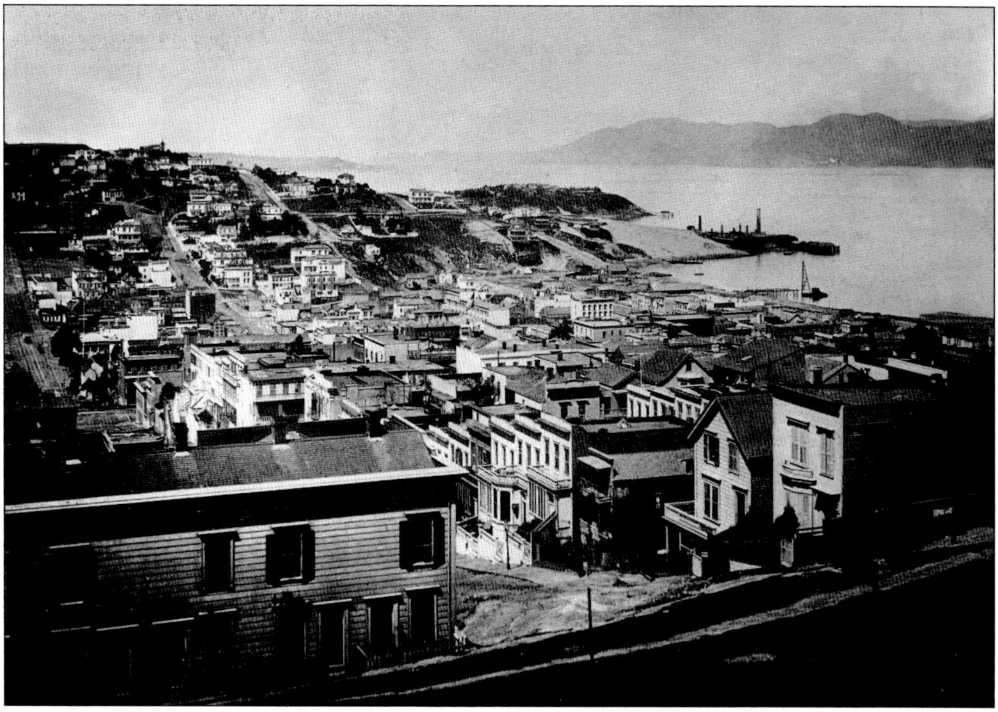

Looking northwest toward the Marin headlands from Telegraph Hill prior to 1906, a portion of the beach that gave North Beach its name can be seen. The shoreline and north beach was at one time about 200 acres. By January 28, 1884, North Beach had grown from Broadway to the high-tide mark. (JBM.)

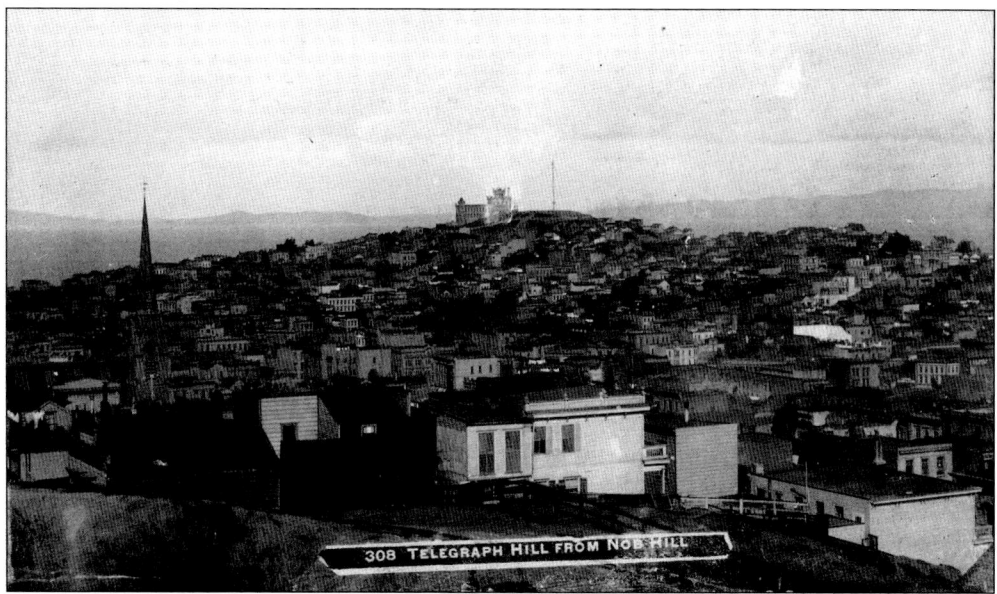

This image shows a view of Telegraph Hill from Nob Hill in 1884. St. Francis Church is visible in the center at Vallejo Street and Columbus Avenue. There is also a windmill on the roof of a building at center right. It was on top of the New Buon Gusto Restaurant on Broadway. There is a closer look at that area later in this chapter. (SFHC.)

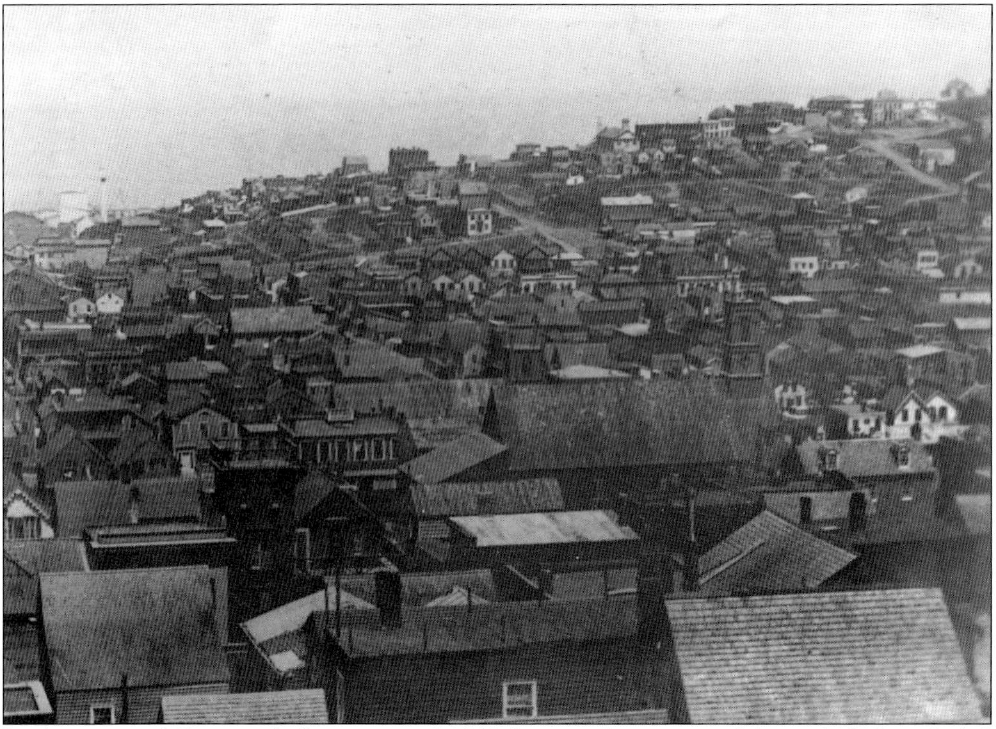

Looking toward Greenwich Street around 1864, historical accounts of the mid-1800s included the following: "June 11, 1864—A portion of Meigg's Wharf tumbled down; July 16, 1865—A fire occurred at 12 o'clock p.m. in the Pacific Warehouse, on the corner of Broadway and Battery Streets. The building, with the greater portion of its contents, were entirely destroyed. Estimated loss about $100,000." (SFHC.)

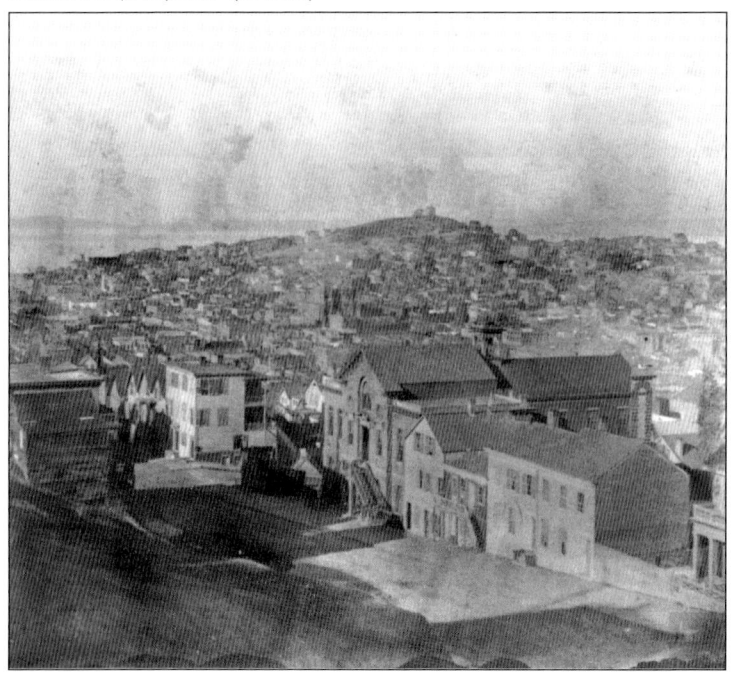

This is Telegraph Hill as seen from the corner of Sacramento and Powell Streets around 1866. The image is one of several in a collection titled "Gems of California Scenery." Keeping this gem safe was the newly established (December 1866) San Francisco Fire Department, consisting of 156 paid members, 6 steam engines, 493 hydrants, and 50 cisterns. The new department replaced the original volunteer organization. (LOC.)

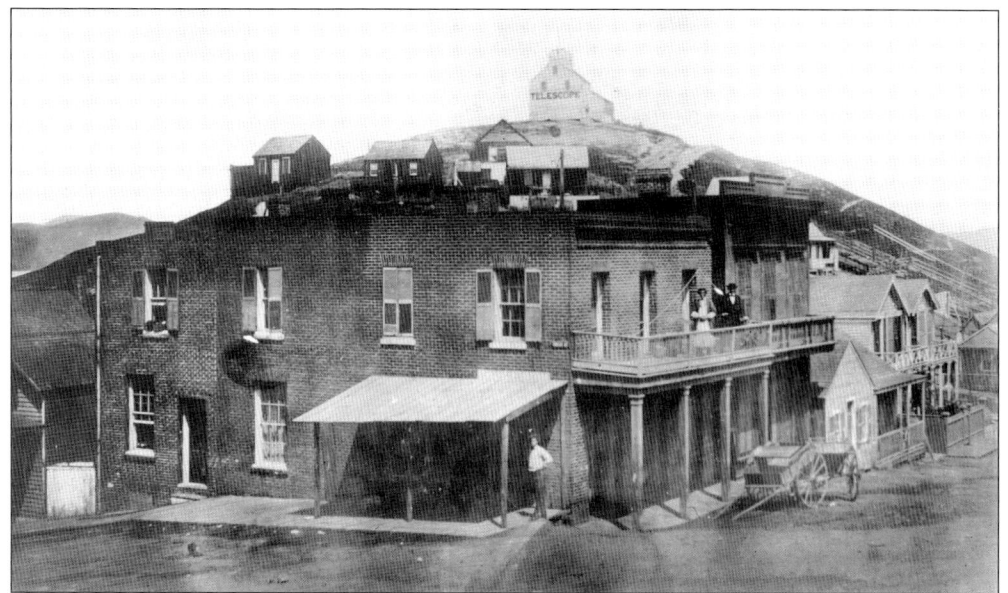

This 1882 view from the corner of Union and Montgomery Streets is just a few streets away from the observatory in the previous image. The side of the observatory reads "telescope" in large letters. In the foreground is 1301 Montgomery Street, possibly the oldest brick building in San Francisco, and one of the first structures constructed around 1850. It was a grocery store from approximately 1854 to the 1880s. The building housed a barbershop in 1915, a pool hall in the 1920s, and finally a residence. (SFHC.)

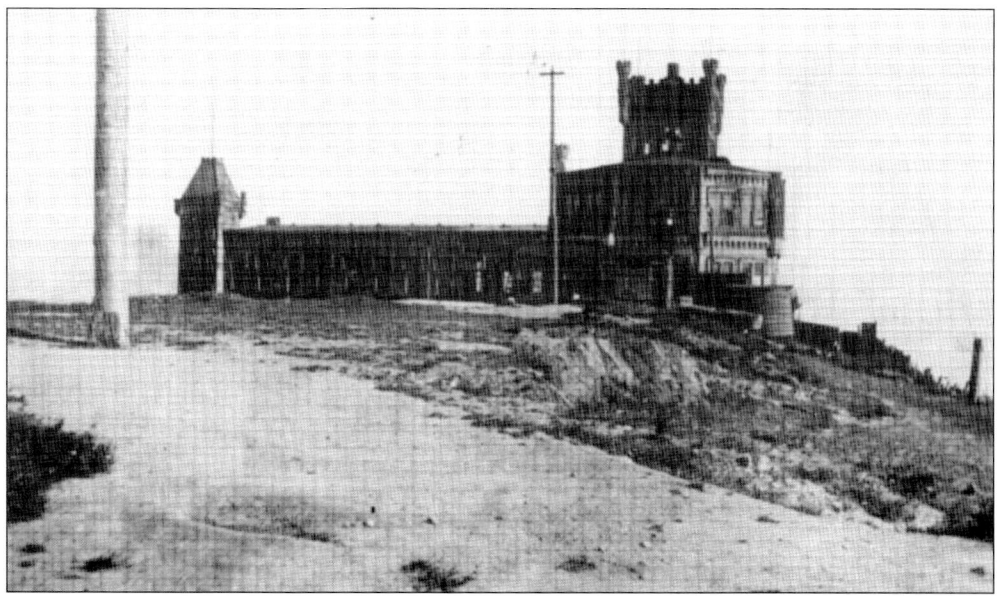

Here is a closer look at the "castle," also called the observatory, and the Temple of Gambrinus. Gambrinus was a legendary king of Flanders and an unofficial patron saint of beer. The 1855 *Annals of San Francisco* read, "September 22d. Opening of the first electric telegraph in California celebrated. This extended eight miles, between San Francisco and Point Lobos, and was erected by Messrs. Sweeny & Baugh . . . Early in 1849 this enterprising firm had erected a station-house on Telegraph Hill." (SFHC.)

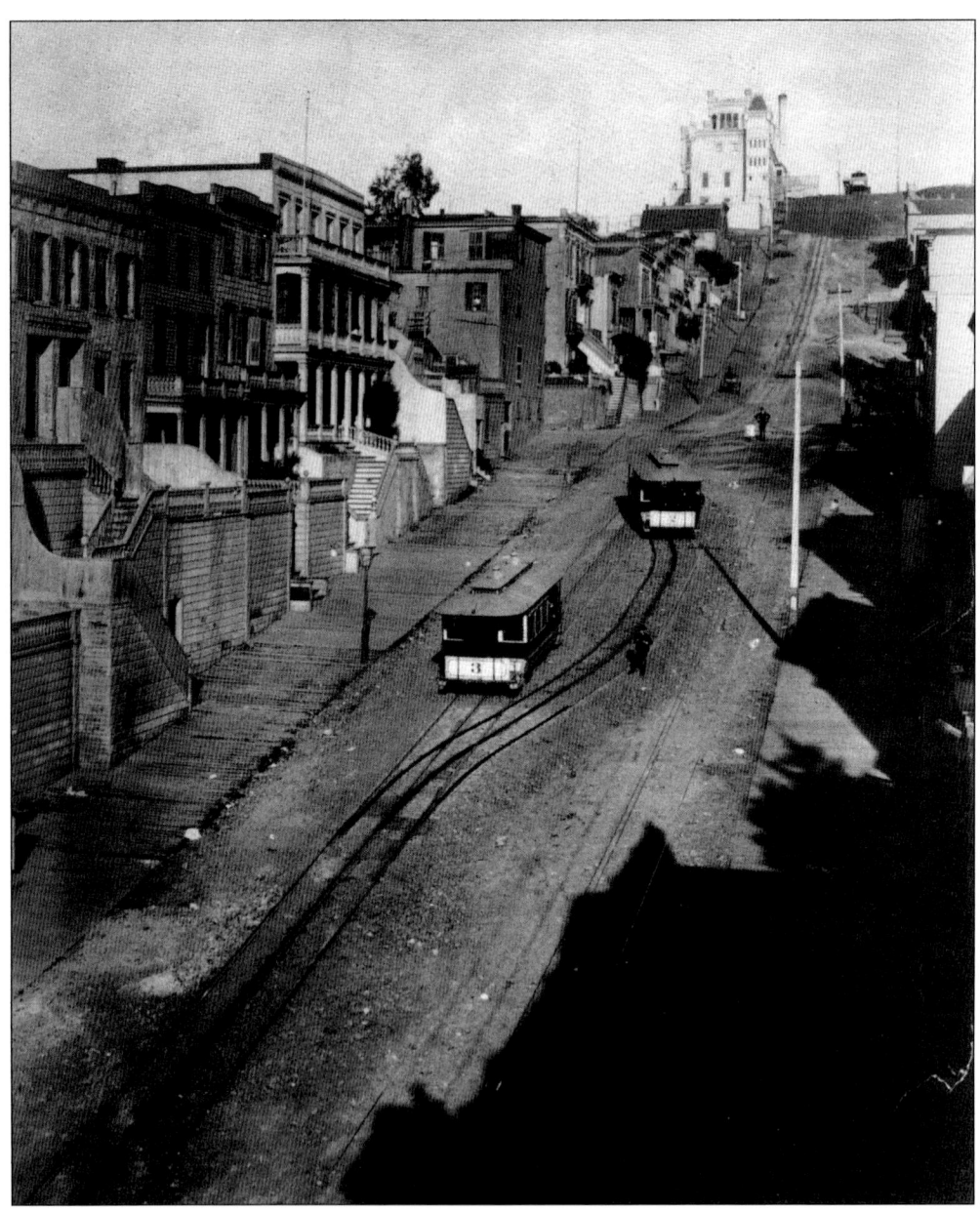

Here is one of the ways people trekked up North Beach hills in 1884. The image reads, "Telegraph Hill Cable R.R." Some say this was not a cable car in the true sense of the word—it was a funicular railway using two cars attached to a cable. It was the idea of Frederick O. Layman, who expected hundreds of people would flock to the top of the hill to enjoy the resort and observatory. Rand McNally and Company's 1886 *Guide to Southern California Direct: Narrative, Historical Descriptive, with Notes on California at Large*, by James William Steele, read, "A remarkable elevation, both in the old times and now, is the small mountain called Telegraph Hill, standing immediately south of the entrance to the harbor (Golden Gate). It has not been long since it was necessary to climb the steep ascent on foot if you wished to enjoy what is, on a clear day, a fine prospect . . . The observatory on Telegraph Hill is very completely furnished with telescopes, field-glasses and other conveniences, and has also a restaurant, and is used by the population as a pleasure resort." (SFHC)

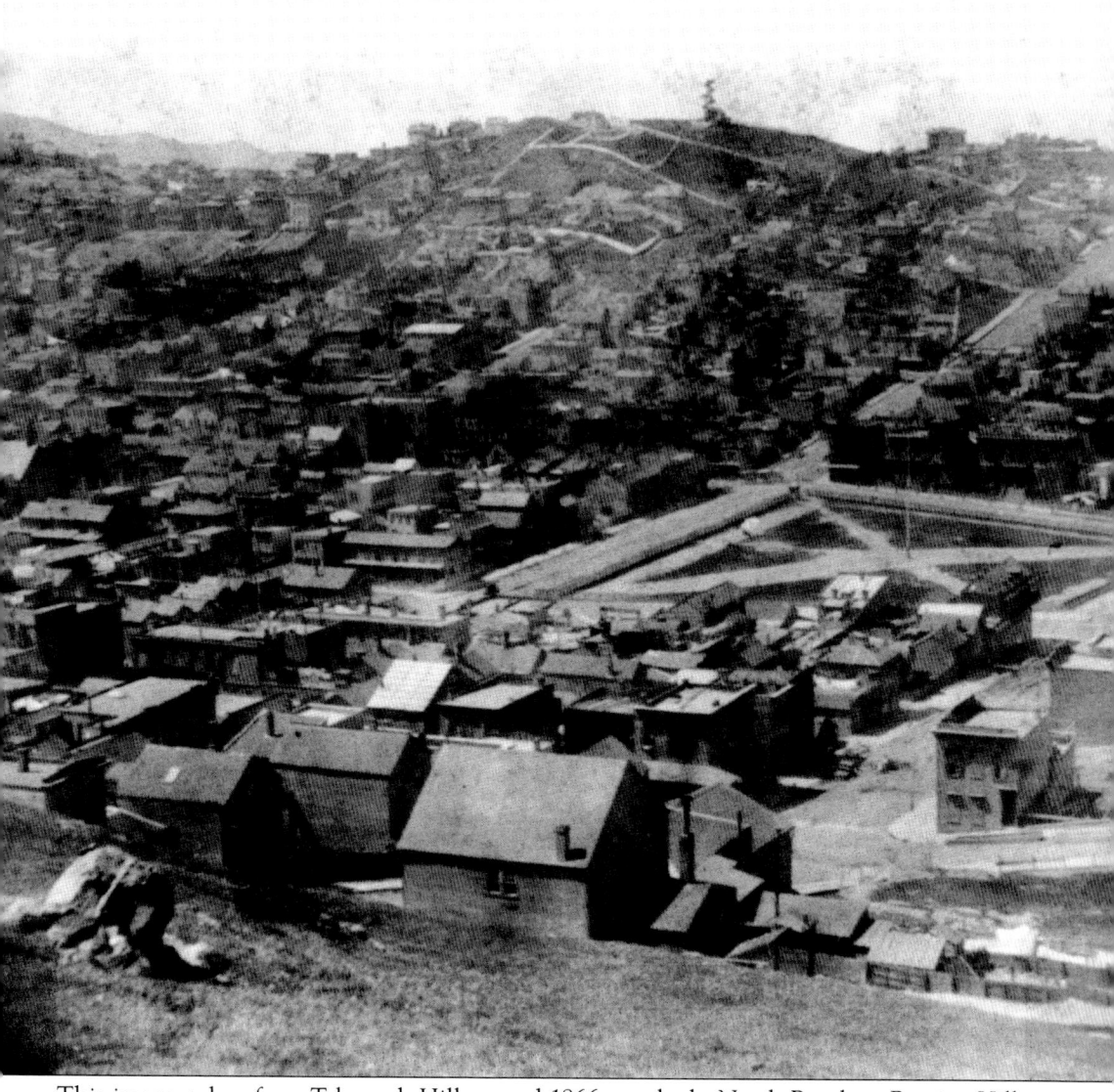

This image, taken from Telegraph Hill around 1866, overlooks North Beach to Russian Hill. In the center is Il Giardino ("The Garden"), as it was called by local Italians. In 1850, the first mayor of San Francisco, John W. Geary, declared the land a public square. The square's many uses over the years included goat pasture and cemetery. In later years, after it was renamed Washington Square, it served as quintessential neighborhood park, a meeting place for both local residents and weary tourists. The square is known as "the park in front of the church," the location of occasional outdoor art galleries, the place where Ferraris are on display during the annual North Beach Festival. The patch of land seen here in 1866 has come a long way over the past 144 years. (SFHC)

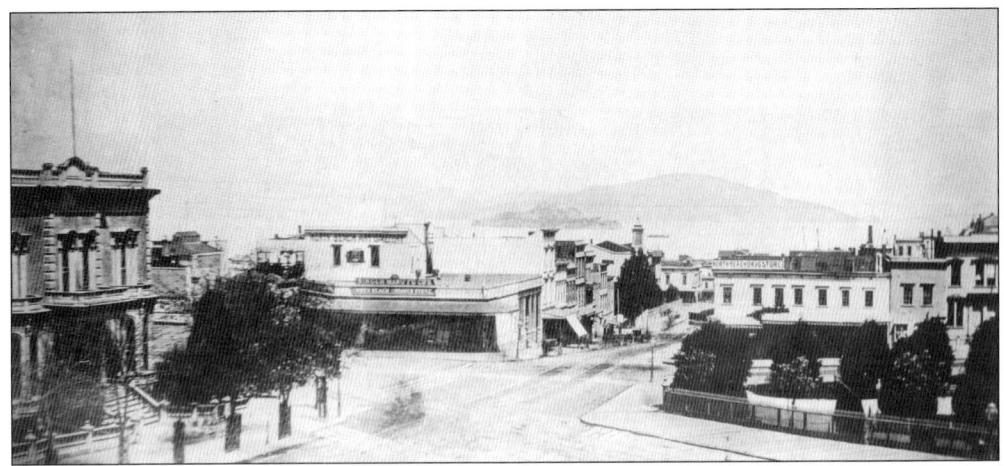

A portion of Washington Square (at right) is pictured here as it was in 1878. Several signs can be seen on the building in the center. The sign on the roof reads, "North Beach Art Gallery," one at the entrance to the storefront reads, "Singer Manufacturing Company's North Beach Store," and on the building at the far right the sign reads, "North Beach Drug Store." (SFHC.)

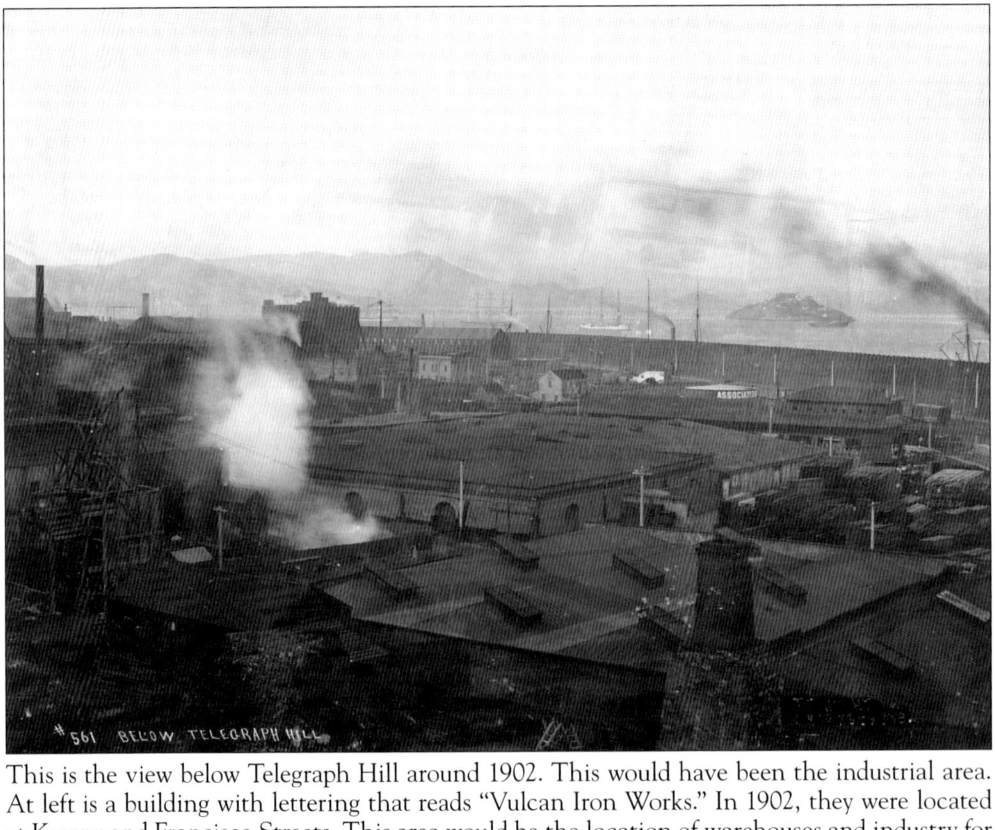

This is the view below Telegraph Hill around 1902. This would have been the industrial area. At left is a building with lettering that reads "Vulcan Iron Works." In 1902, they were located at Kearny and Francisco Streets. This area would be the location of warehouses and industry for many years to come. (SFHC.)

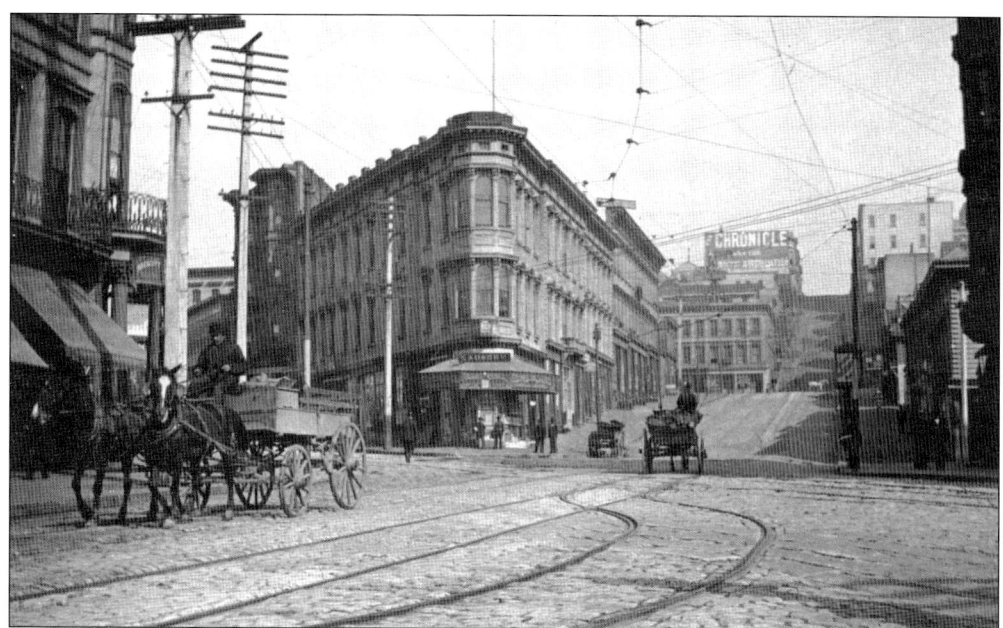

This would be a typical 1902 scene in the business section of North Beach. A large building has a roof sign reading "The Chronicle." Even then, the *San Francisco Chronicle* newspaper was a big deal. The August 1, 1902, issue reported, "Terror reigns in Los Alamos Valley!" describing a series of earthquakes that struck the small town of Los Alamos in northern Santa Barbara County. Little did the people in this photograph realize that four years later an earthquake would rock their own neighborhood. (JBM.)

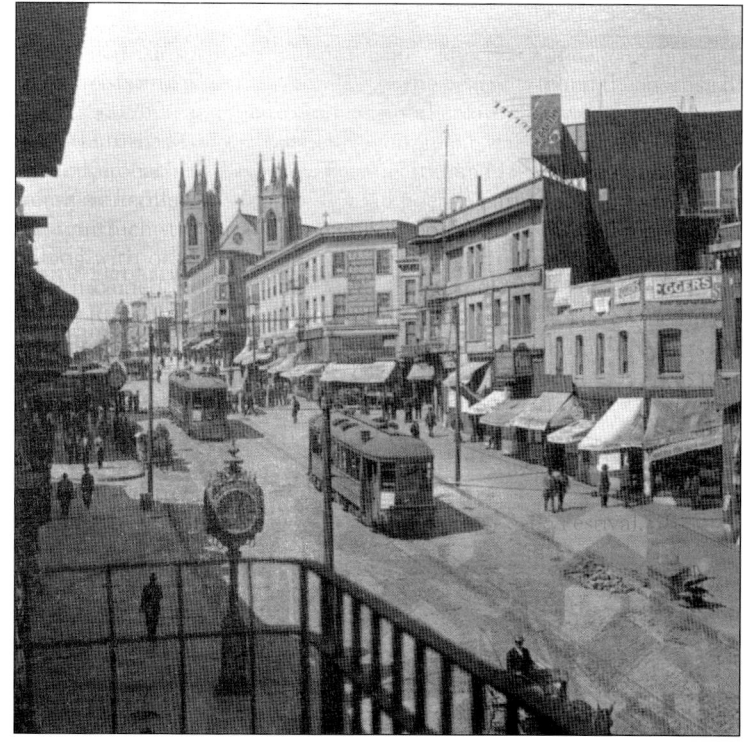

This view looks north on Montgomery Street near the intersection with Broadway around 1900. Montgomery Street's name was changed in 1909 and is now called Columbus Avenue. At the top of the photograph is St. Francis Church, one of the two major Catholic churches in the area. It is San Francisco Landmark No. 5, at 610 Vallejo Street. The church on this site was gutted by the 1906 fire, leaving only the brick walls and towers intact. (JBM.)

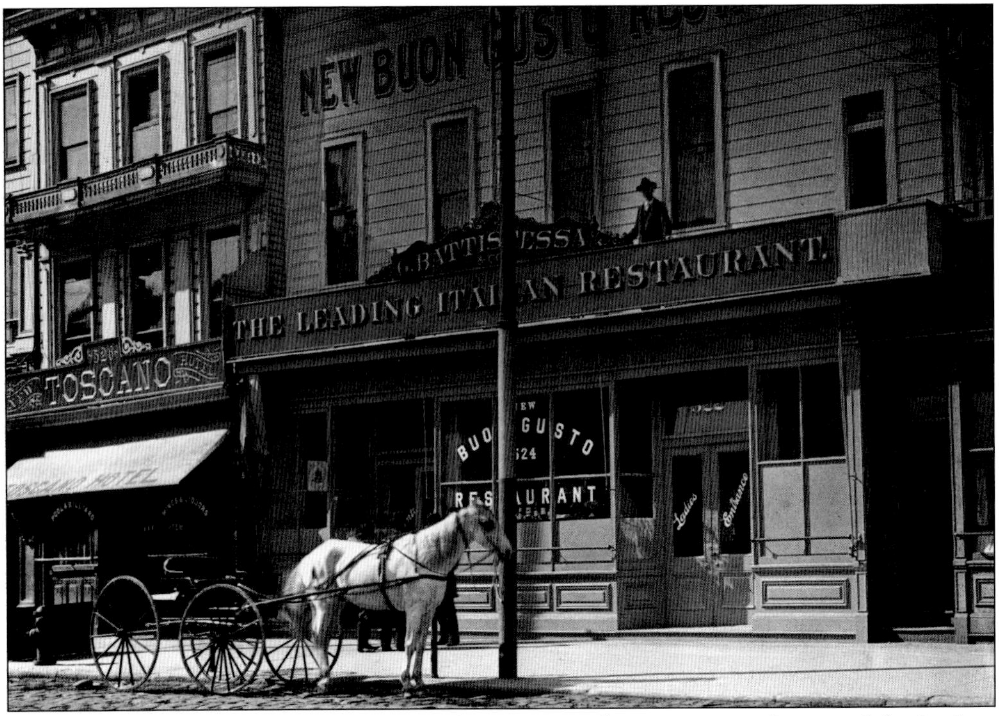

The New Buon Gusto Restaurant was, as the sign over the entrance reads, one of the leading Italian restaurants in North Beach during the late 19th century. This is the restaurant where the noted photographer J. B. Monaco met his future wife, Katherine Battistessa. Next door is the Toscano Hotel. Just down the street on the right, out of view, was the Broadway jail. (JBM.)

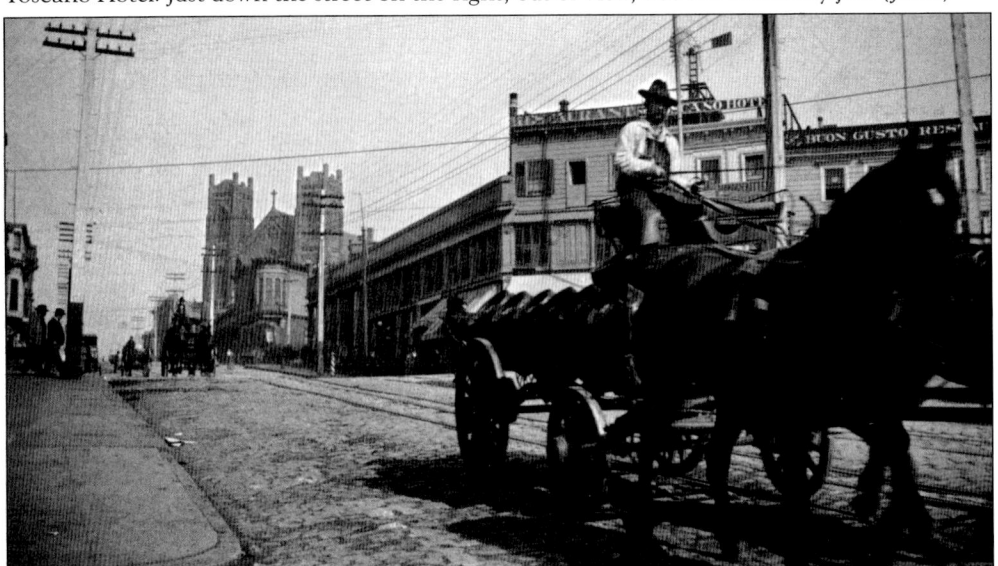

The wagon, carrying barrels, is traveling down Montgomery Street near Pacific Street. It has probably just delivered beer or wine to the New Buon Gusto Restaurant just behind it. The Toscano Hotel can be seen over the top of the wagon. Raphaelo Petri, a native of Tuscany, came to San Francisco with his family in the early 1800s. He also brought with him the family tradition of hospitality, good food, and wine. (JBM.)

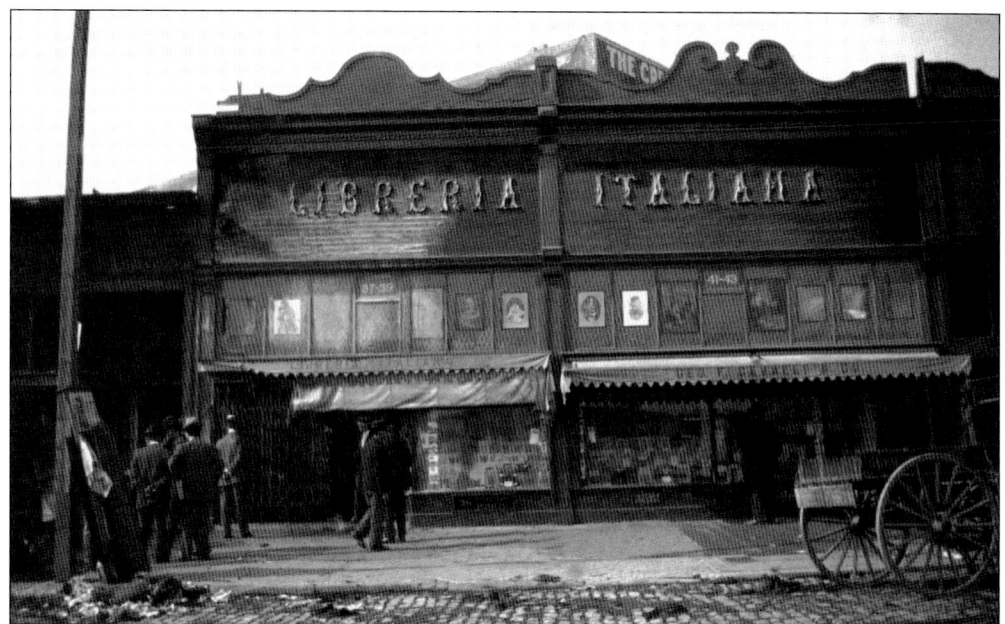

George Favius Cavalli established the Liberia Italiana and Cavalli Bookstore, pictured here. In 1880, he founded one of the most important cultural resources in North Beach, the first Italian-language bookstore. The bookstore did, and still does, provide Italian books, magazines, and phonograph records. Cavalli was from the little village of Verscio, a municipality in the district of Locarno in the canton of Ticino, Switzerland, close to the border with Italy. (JBM.)

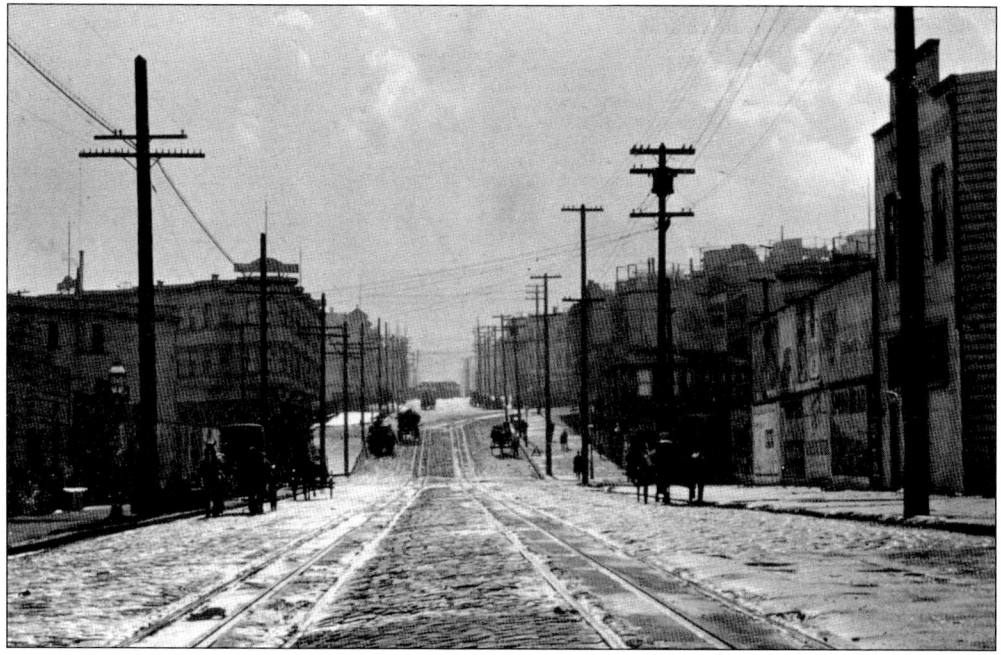

This is Columbus Avenue from Chestnut Street looking south before 1906. Cobblestones make up the street for horse-drawn carriages and wagons. The wall on the right sports several large advertisements. One appears to be for Spear Head plug tobacco. The streetcar tracks are a reminder that North Beach and much of San Francisco, at that time, was crisscrossed with tracks and streetcars. (JBM.)

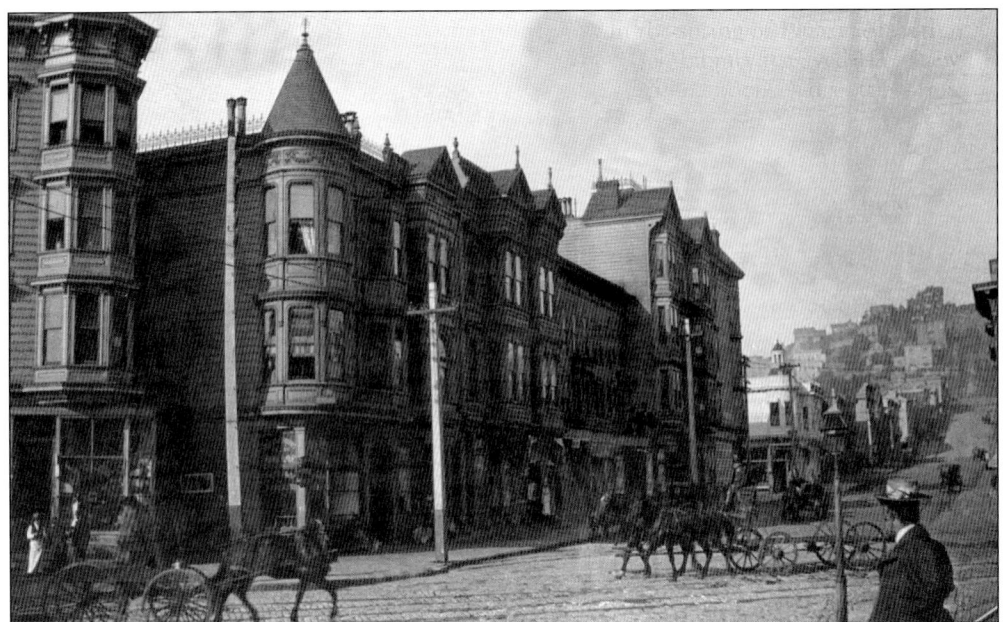

Above is the residence of renowned photographer J. B. Monaco at the corner of Vallejo and Montgomery Streets in 1900. This is where his only son, Dante, was born on November 12, 1900. Dante became a motion picture engineer and technician of considerable prominence. This Monaco image depicts a typical neighborhood prior to the 1906 earthquake and fire. (JBM.)

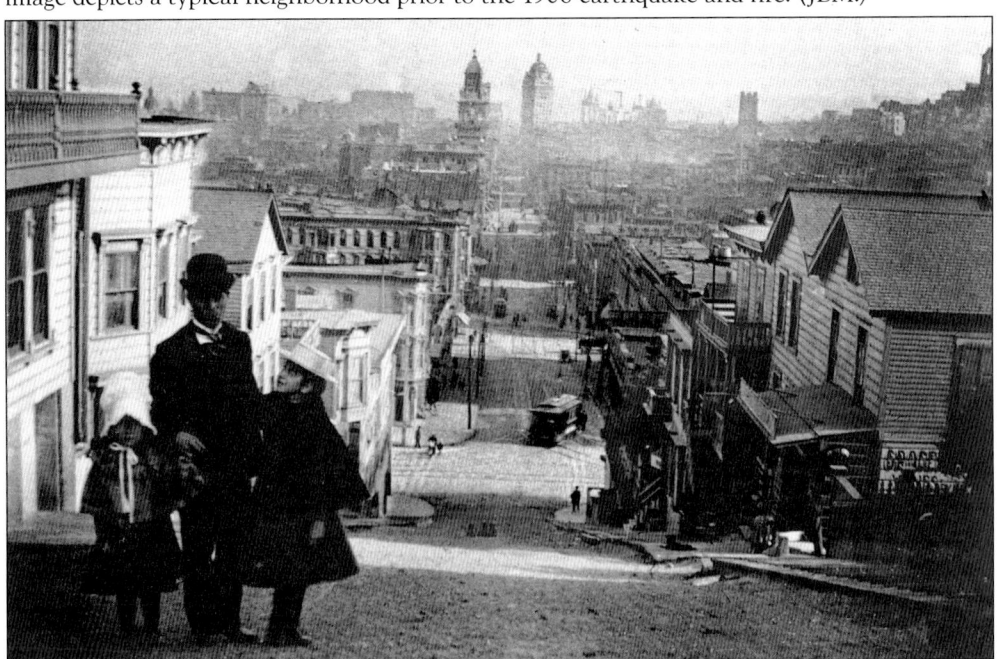

The photographer is standing on Vallejo Street looking down Kearney Street toward Broadway. Notice the children sitting in the middle of the hill and the dog lying on the sidewalk near the neighborhood grocery store. It is another day in North Beach. Before the 1906 earthquake and fire, the area was made up of families, many of them captured in time by photographer J. B. Monaco. (JBM.)

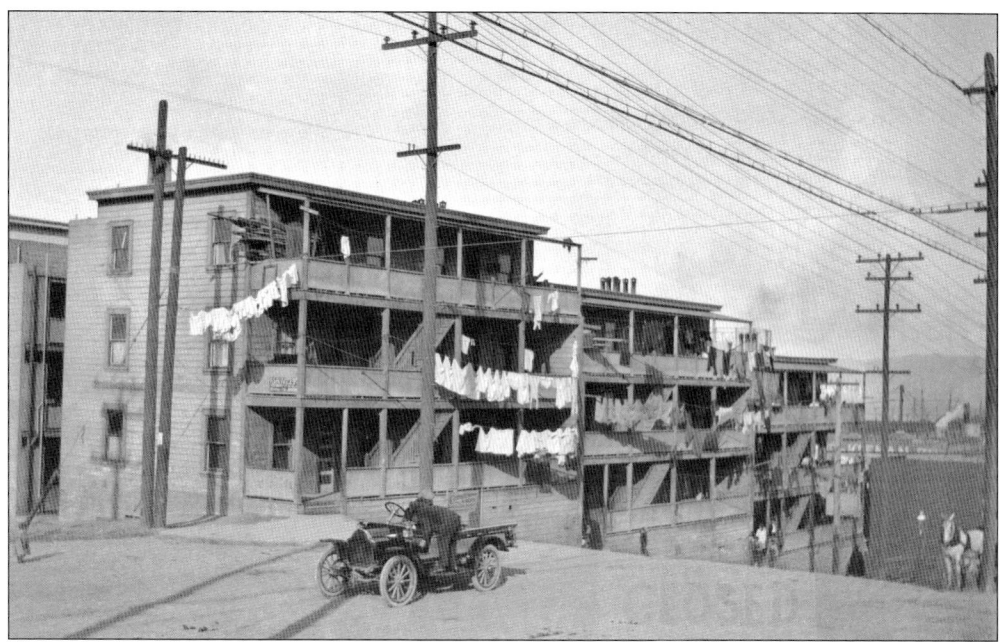

These are the Cuneo Flats at Bay and Leavenworth Streets around 1904. Although the flats were near Russian Hill, Joseph Cuneo was an important figure in the neighboring North Beach district. Cuneo was born in Italy in 1839. He had a successful real estate career, including this property. The sign on the left side of the building reads, "2, 3, 4, 5 room flats to let." (JBM.)

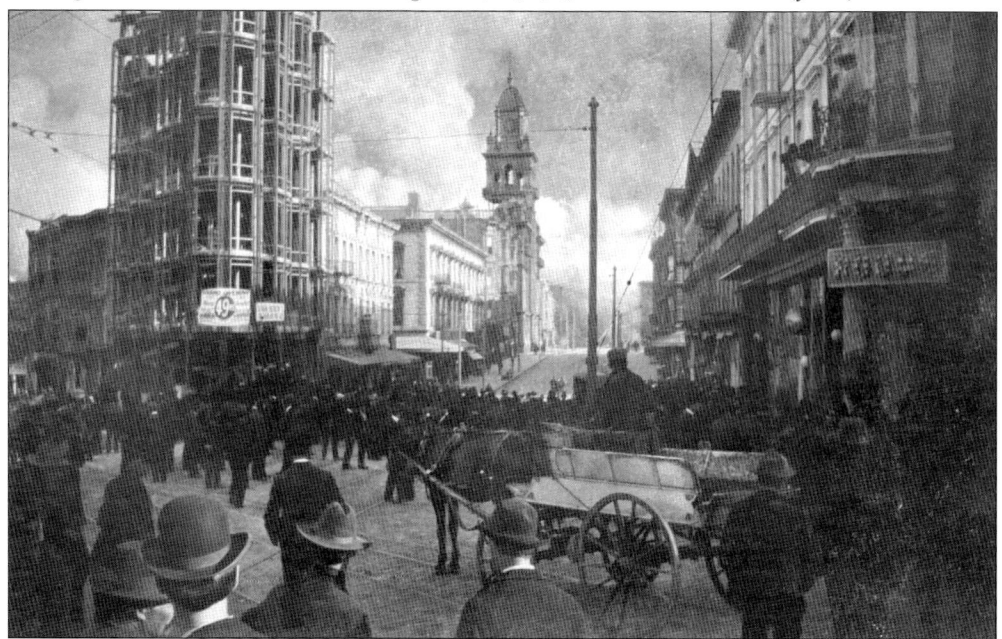

Then came 5:13 a.m., April 18, 1906. The fire caused by the great earthquake is burning up Kearny Street towards the Hall of Justice. The Sentinel building, on the left, was under construction at the time. The building is now called the Columbus Tower. Nearby, at Kearny and Pacific Streets, one of many firebreaks failed, and the flames moved through buildings on their way to North Beach. (JBM.)

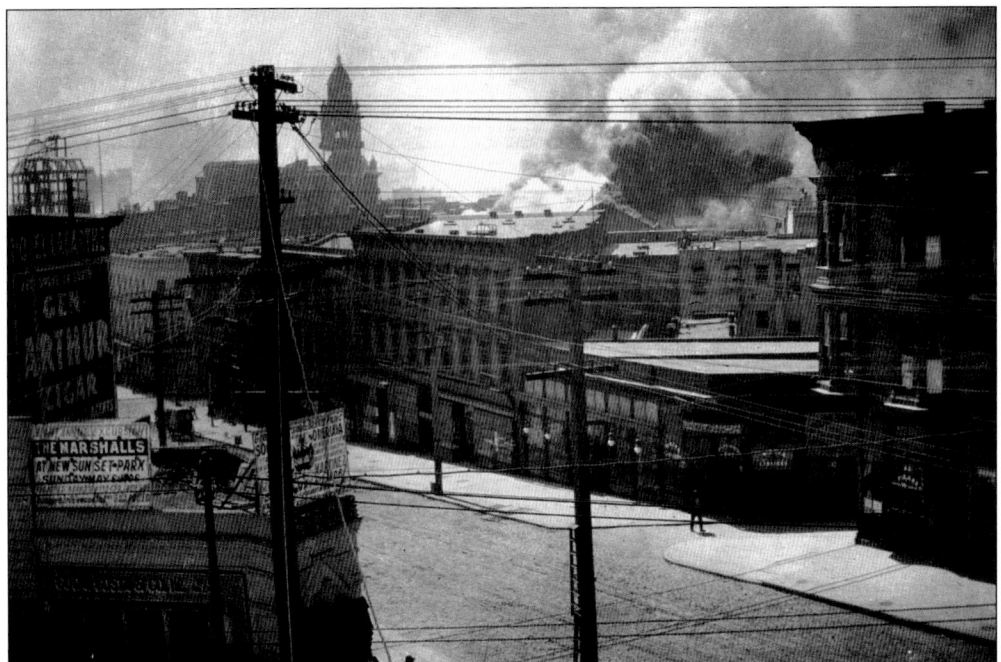

Here comes the fire up Broadway at Columbus Avenue. In the early evening of April 19, 1906, the fire jumped Washington Street and began its way up most of the streets in North Beach. According to the San Francisco Relief Survey, the multiple fires consumed 490 city blocks, another 32 blocks were partially burned down, and 28,188 buildings were destroyed. (JBM.)

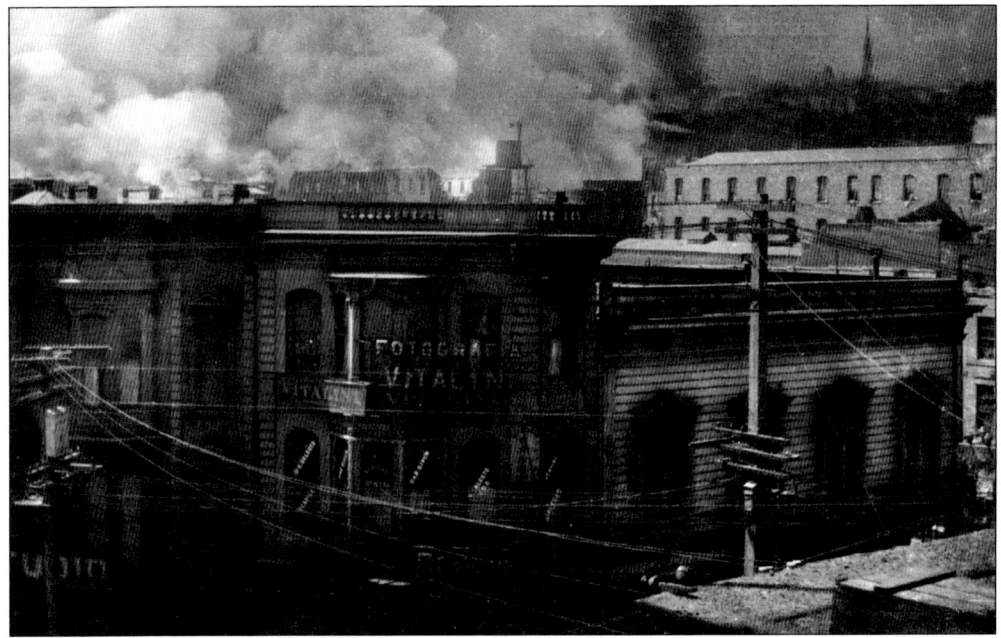

Just over the hill, flames eat up Russian Hill and move towards Columbus Avenue. One resident described the scene, saying, "All Telegraph Hill seemed to be on fire." At this point, firefighters allowed residents to douse flames with anything available, including wine-soaked burlap bags. There are reports that this method of beating out flames really did work. (JBM.)

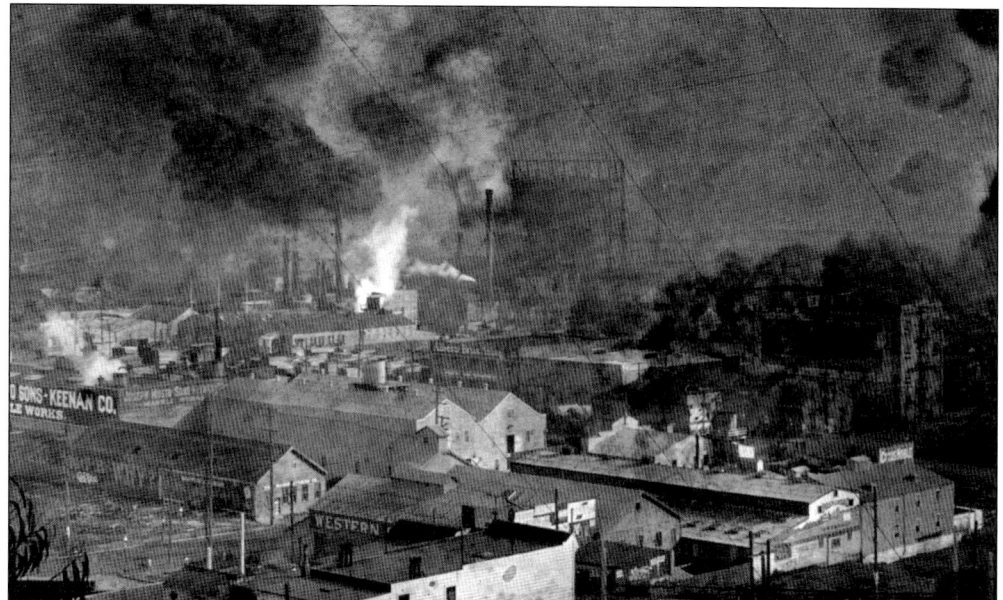

North Beach and Fisherman's Wharf are burning. Scenes like this drove many residents out of San Francisco. Many families decided to flee east to Oakland and Alameda or north to Santa Rosa and Sacramento, climbing aboard ferryboats crossing the bay to safety. Some climbed over the hill and then descended the Filbert and Greenwich stairs to the waterfront. There they boarded boats to Marin County, sadly leaving behind a city without water, with twisted streets, piles of rubble, and smoldering dreams. (JBM.)

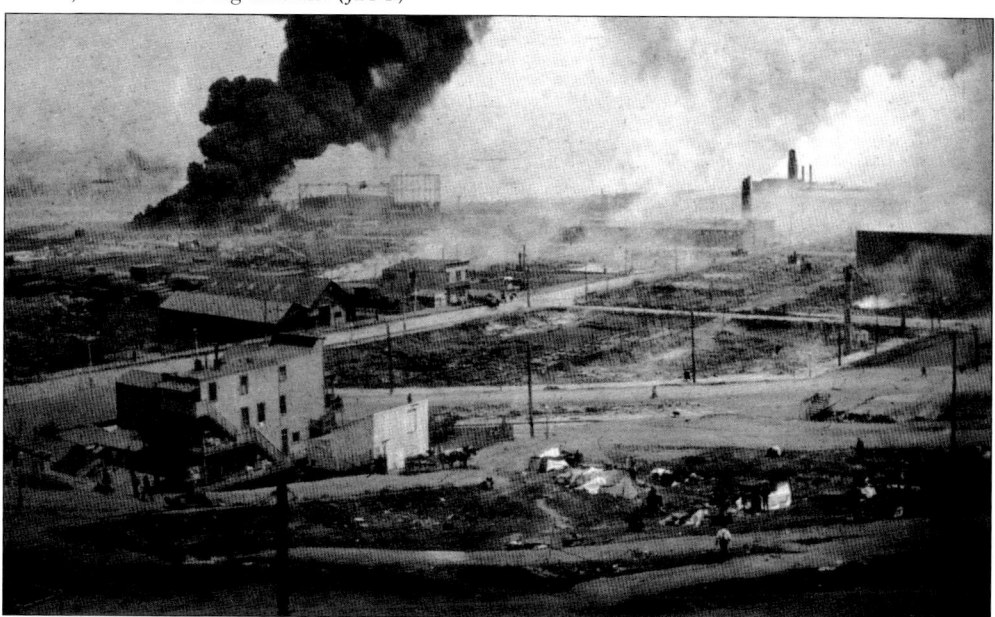

The North Beach district was one of the last in the city to deal with the fires. The aftermath of the fire is visible above. This image was taken from the photographer's home on Russian Hill. Some refugees are starting to camp out on the vacant lot in the bottom right of the photograph. That vacant land is now the site of the San Francisco Art Institute on Chestnut Street between Jones and Leavenworth Streets. (JBM.)

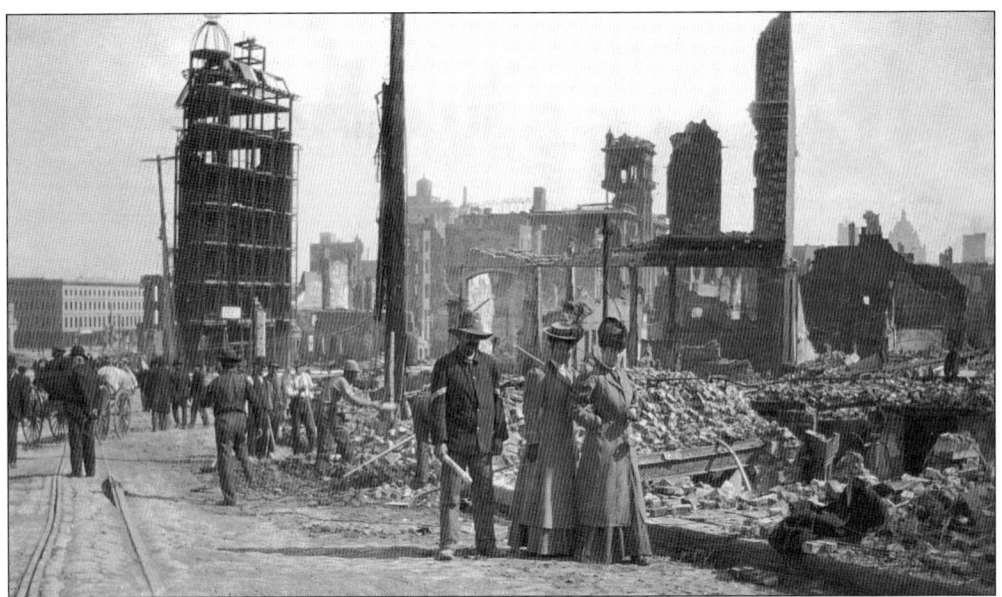

Frank Giovanessi, Lydia Cavalli (center), and Nina Monaco (right), relatives of photographer J. B. Monaco, pose in the rubble of the Monaco Studio on Market Street. The shell of the Columbus Tower is in the background. Even during this devastation, ladies and gentlemen wore their hats. (JBM.)

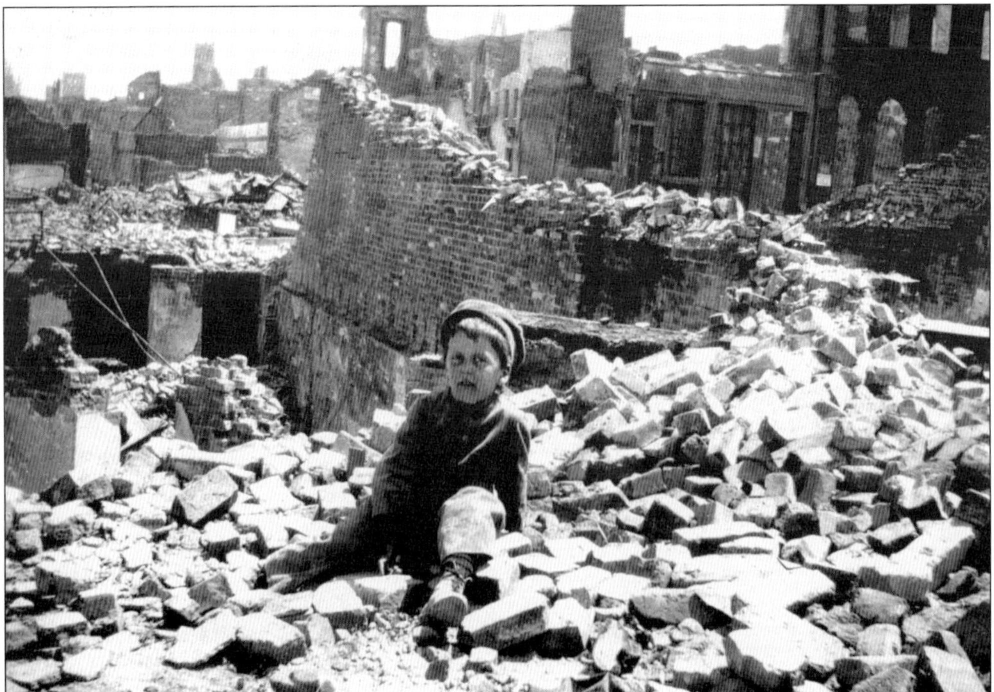

Dante Monaco, the son of the photographer, sits in the ruins of his father's studio, now just rubble at 702 Market Street. The image so poignantly depicts the devastation caused by the 1906 earthquake and fire. Most buildings in early San Francisco were constructed of either wood or brick, thus, unreinforced masonry structures collapsed. A rain of bricks fell all over North Beach. (JBM.)

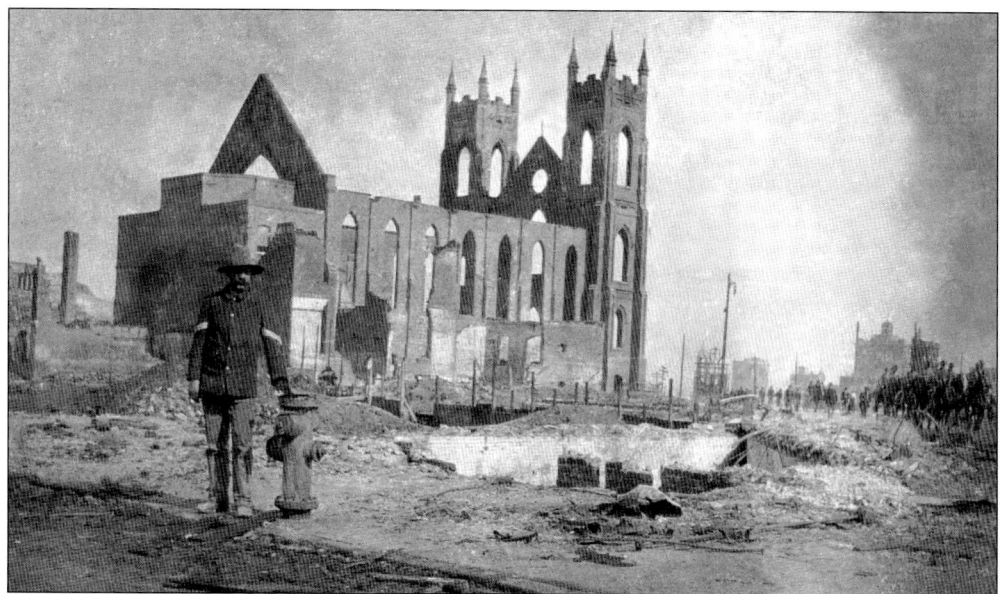

Frank Giovanessi ironically stands next to a fire hydrant with the ruins of St. Francis Church in the background. An account of the day relates, "Four or five days later, we went back and wandered among the ruins of what had been the Italian District, looking with heavy hearts for something in the smoking remains that would remind us of our home and the things dearest to us." (JBM.)

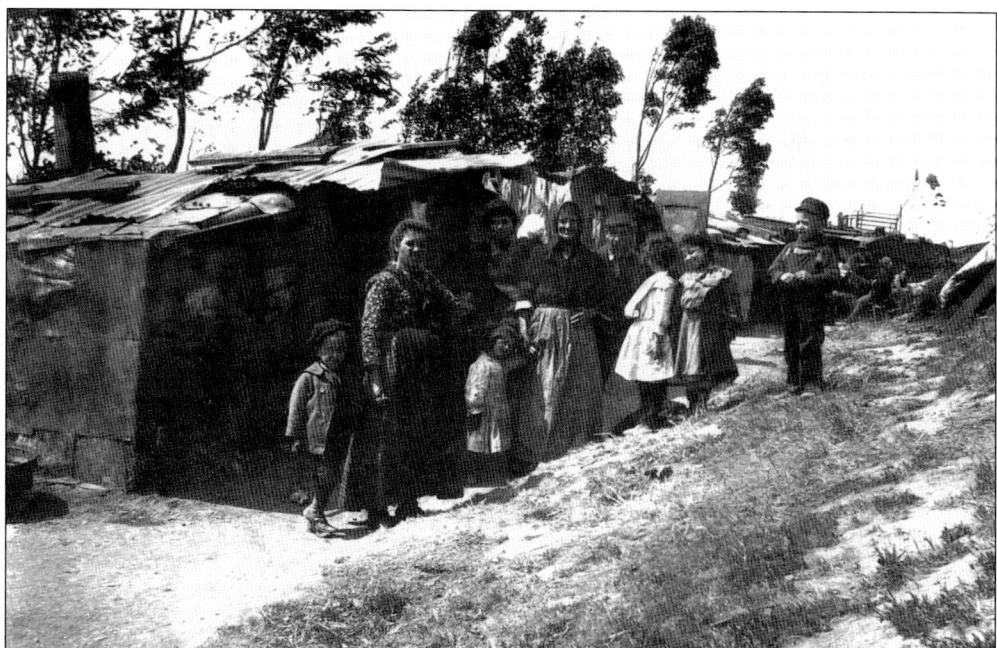

Refugees find shelter on Telegraph Hill in their shanty village. Residents of North Beach who had not evacuated north, east, or south via ferryboats set up camps. Accounts report people pushing chairs and carts piled high with belongings singed by fire, as if they were the finest and most expensive items. Perhaps this is where Larry Harris's famous verse—"The Damnedest, Finest Ruins"—on the description of post-1906 San Francisco found its inspiration. (JBM.)

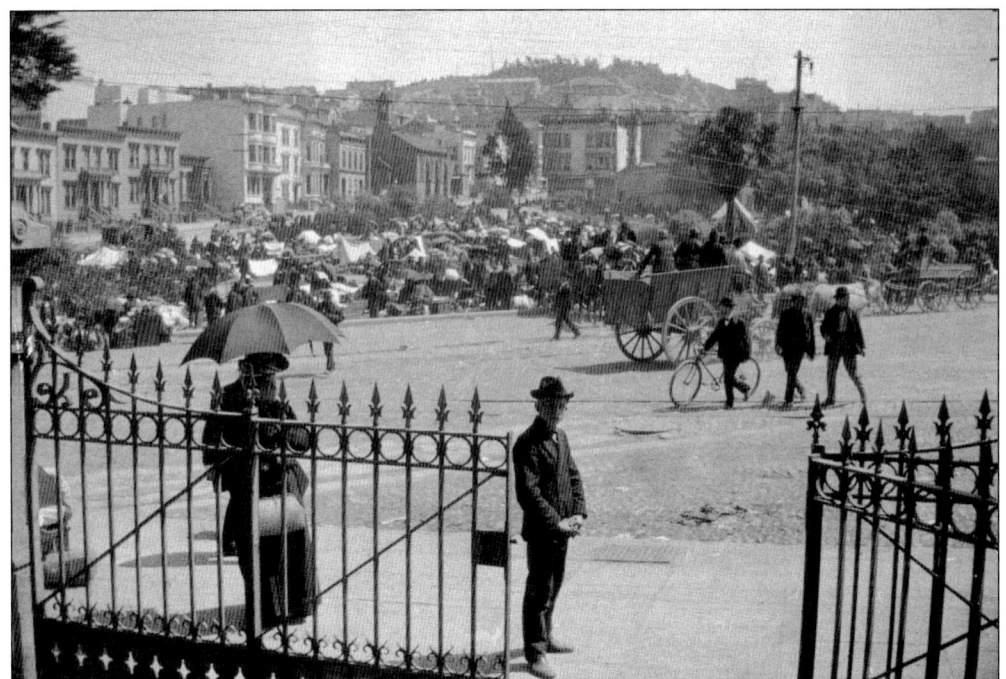

Refugees made temporary camps in the plaza now called Washington Square in the heart of North Beach. More than 600 refugees lived in the square for over one year. Originally, army tents sheltered 40,000 of the 300,000 homeless in 25 refugee camps all over the city. Camps were replaced by small "earthquake cottages." The last camp in the city came down in June 1908. (JBM.)

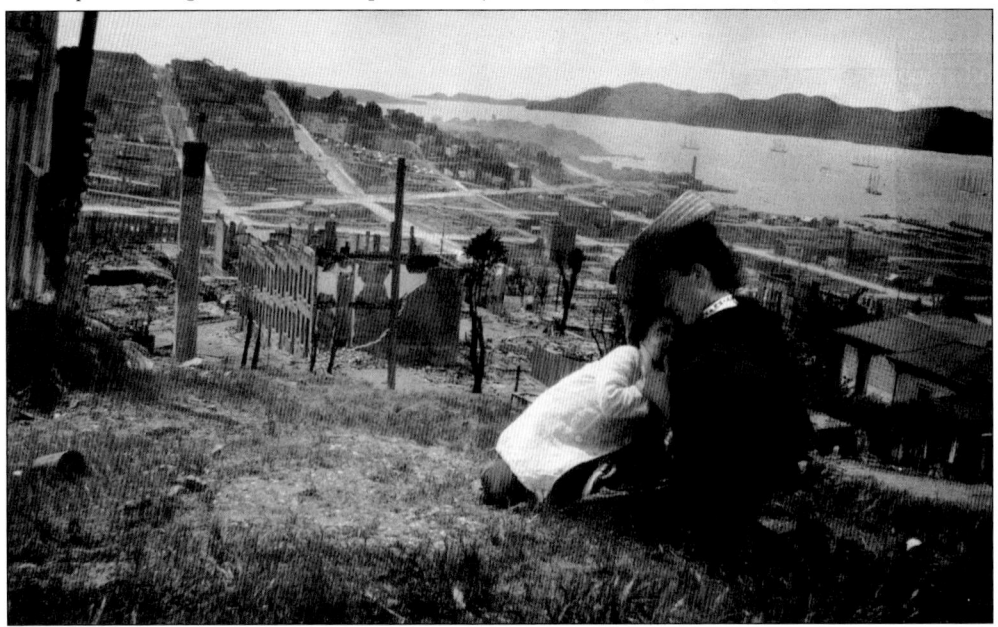

The fire was out, but smoke hung heavy over the city for days. This is Catherine Monaco, wife of the photographer, and their son, Dante, on Telegraph Hill over looking Columbus Avenue. This is possibly one of the most poignant images available. It says everything needed to know about devastation, tragedy, and the spirit to live. (JBM.)

Two

FROM THE BEACH TO THE HILL

In 1914, Clarence Edwards said of the North Beach area, in *Bohemian San Francisco*, "this area was the first part of San Francisco to rebuild after the great fire, and in its rebuilding, it recovered all of its former characteristics, which is more than can be said of any other part of the rebuilt city." After the 1906 earthquake and fire, many German, Russian, and Eastern Europeans moved out of North Beach, while Italian in-migration continued. According to historical records, the Italian influence on North Beach peaked between the two world wars, when over 60,000 noted their ancestry as Italian. By the 1920s, the area was known as "Little Italy."

While cost of living in the area has been high for years, new development is, and always has been restricted by topographical constraints. Construction has also deferred to the cliffside location, resulting in steps, wooden walkways, footpaths, and winding streets. Street paving of Montgomery and Alta Streets did not occur until 1931, or on Union and Calhoun Streets until 1939.

During Prohibition there were speakeasies, and in the 1950s and 1960s there were nightclubs and renowned restaurants, mostly on Columbus Avenue and Broadway. Other streets, such as Vallejo, Grant, Union, and Green, provided neighborhood services, such as barbershops, shoe repairs, groceries, and pharmacies. Slowly but surely, immigrant families—the blue-collar workers—moved out into the Sunset or Richmond districts, or just out of town. Luckily, the struggle to save North Beach and Telegraph Hill from major redevelopment has been largely successful. Rents and home values escalated after the 1970s, and now Telegraph Hill is home to wealthy and successful individuals attracted by the cosmopolitan feel and breathtaking views. Beginning in the late 1970s and continuing today, San Francisco's central business district proliferated. The neighborhood became much sought after by an increasing influx of well-paid white-collar workers. An example of tremendous change was replacement of the historic Montgomery block (also known as the Monkey block) with the Transamerica Pyramid in 1972.

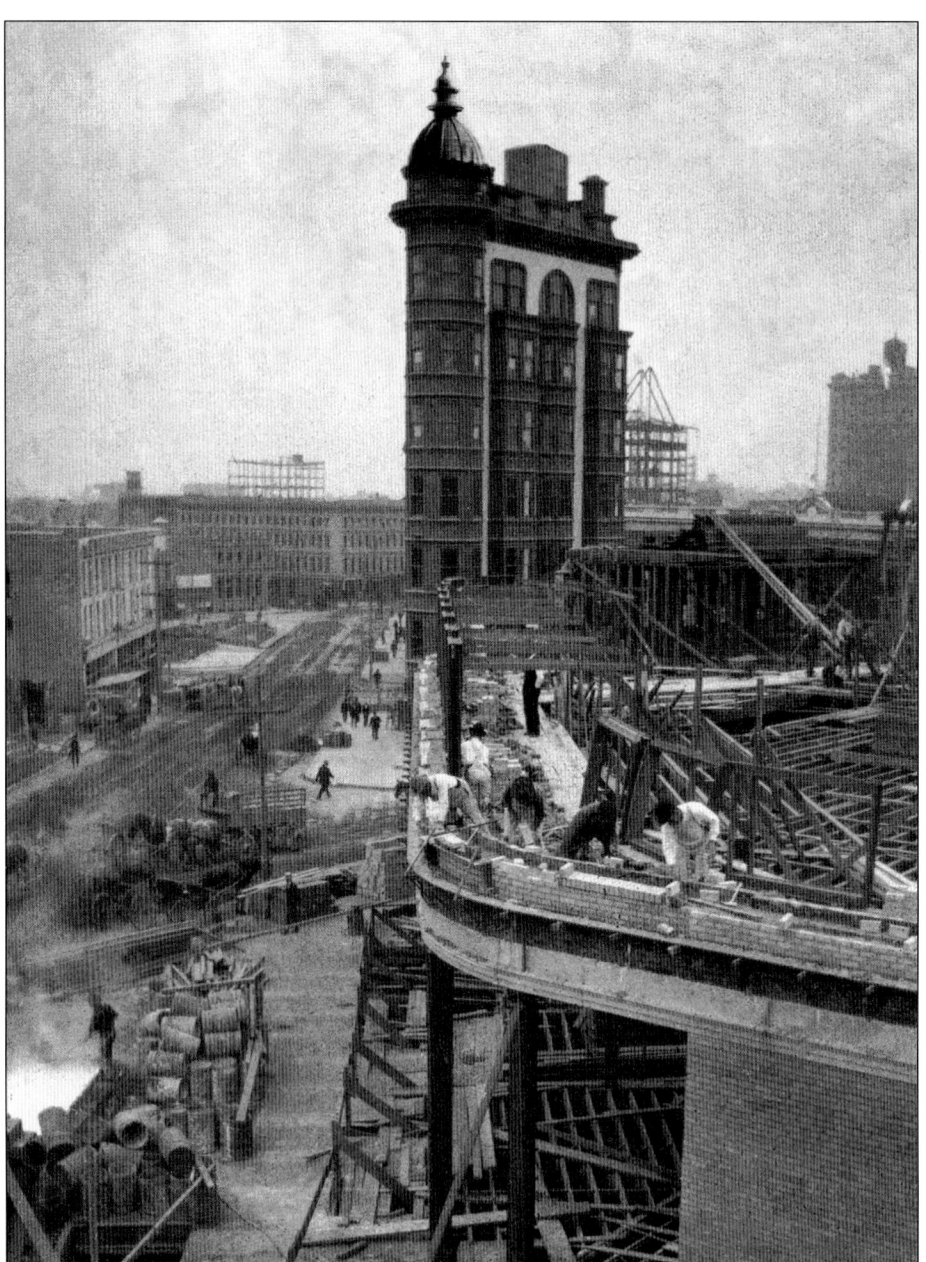

In the foreground is reconstruction of the St. Paul Hotel after the 1906 earthquake and fire. It is still a hotel located at 935 Kearny Street. In the background is the famous Columbus Tower building at 916 Kearney Street, which occupies the block surrounded by Columbus Avenue, Kearny Street, and Jackson Street. Also known as the Sentinel building and the San Francisco Flat Iron building, construction began prior to the 1906 earthquake and fire. Only the frame survived, and the building was ultimately completed in 1907. It is designated San Francisco Landmark No. 155. The top floor initially housed the headquarters of the notorious Abe Ruef, a local political figure at the time. At one time it housed Caesar's, the restaurant credited with creation of the caesar salad. Film director Francis Ford Coppola purchased and renovated the structure, which houses his American Zoetrope Studio. (JBM.)

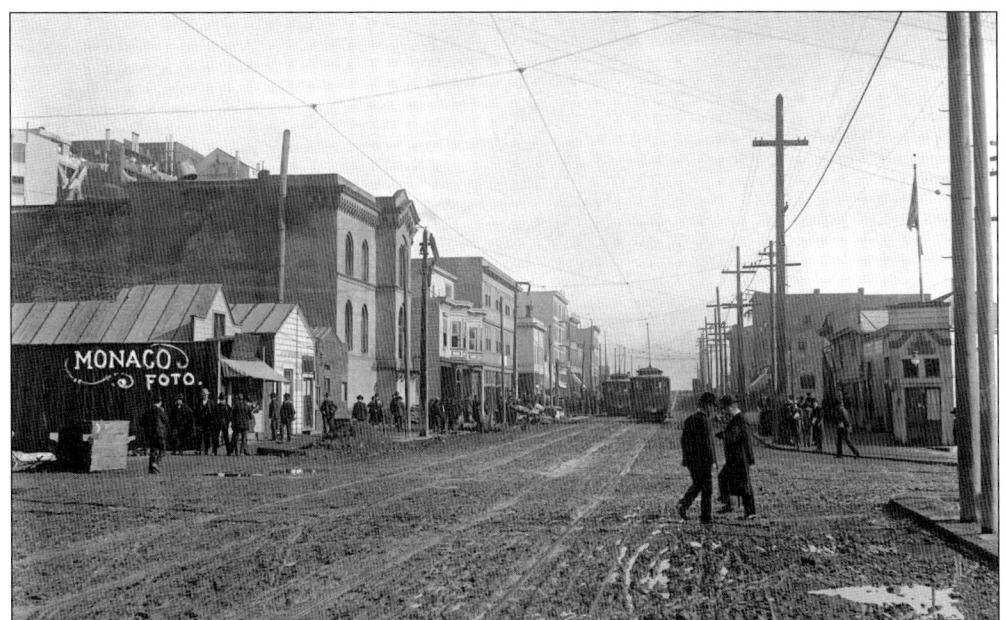

After the 1906 disaster destroyed the Monaco Photographic Studio, it was relocated here on Broadway at the corner of Columbus Avenue. The logo on the side of the building is actually etched onto the glass negative and not on the building itself. This site is now the Condor Club, where topless dancing began. (JBM.)

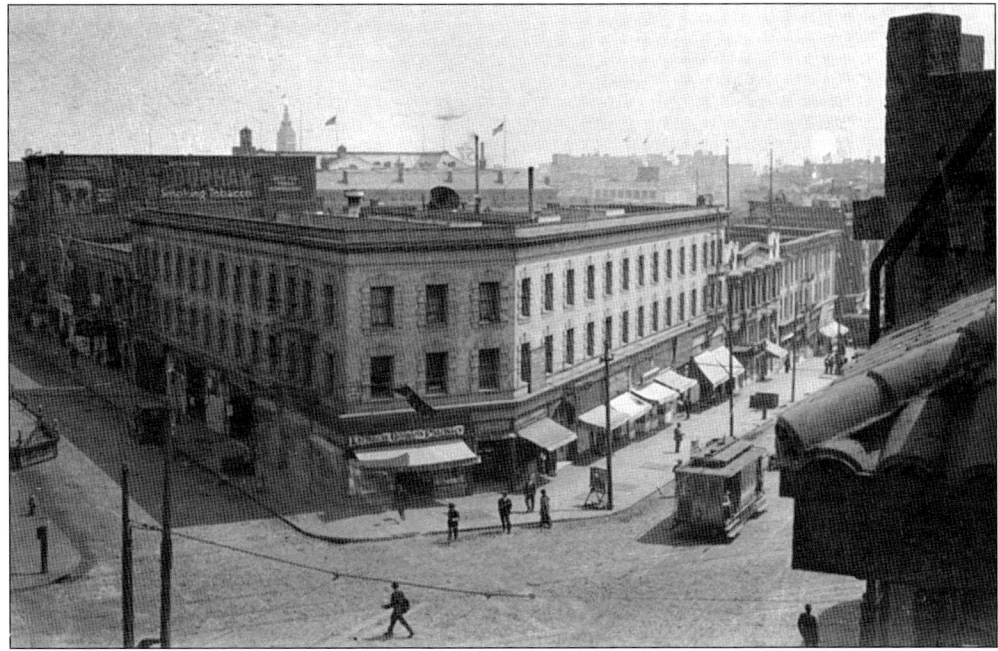

Pictured here is Columbus Avenue at Pacific Street with the Commercial Hotel and the Calegaris Pharmacy on the corner. Joseph Calegaris was Genoa-born in 1835, becoming a university graduate in chemistry and pharmacy. After arriving in the city, he became a prominent pharmacist, importing medicines from Italy, France, and Germany. At one time, the Commercial Hotel advertised 200 sunny rooms for 50¢ per day or $1.50 per week. (JBM.)

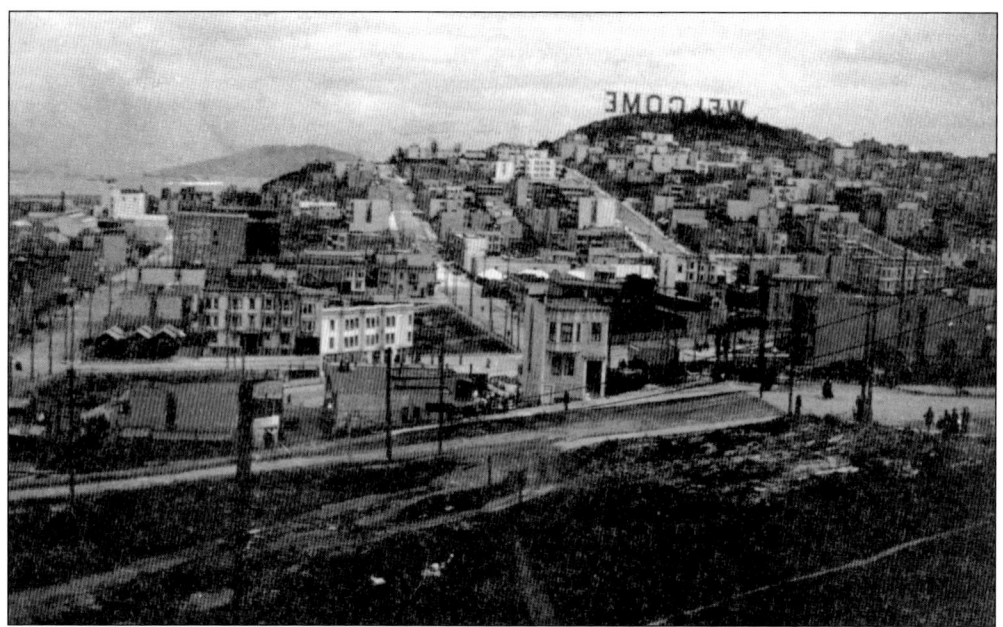

A large welcome sign sits atop Telegraph Hill in 1908. It was constructed to welcome the Great White Fleet. The 50-foot-high letters could be seen 30 miles away. When the fleet arrived in San Francisco on May 6, the hills surrounding the city by the bay were packed with thousands of greeters. (JBM.)

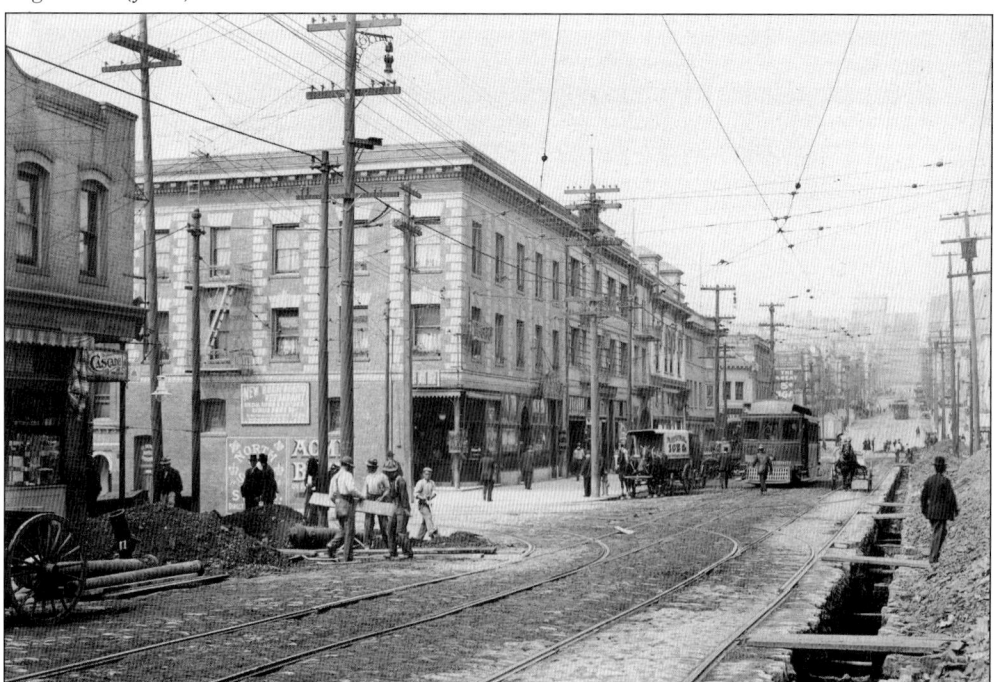

This is Broadway at Kearny Street in 1910. At the far left is the Mint Saloon, at the center left is the New Buon Gusto Restaurant building with a sign reading "Regular dinner 50 cents." This portion of Broadway was primarily grocers, restaurants, lodging houses, hotels, and saloons. Pacific Street, just south of Broadway, was the center of the notorious Barbary Coast. (SFHC.)

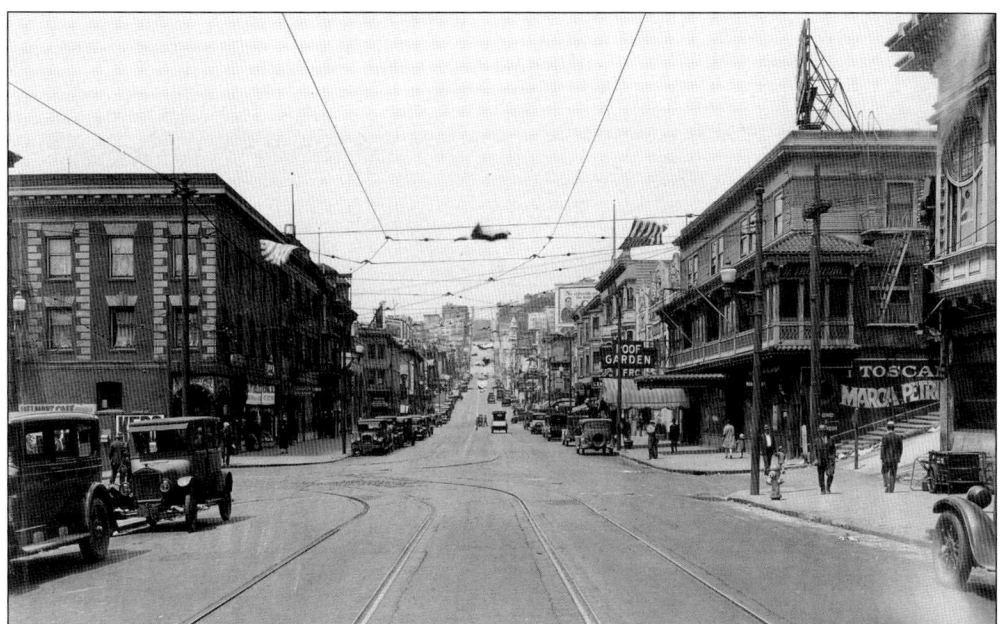

Here again is the corner of Broadway and Kearny Street, now in 1929. On the right is Il Trovatore and a corner of the Fior d' Italia. The establishment eventually grew to a size that could seat 750 and serve 1,500 meals a day. Il Trovatore was established by Archimede Puccinelli, who came to San Francisco alone at the age of 11. (SFHC.)

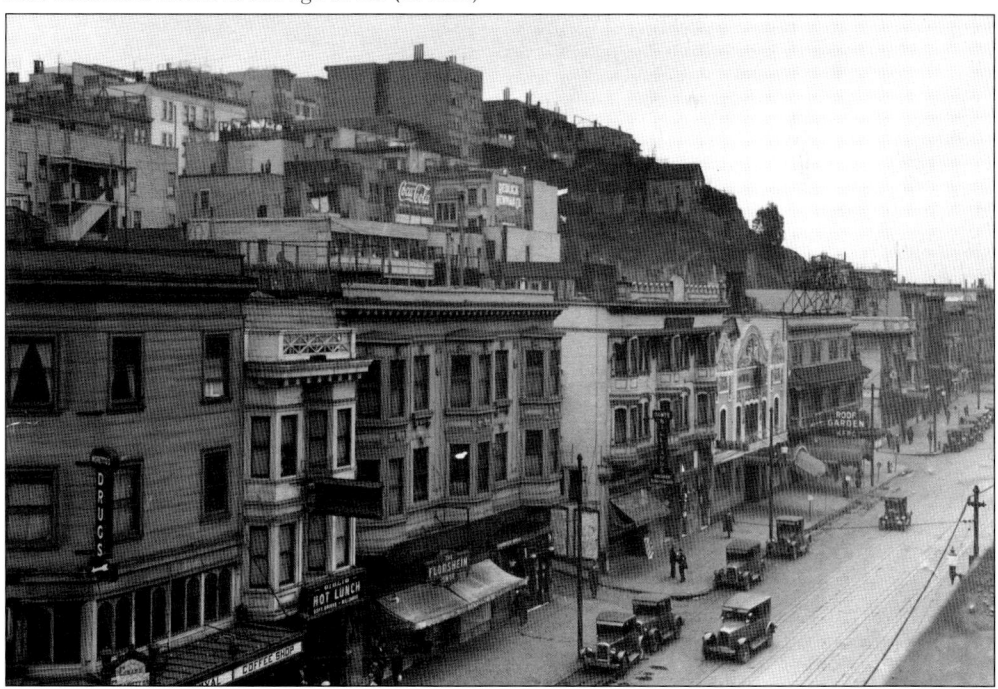

On Broadway, a major neighborhood street, in the 1920s are Moretto's drugstore, Giglio's Hot Lunch spot, a Florshein shoe store, and Dante Billiards. This daytime image belies the fact that there were hundreds of speakeasies throughout San Francisco, including a number in this area. (SFHC.)

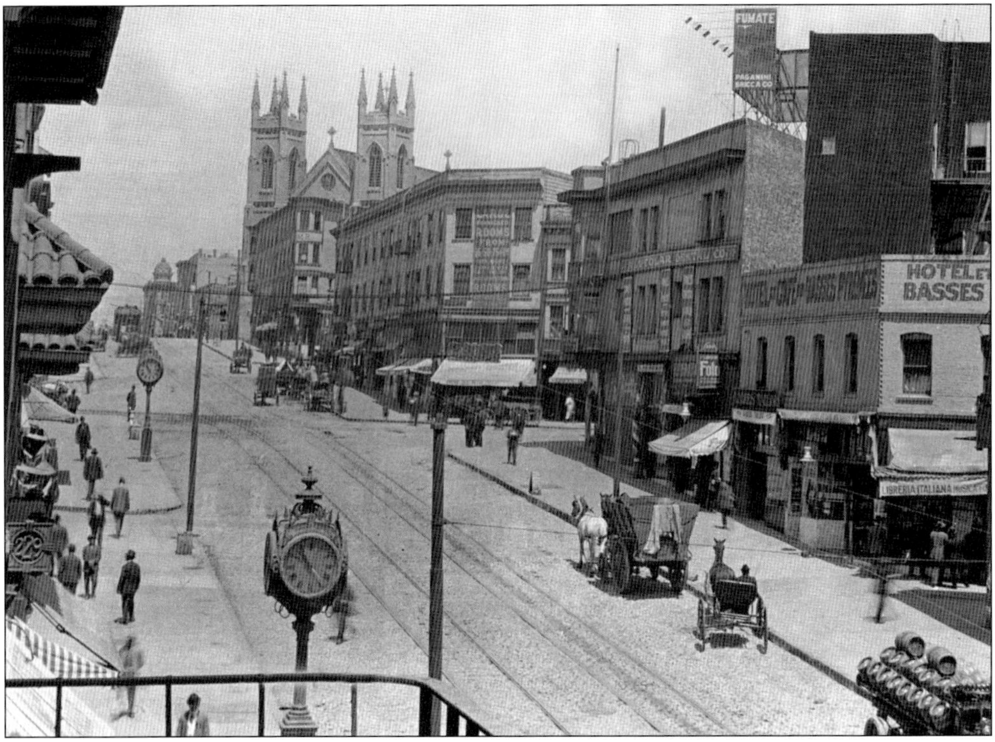

This view looks north on Columbus Avenue in 1910. The photograph was taken from the J. B. Monaco studio at 205 Columbus Avenue at 10:53 a.m., as shown on the beautiful ornate clock. This street began as the old Presidio trail in 1776. The trail was developed into Montgomery Street in 1873. In 1909, in honor of the heroic Italian efforts during the 1906 disaster, it was renamed Columbus Avenue in honor of the Italian explorer. (Both, JBM.)

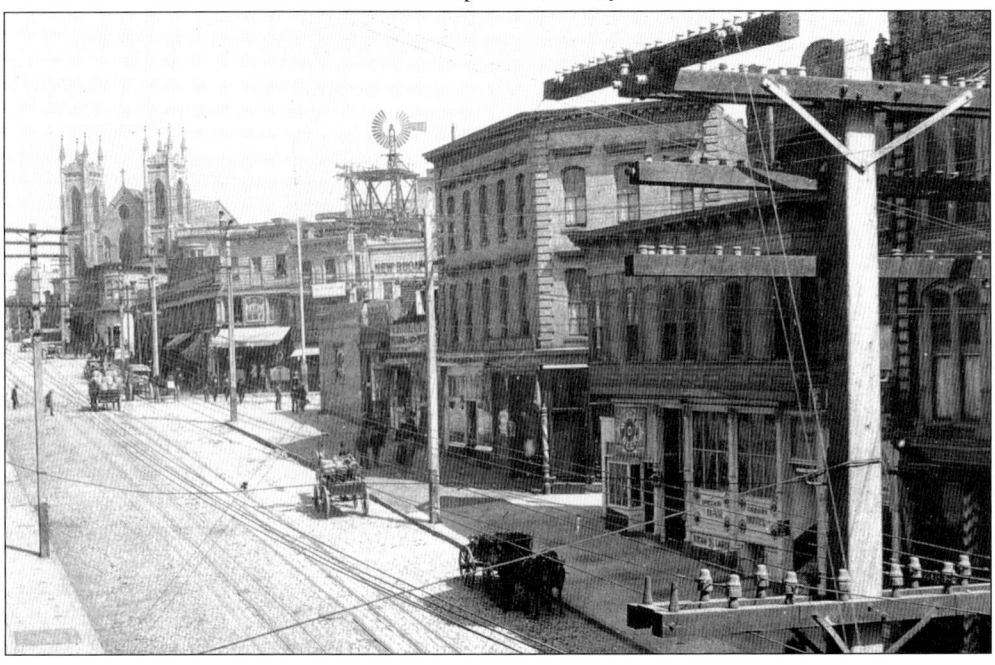

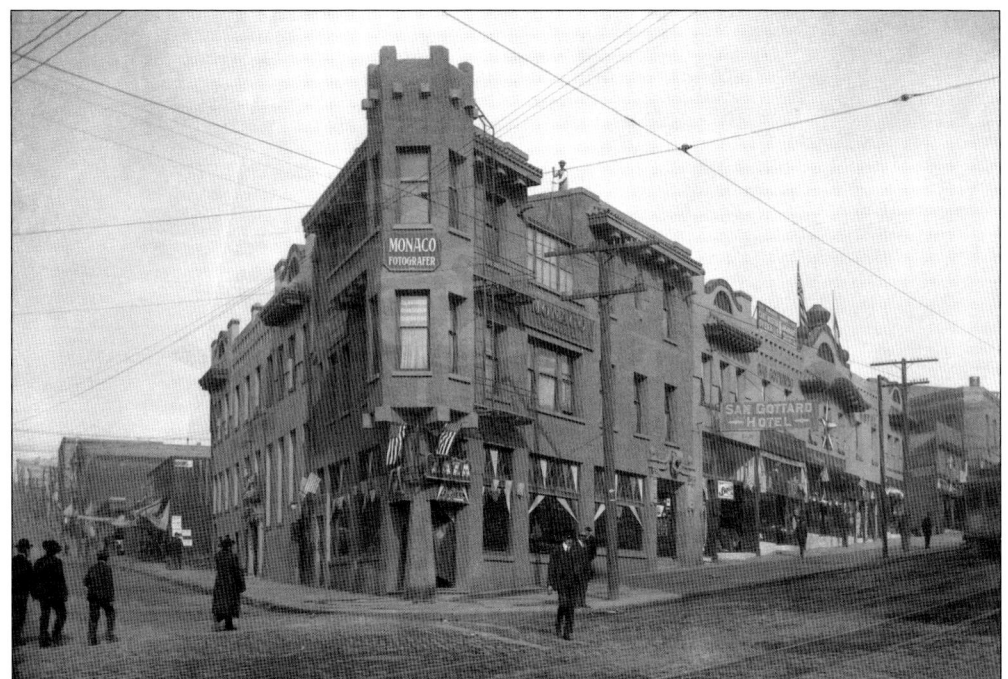

When the Monaco Studio near Market Street was destroyed by the 1906 fire, the photographer moved his business to Broadway temporarily then here to 205 Columbus Avenue. The St. Gottard Hotel is to the right. Also pictured is the Franzi Brothers shop, with many American and Swiss flags. Records indicate a Swiss population of 1,696 in 1890, of 2,806 in 1920, and 8,120 in 1930. (JBM.)

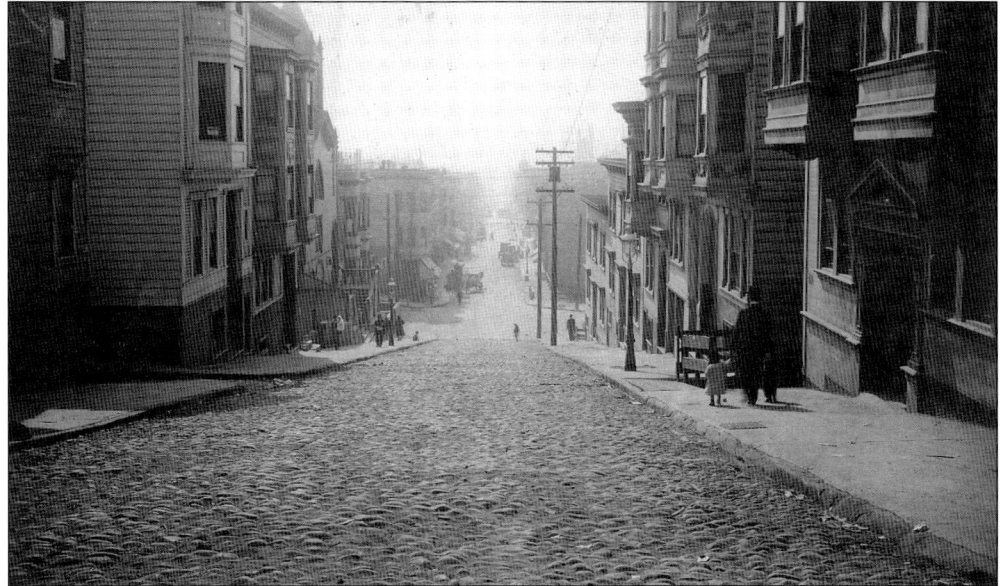

This is Grant Avenue, looking south from Greenwich Street on October 14, 1915. Most of the earthquake reconstruction is complete. However, the autumn months of 1915 were rife with earthquakes—October 1 at 7:26 a.m. on the San Andreas fault and October 7 at 9:26 p.m. on the Hayward fault. (JBM.)

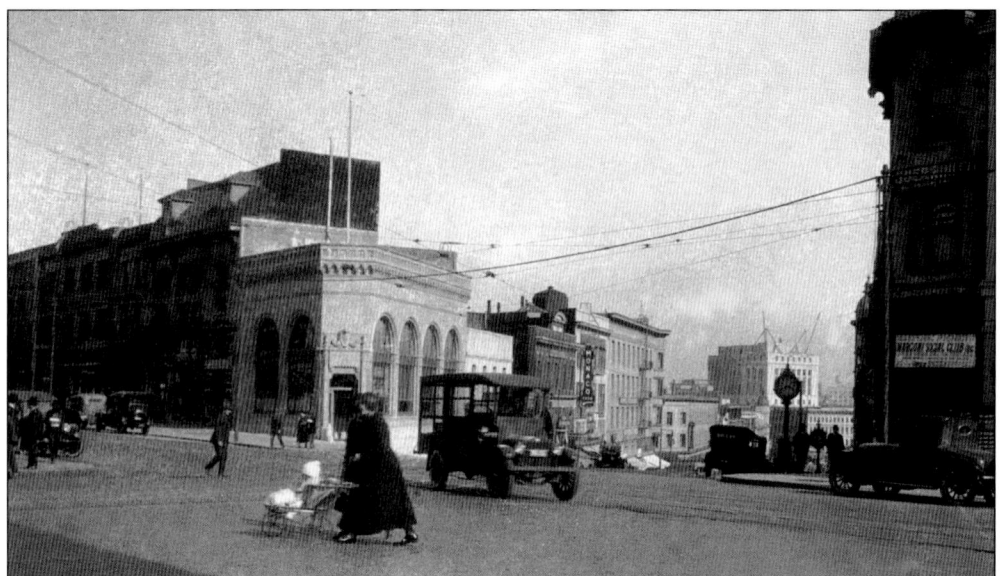

Here is Columbus Avenue at Broadway in the 1920s. The clock reads 3:40 p.m. The building on the right housed the Guerrini Accordion Factory. Guerrini accordions are considered some of the finest around the world. The company was founded in 1903 by Paul Guerrini and Rafaelo Carbonari, who sold the company to Pasquale Petromilli and Colombo Piatanesi in 1907. (JBM.)

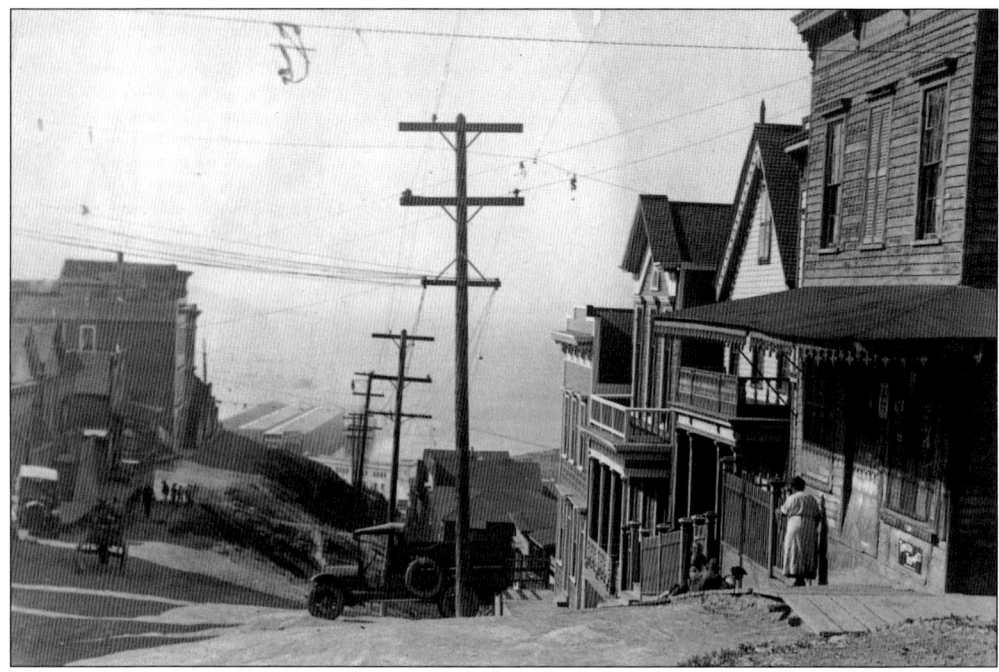

Here is Montgomery Street near Union Street in 1920. The woman is standing in front of Meisel's store. German immigrant Herman A. Meisel opened his store in 1881, selling groceries, sundries, and whisky. Years later, it became the Dead Fish Café, run by Honore Gledhill. An article in the November 11, 1933, *Berkeley Daily Gazette* reported that a Mrs. Gledhill "stood last night in front of the Dead Fish Café, artist colony rendezvous, and took pot shots at Coit Memorial Tower with a 22-caliber revolver." (SFHC.)

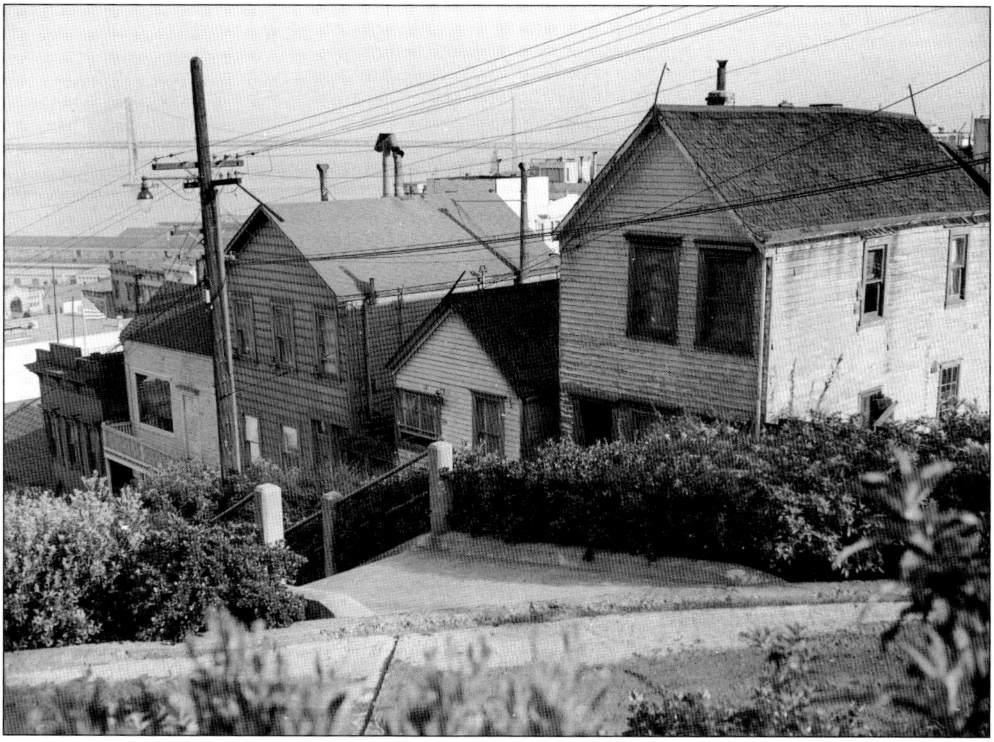

These houses are on the 300 block of Filbert Street in 1940. In the distance are docks and the San Francisco–Oakland Bay Bridge. Note the stairway down the hill just below Telegraph Hill Boulevard and Coit Tower. The Filbert steps meander through several blocks of hillside dwellings and spectacular views, ending up on Sansome Street at the base of Telegraph Hill. (LOC.)

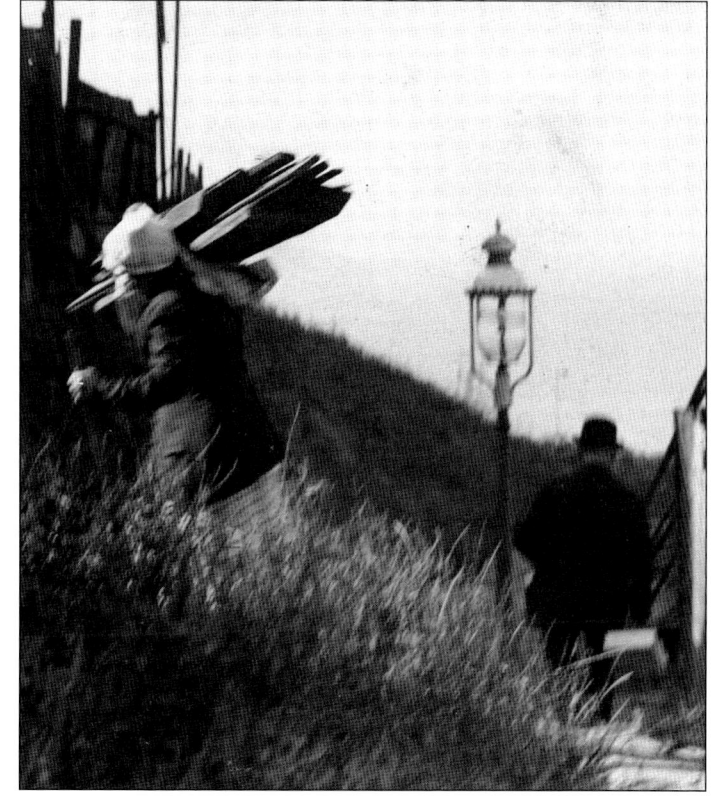

Hard work was the standard of the day. Here, on June 3, 1932, a woman carries wood while a man, the usual hat atop his head, walks past on a dirt path towards one of the many stairways that provided access to Telegraph Hill. (SFHC.)

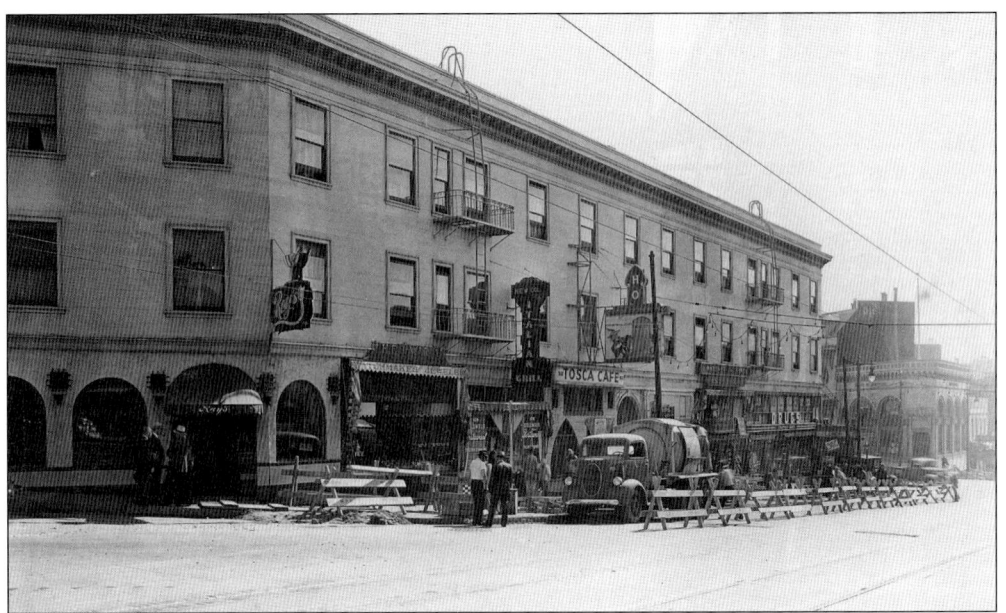

This is an image of Broadway that Herb Caen refers to in his newspaper column of March 14, 1996, which reads, "Talk of the North Beach saloon set: May Ditano, owner of the 70-yr-old Columbus Restaurant at 611 Broadway, being told by her landlord that she'll have to move out May 31." (SFHC.)

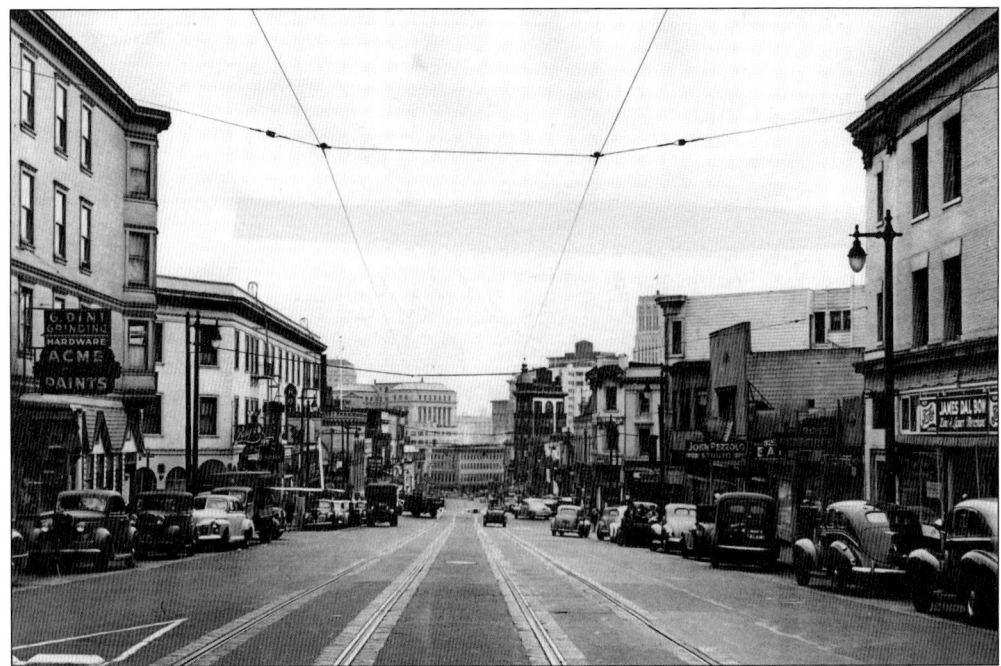

This view looks south down Columbus Avenue on August 19, 1944. Down the street, at 414 Columbus Avenue, was the Nebbia Pastry Shop. *Nebbia* means fog in Italian—appropriate for San Francisco. The storefront is still there and so are the frescos of angels on the ceiling, dating back to the early 1900s. These lovely murals are of rosy cherubs baking, rolling pastry dough, and serving coffee. (CAA.)

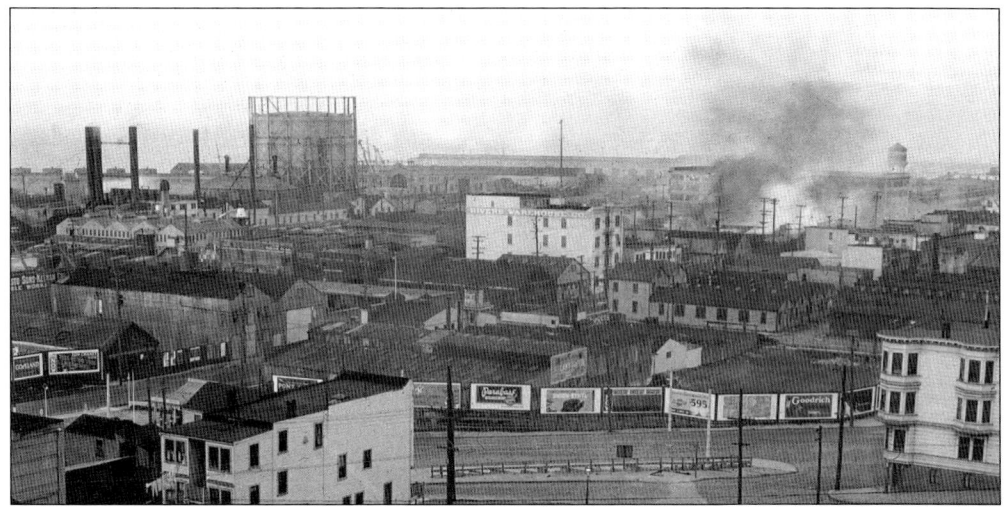

On the eastern side of Telegraph Hill was the industrial area of North Beach. There was a horse lot in the center at one time. Large signs advertise Beech Nut Fruit drops and Can't Bust 'Em overalls. One of the major businesses in the photograph above is the Musto Sons Keenan Company at the far right. Their marble works supplied the new San Francisco City Hall building. The family business was begun in San Francisco in 1868 by Joseph Musto, a fifth-generation Italian stonecutter and tile setter. He brought with him the skills of his forefathers and established the Musto Steam Marble Mill. By 1949, the newly named Musto-Keenan Company had gained a reputation for making top-quality diamond tools to cut marble and tile faster and more efficiently. (Both, JBM.)

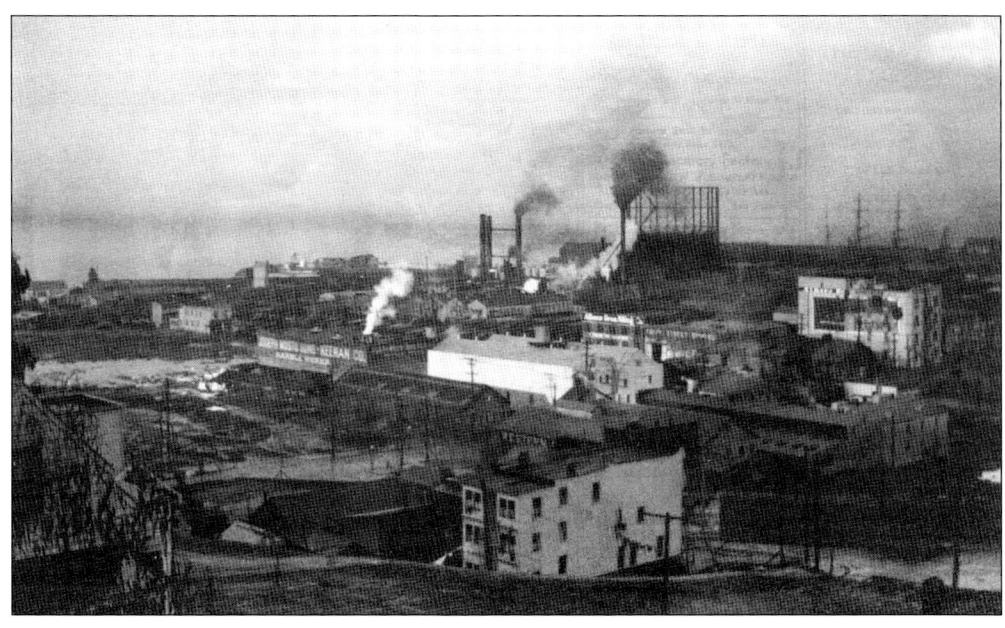

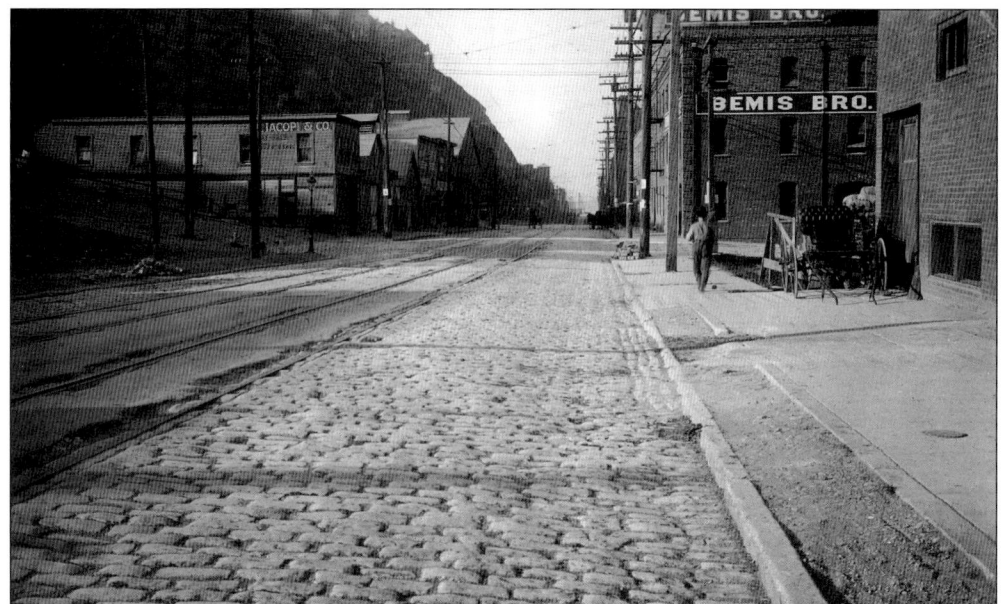

Another industrial area was this one on Sansome Street, looking north from Broadway on October 15, 1915. The Bemis Brothers Bag Company is on the right at 1000 Sansome Street. The company made burlap and cotton bags. Just down the way at 202 Green Street, in a simple laboratory, Philo Taylor Farnsworth, U.S. pioneer in electronics, invented and patented the first operational all-electronic television system on September 7, 1927. (SFHC.)

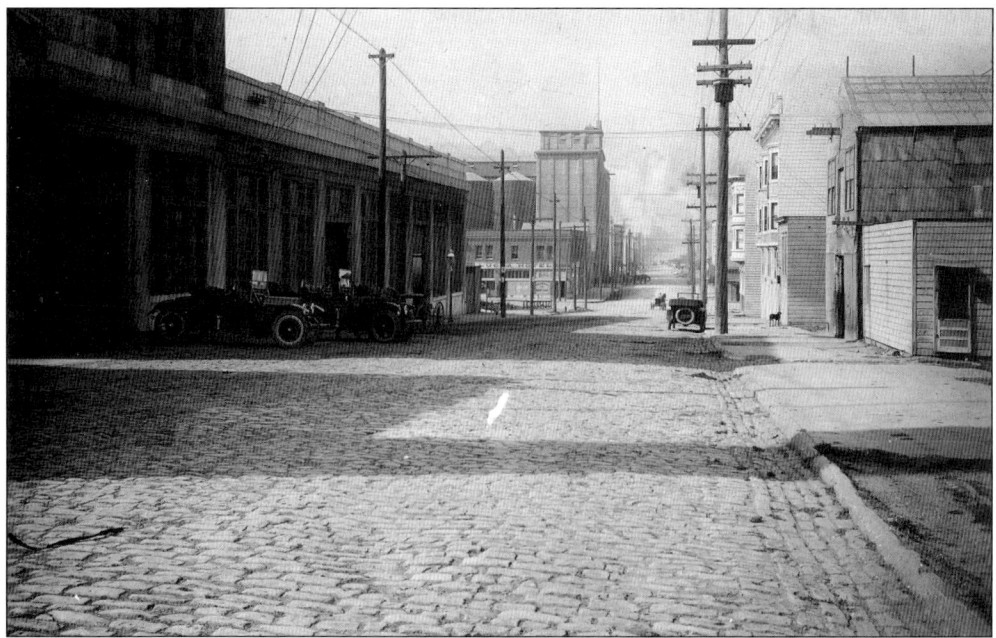

This is Francisco Street, looking west from Stockton Street, on October 14, 1915. The large structure down the street was the North Beach Malt House. It is Historic Landmark No. 129, located in the city block of Francisco, Mason, and Powell Streets. The Malt House served as a malting factory and brewery for 40 years. Nearly destroyed by fire in 1906, it was rebuilt by George W. Bauer. (SFHC.)

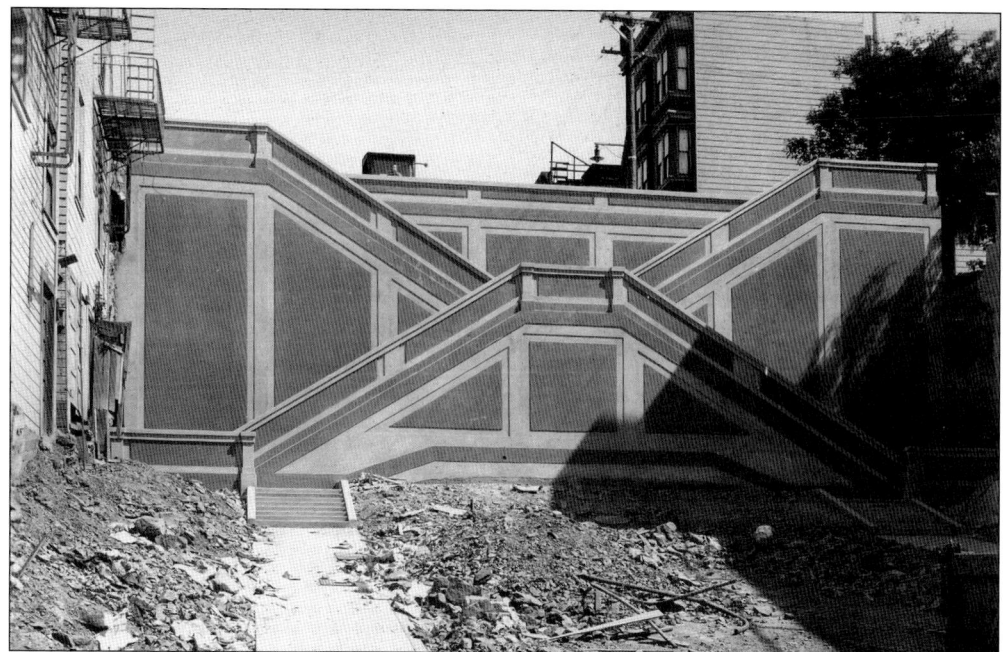

These are the fabulous steps on Montgomery Street, just north of Green Street. This department of public works photograph was taken on June 5, 1928. These steps are a graceful alternative to the steep climb up a hill. (SFHC.)

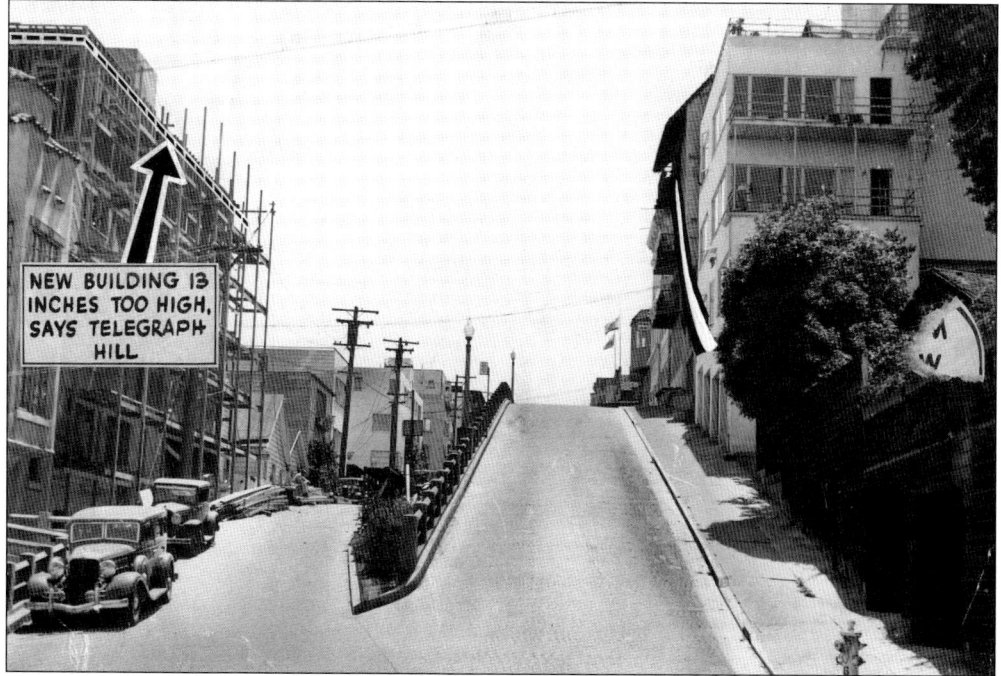

This view is from the top of the Montgomery Street steps in this image taken on September 10, 1940. Two buildings have signs posted for apartments to rent. Local residents likely did not realize how the rents of this picturesque area of San Francisco would skyrocket in the next few decades. (SFHC.)

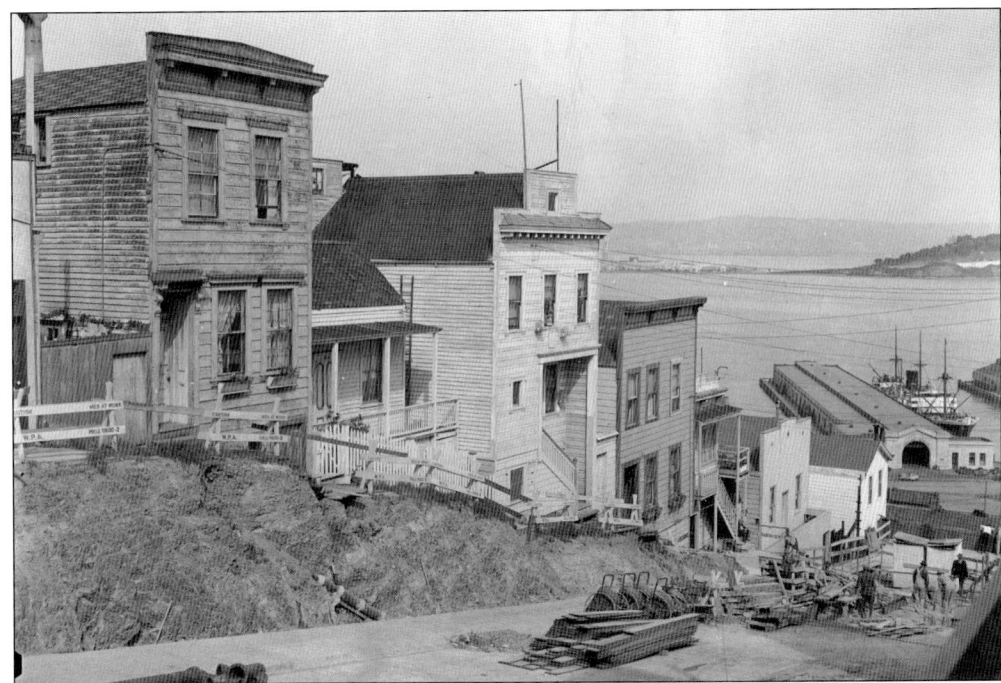

These two photographs are of Union Street in 1940. Above is the north side, east of Montgomery Street, and below is the south side, east of Montgomery Street. Most of these houses date back to the 1800s. The department of public works is upgrading the street. At the end of the street and to the right is Pier 19, with a large ship docked, and in the distance is Treasure Island, complete with the ongoing Golden Gate International Exposition. Below is the south side of Union Street. What a charming view of three historic gems. In the center is the former Cooney home at 291 Union, one of the oldest in San Francisco. Built in the mid-1800s by John Joseph Cooney, an Irish immigrant, it had a grocery store on the bottom level until 1906. The cottages adjacent were built around 1857. Very close to the smaller structure at the far right was H. C. Hudson's coffee and spice mill, in operation between 1851 and 1855. (Both, LOC.)

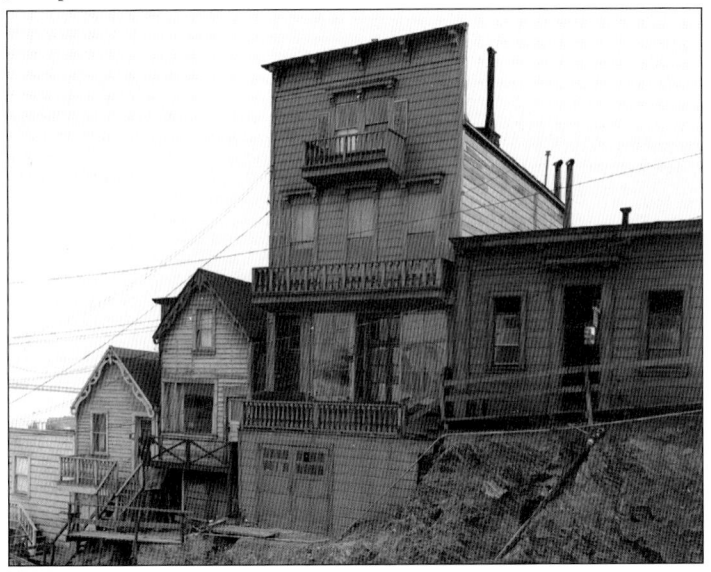

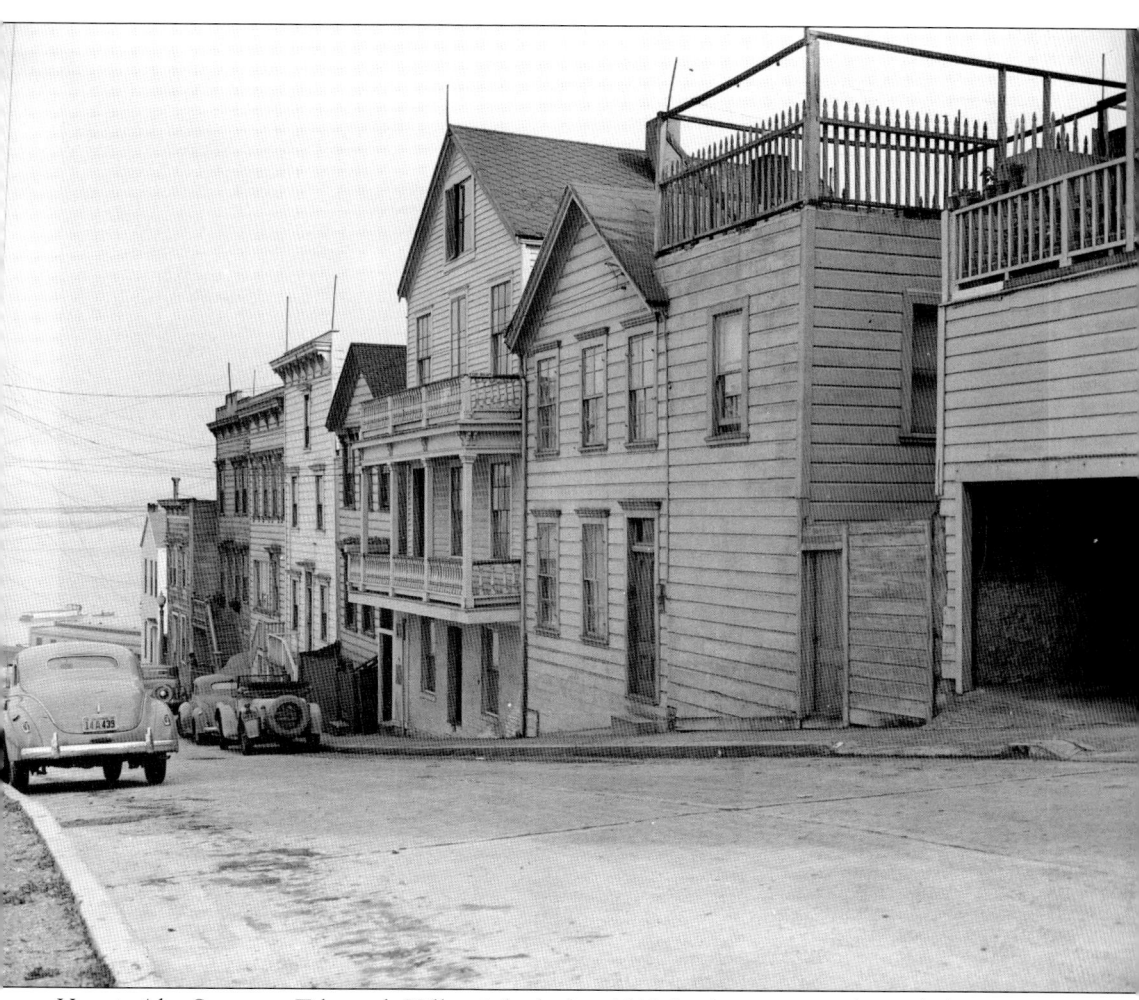

Here is Alta Street on Telegraph Hill as it looked in 1940. In the center, with two balconies, is 31 Alta, built by Captain Andrews around 1852, and said to be the oldest house on the street. In the 1920s, the then-current owner's wife converted the lower level into a tavern, causing quite a stir in the neighborhood. From its earliest days, Telegraph Hill attracted working-class immigrants from around the world. Workers' homes were affordable, because at the time wealthier citizens did not care for the steep climbs up precarious hills. The hill was mostly occupied by Irish immigrants from the Gold Rush days until the late 1900s. (LOC.)

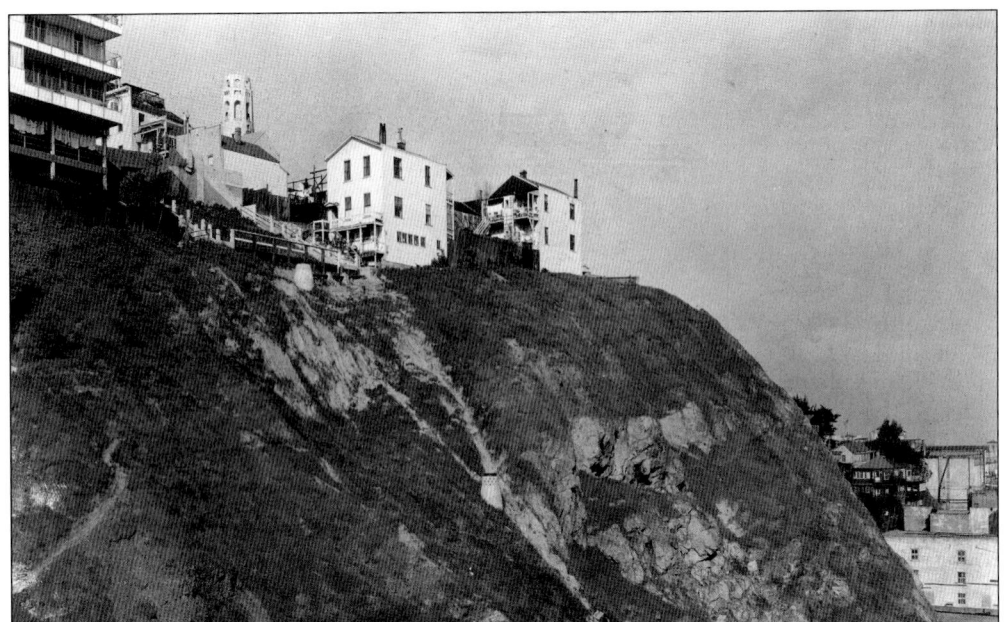

The February 17, 1942, image above shows the west side of Sansome Street below Union Street. Clearly the crumbling hillside is sensitive to erosion and landslides. This unstable area of Telegraph Hill is due in part to the extensive quarrying that took place around the start of the 20th century. Sailing ships brought cargo to San Francisco, and when leaving the port empty, rocks from the hill were used for ballast. The image below is of the cliff near the Filbert Street stairway below Alta Street. (SFHC.)

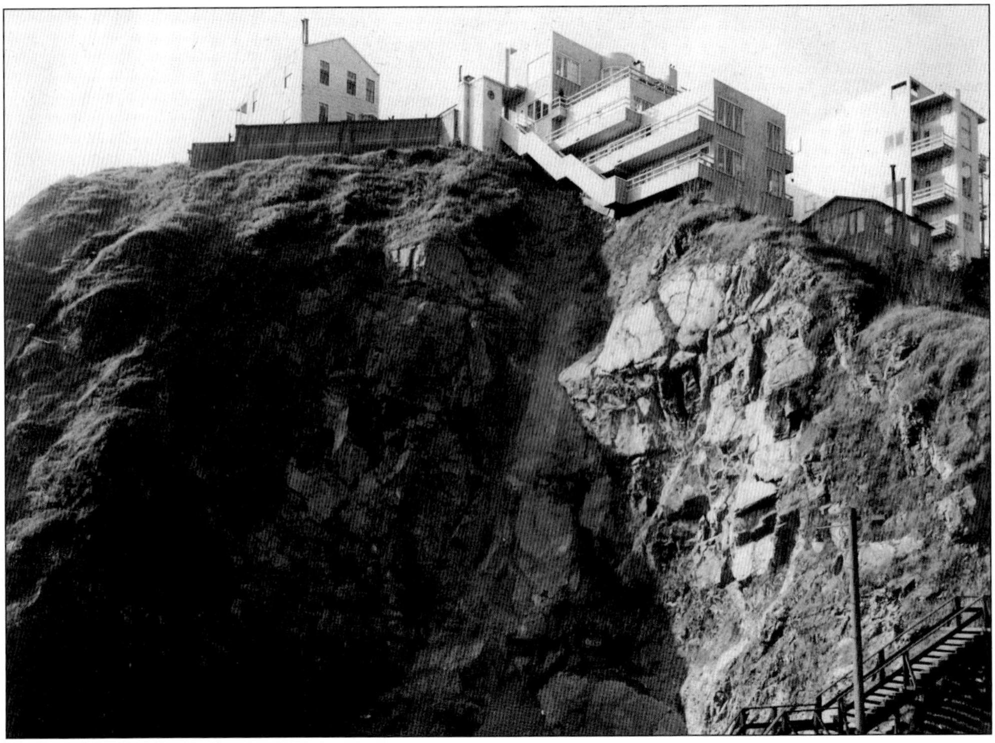

Six years later, on January 2, 1948, police offers inspect a car damaged by a Telegraph Hill rock slide. They are standing on Sansome Street at the east side of the hill. Over the years, a number of rock and landslides would traumatize the neighborhood. (SFHC.)

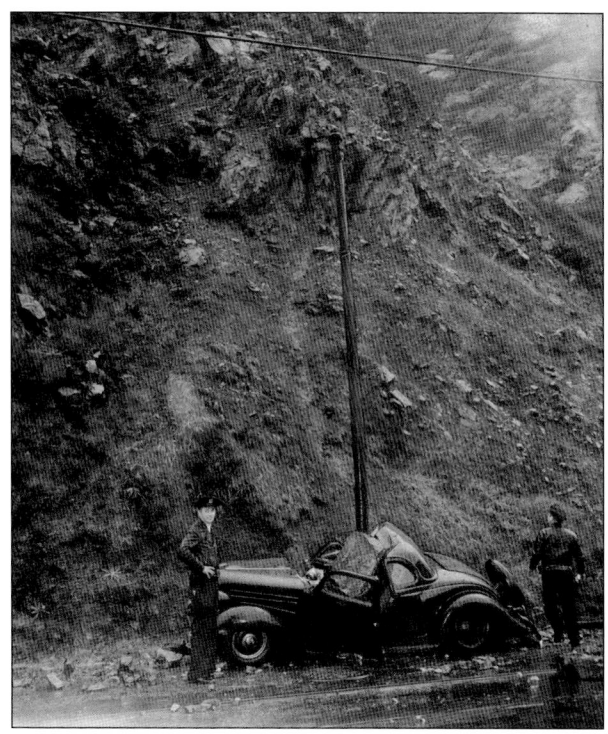

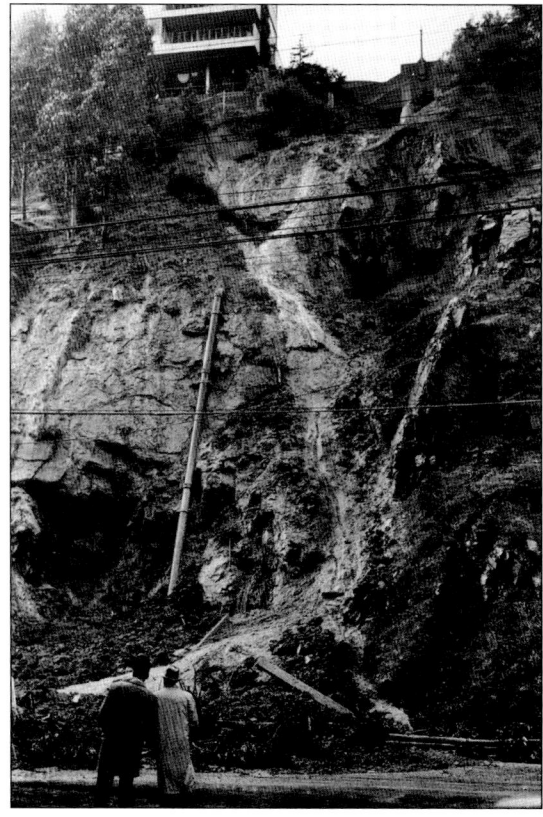

On January 14, 1952, slippery slopes sent tons of earth down the east side of the hill at Union and Sansome Streets, along with bushes and trees, some landing on a 1951 Nash. The home at the top at 66 Calhoun Terrace was not believed to be in immediate danger at the time. (SFHC.)

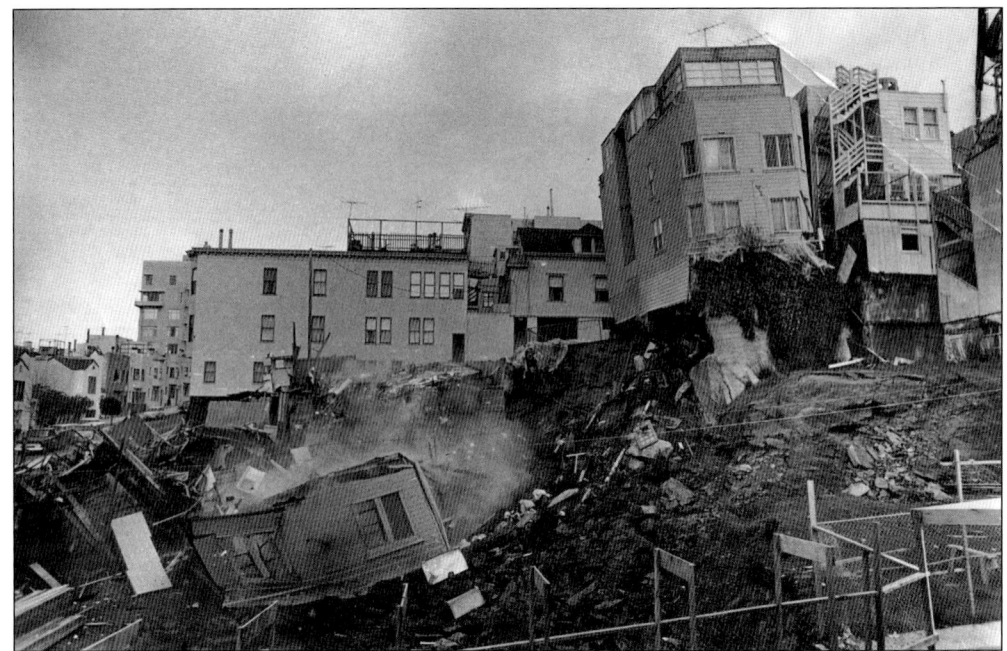

A building collapses down the hillside from Child Street on the western slope of Telegraph Hill on December 29, 1964. This was quite the event. Streets were closed off due to safety concerns and residents of several nearby homes were evacuated as the hillside's safety was assessed. To this day, house foundations are visible down the slope. The street has since been rebuilt, and a new balustrade is in place. (SFHC.)

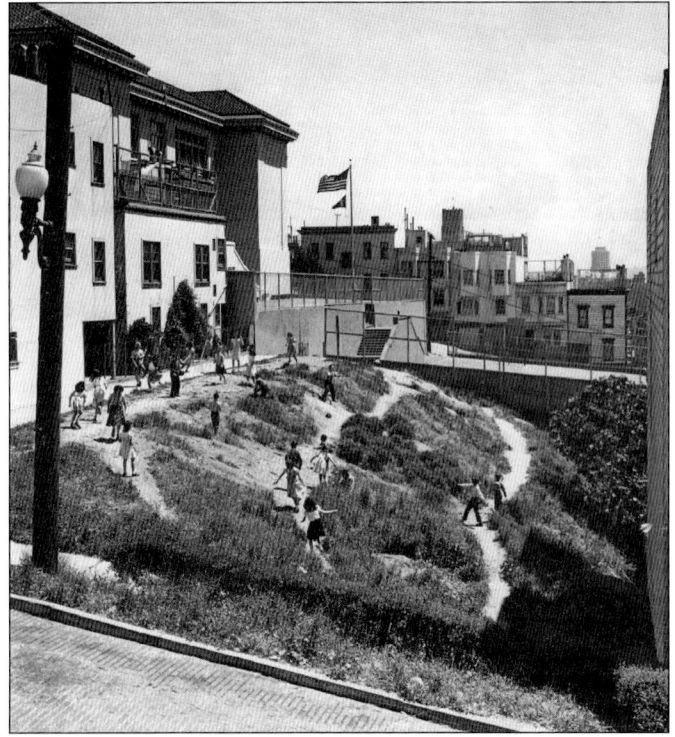

These children are playing on another steep slope in a vacant lot next to Garfield School on May 17, 1948. The original Garfield School at this location dates back to the early 1900s. Located at the top of one of San Francisco's steepest hillsides, the Garfield School sits at the base of Coit Tower on Filbert Street. (SFHC.)

The notation for this image reads, "crib house on Telegraph Hill." The term crib house seems to have several connotations. Whatever this house may have been, it was a dwelling on the hill in 1955. (SFHC.)

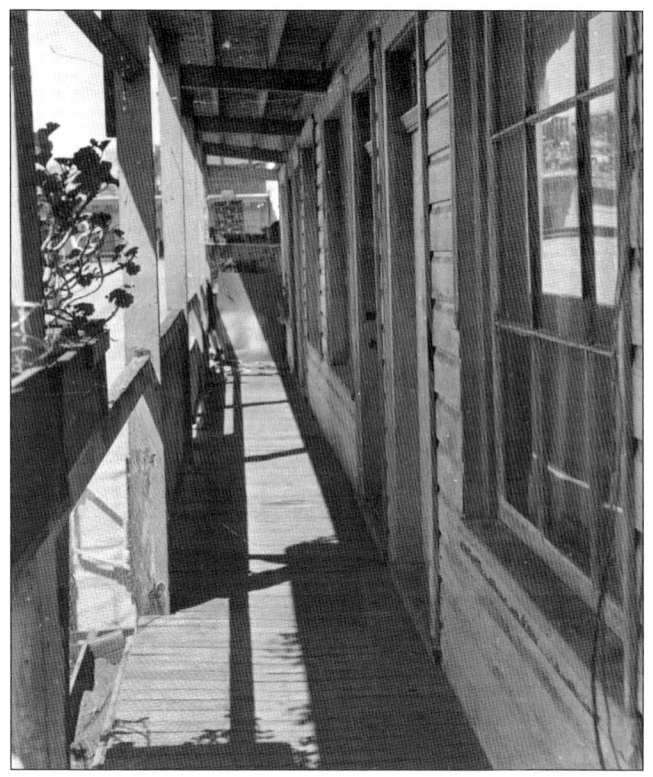

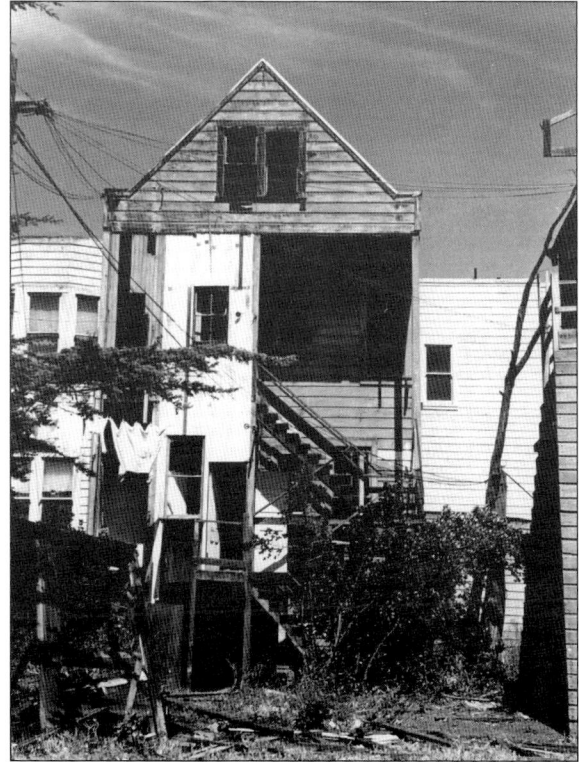

This images shows the back of a house in the 1960s. Ransacked might describe this edifice, or, perhaps, a touch bohemian. The 1960s were the days of flower children, or hippies. Although most of their happenings centered around the Haight–Ashbury district, plenty of similar activity happened in North Beach. (SFHC.)

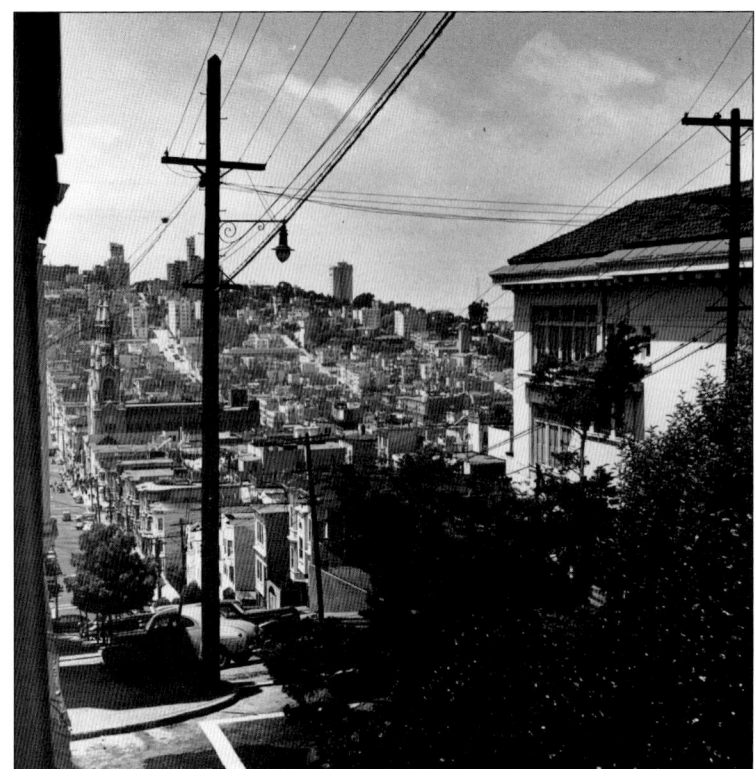

Not far away, at the top of Filbert Street, is a pleasing North Beach view looking toward Russian Hill. Just to the far right is the Garfield School. At the bottom center is SS. Peter and Paul Church. The concept of urban area being grand while quaint at the same time is thoroughly San Francisco. (SFHC.)

This is a typical North Beach street that has not changed much in the last 50 years. It is true that in the years between 1850 and 1900, the neighborhood's inexpensive land values and low rents attracted working-class people. By the 1920s, artists and writers enjoyed the quiant urban ambience. (CAA.)

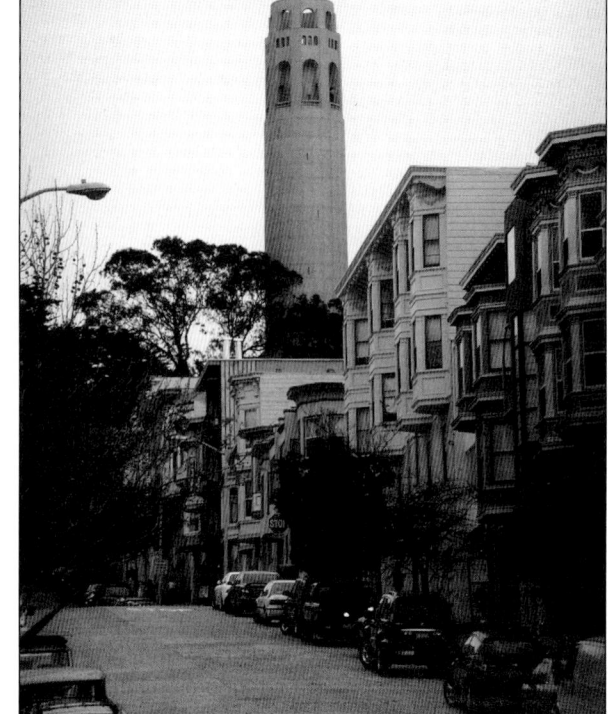

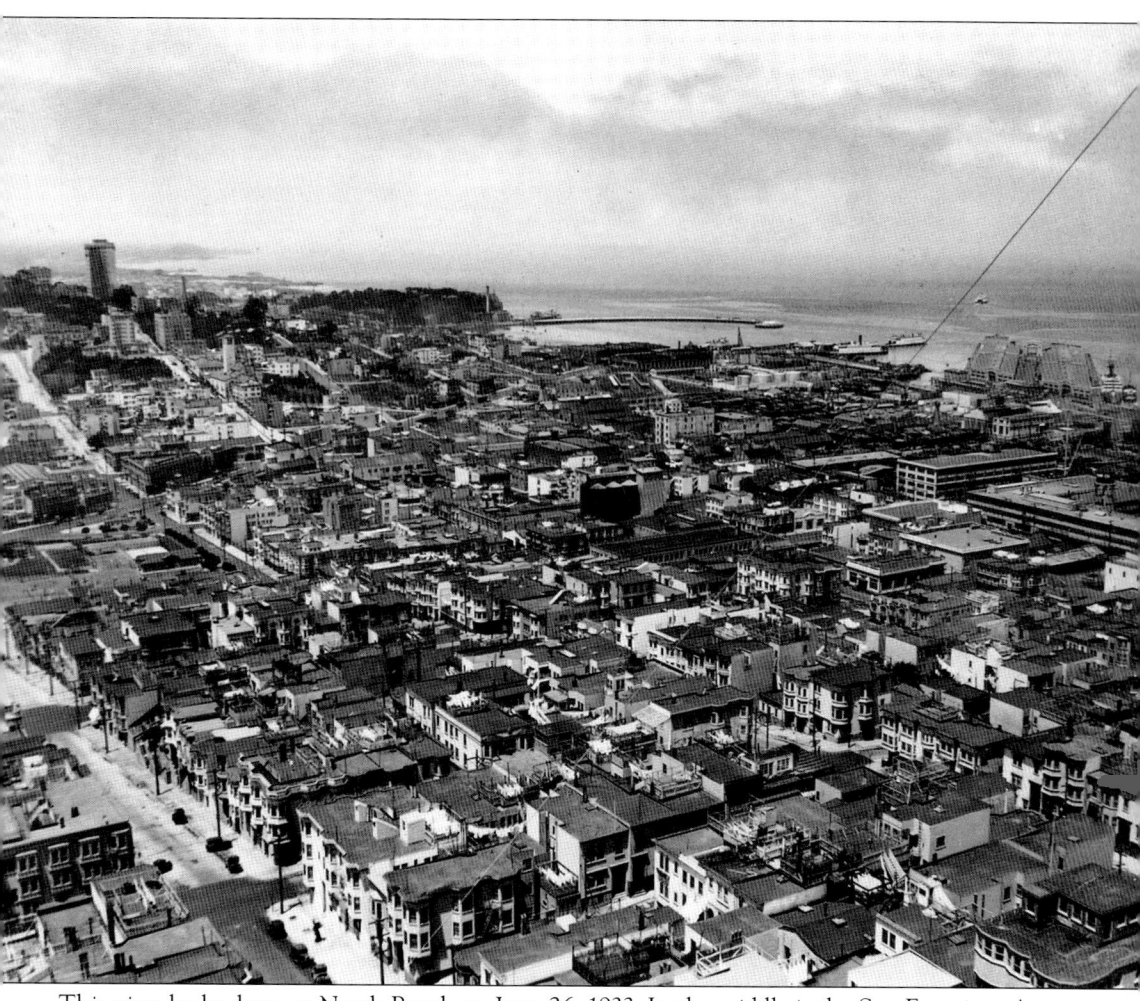

This view looks down at North Beach on June 26, 1933. In the middle is the San Francisco Art Institute, with its distinctive tower, located at 800 Chestnut Street. At one time, the institute was called the California School of Fine Arts. It has a long history dating back to the early 1870s, when a group of artists, writers, and community leaders had an idea, a cultural vision for San Francisco and the entire West. Over the years, notable artists contributed their art to the school, including Mexican muralist Diego Rivera. *The Making of a Fresco Showing the Building of a City* (1931) is one of four murals in the Bay Area painted by Rivera (1886–1957). This magnificent work covers an entire wall of the gallery with a fresco-within-a-fresco depicting the building of a modern city. Also discernable in this photograph is an area in the distance that would eventually become Aquatic Park. Nearby, construction of the Golden Gate Bridge was only a few months along in 1933. (SFHC).

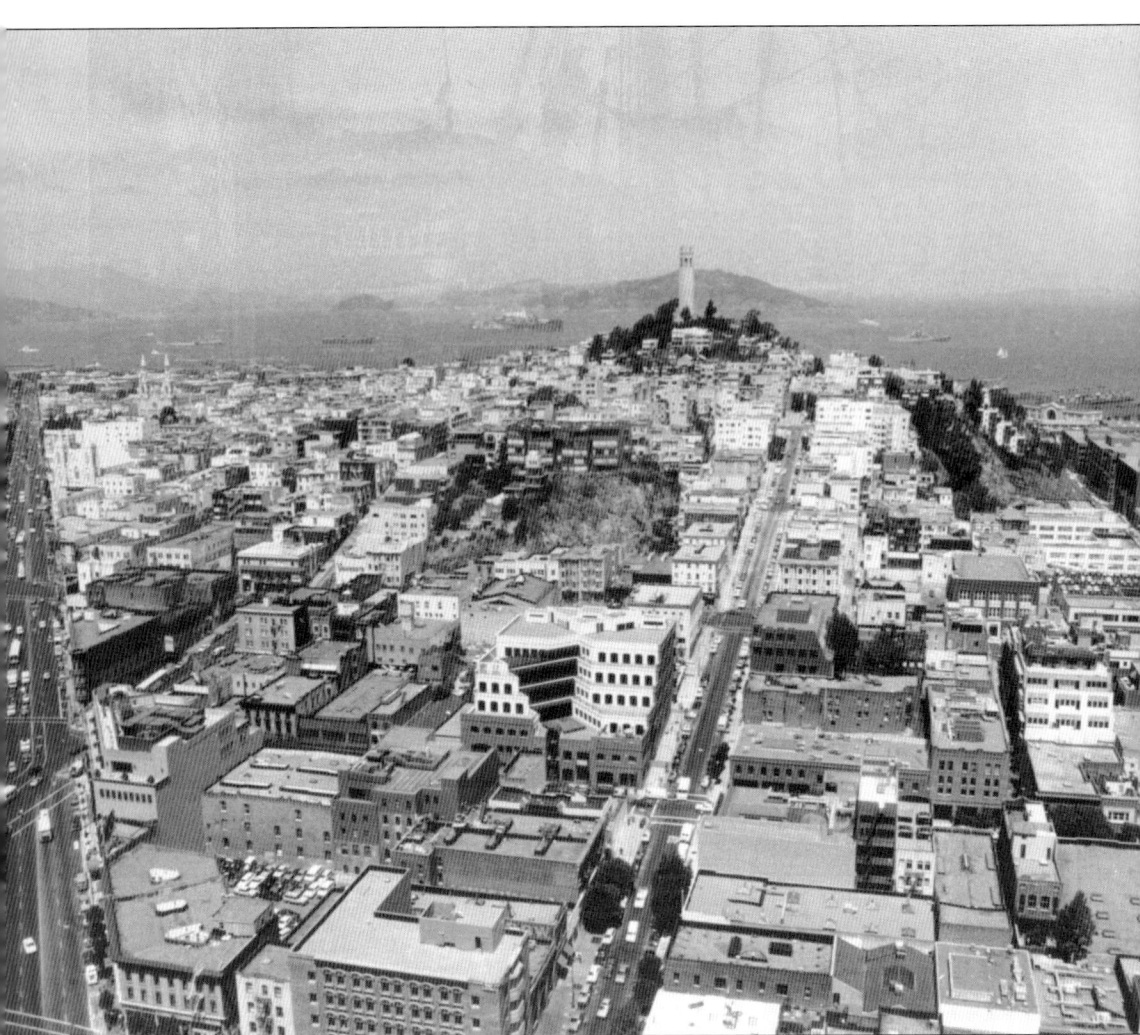

Looking back at the hill with Alcatraz in the background, it is quite easy to see why Telegraph Hill, with North Beach at its base, is such a beloved neighborhood in San Francisco. In this image is the Vanessi's sign on Broadway and Pasquale's Tower halfway up the slope. Just above the tower is a new luxury apartment building, affording its residents stunning views north towards Marin County and south towards the Financial District. North Beach and Telegraph Hill have it all—the culture, the stunning topography, and the intimate neighborhood experience. Dramatic modern architecture coexists with historical cottages, clinging to the very same cliffs. (SFHC.)

Three
NEIGHBORHOOD CULTURE

Culture has been defined as "social and intellectual information; social behavior, arts, beliefs, institutions; and products of human work and thoughts characteristic of a community as their social and artistic expression." North Beach and Telegraph Hill represent the quintessential expression of one of San Francisco's most beloved districts. The area's literature, bookstores, arts, clubs, periodicals, and restaurants are unsurpassed cultural gems. The 1920s and 1930s gave rise to the bohemian movement of artists and writers. In the 1950s, the beatniks found the essence of bohemia. The hippies arrived in the 1960s, and they too added another layer of flavor. Coffeehouses and art galleries continued to flourish. Minimum Daily Requirement was the place to be. The beat generation, including Jack Kerouac and Lawrence Ferlingetti, made North Beach home.

Vesuvio's and Café Treste offered coffee and a place to read poetry. Early bookstores included Cavalli and City Lights, both of which still serve the neighborhood. Music was well represented in Broadway Street clubs, along with other forms of nightlife. Delightful restaurants served its neighbors and tourists. They included Fior d' Italia, the U.S. Restaurant, Julius' Castle, and the Old Spaghetti Factory. The Roma Macaroni Factory, clinging to the east side of the hill at Francisco and Grant, provided Italian pasta for the neighborhood and cities beyond. The arts are represented superbly in the lobby of Coit Tower, with murals and frescoes painted by artists as part of the Public Works Administration projects. Noteworthy films like *House on Telegraph Hill*, *Dark Passage*, and *Basic Instinct* also left their mark. Exceptional architecture, such as Richard Neutra's Kahn House (1939) at 66–70 Calhoun and Irvine Goldstine's art moderne Malloch Apartment building (1936) at 1360 Montgomery Street, add yet another layer of unique character to North Beach. Annual festivities, such as the Columbus Day Parade and North Beach Festival, continue to delight residents.

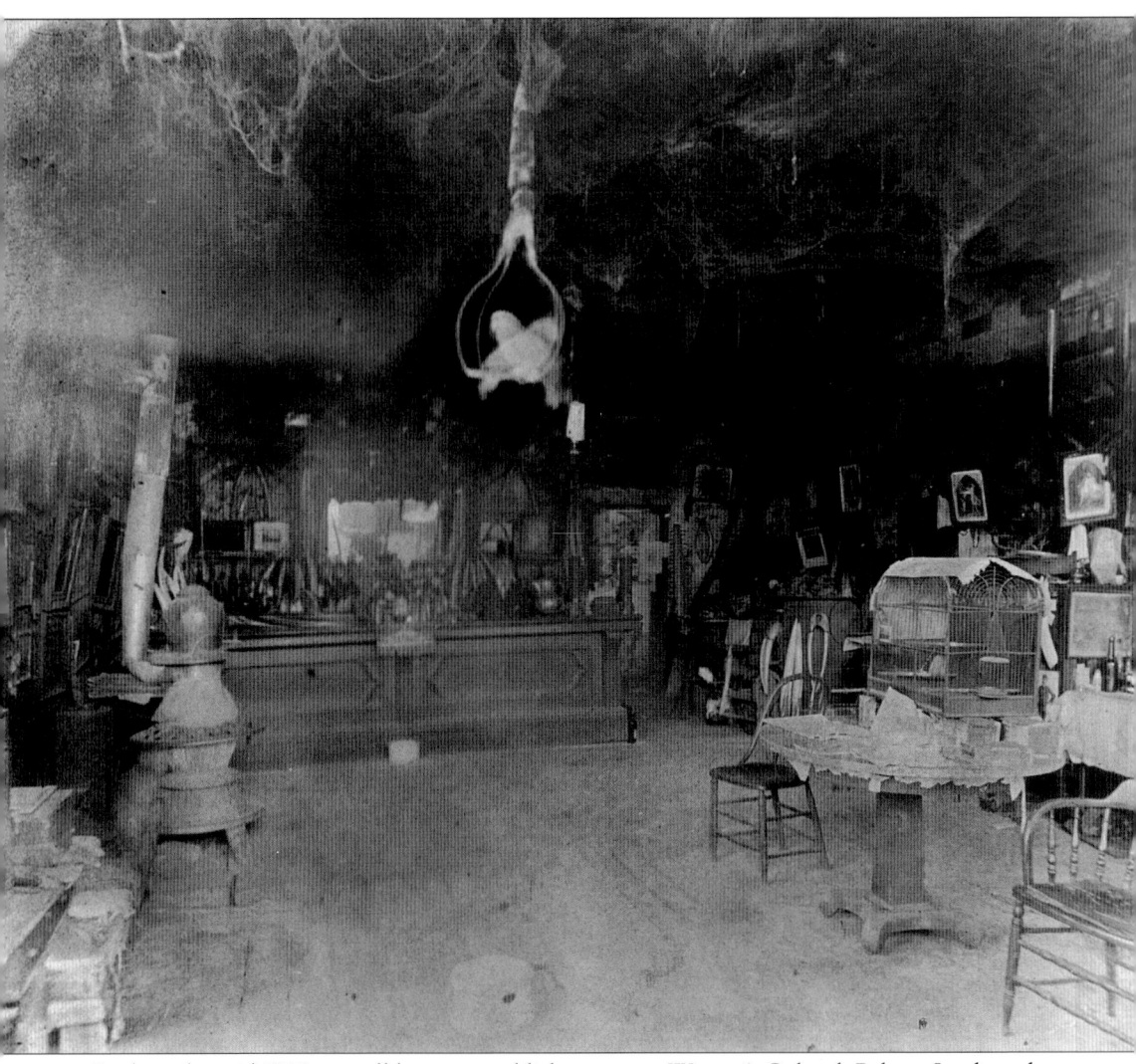

Back in the mid-1800s, a well-known establishment was Warner's Cobweb Palace. Look at those webs hanging from the ceiling. A bird rests in the center on its perch. Abe Warner's Cobweb Palace (formerly a butcher shop) was really a saloon in the true sense of the word. It was at Meigg's Wharf on the corner of Francisco and Powell Streets. A popular gathering place for sailors and gold miners drifting through town, Abe would offer chowder, crabs, mussels, and local French bread. A resident white cockatoo would screech "I'll have rum and gum, what'll you have?" Today the Cobweb's site would be around 2200 Powell Street, now four blocks inland. (SFHC.)

In 1849, a storm blew the ship *Arkansas* aground. It was eventually moved to the shoreline, which was then at Battery and Pacific Streets. Years later, the ship was converted into the Old Ship Ale House, and later still the Old Ship Saloon was built over the site. (CAA.)

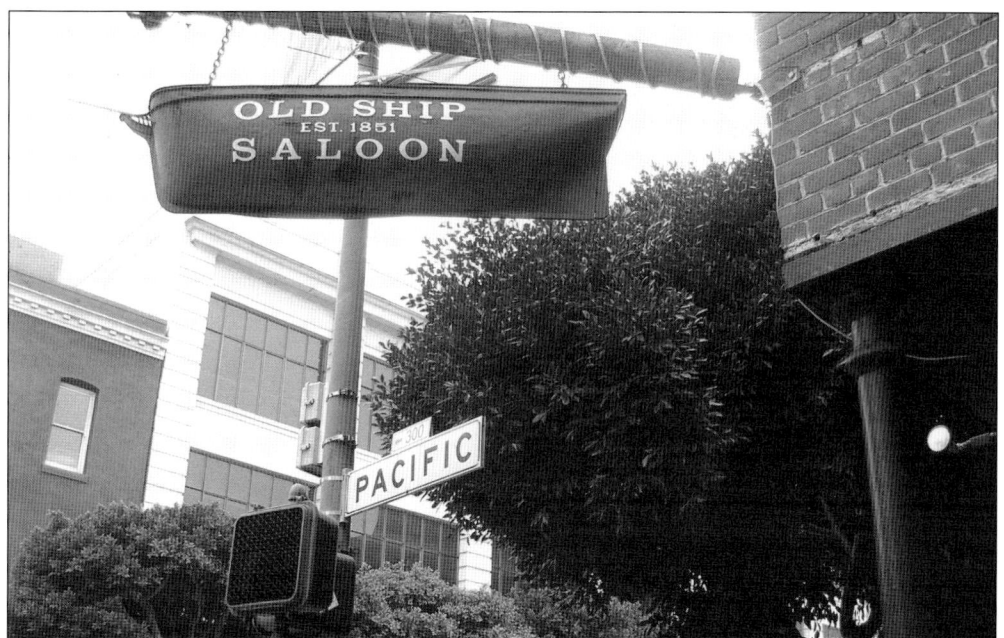

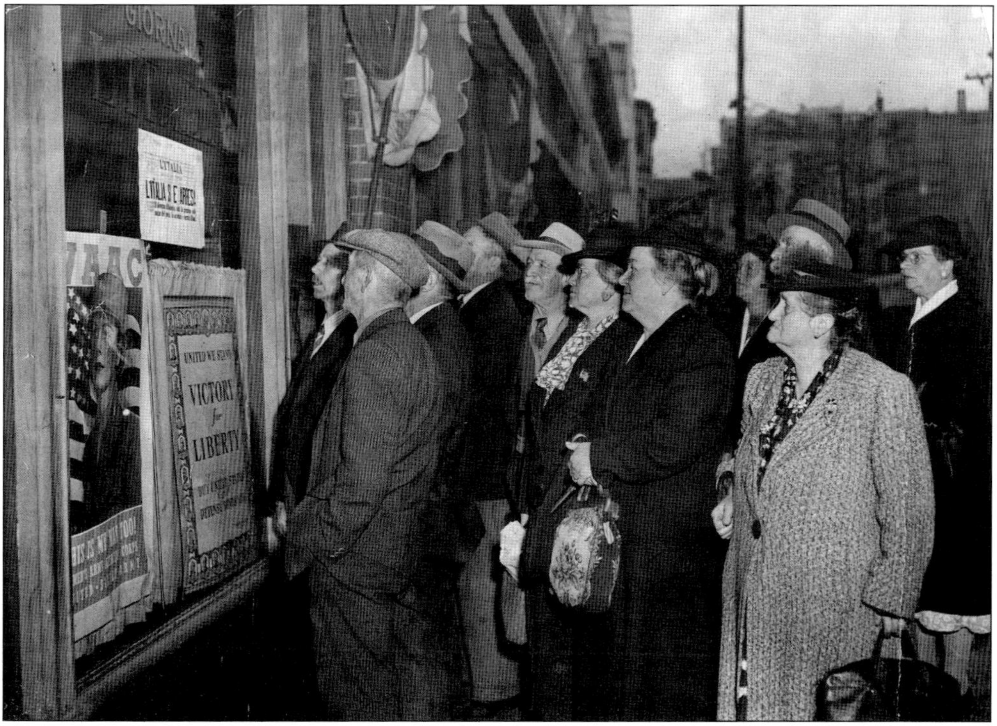

On September 8, 1943, the Italian newspaper *Giornale L'Italia* announced the unconditional surrender of Italy during World War II. These people are reading a notice posted in the window that reads, "L'Italia si è arresa," (meaning "Italy has surrendered"). (SFHC.)

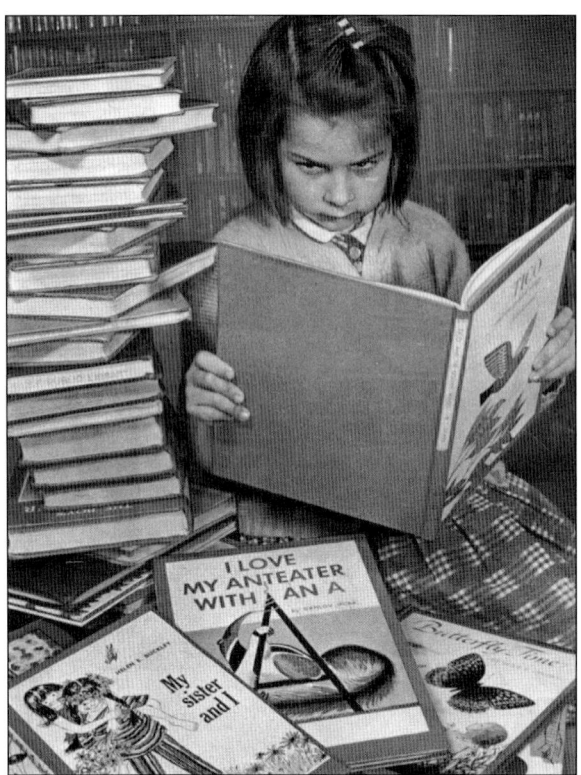

In the spring of 1965, the North Beach Library received 1,200 new children's books. This little girl is reviewing several volumes. The library was completed in December 1958, and opened in January 1959 at a total cost of $220,627. It was the 26th branch established by the San Francisco Public Library system. It is next to the Joe DiMaggio playground. (SFHC.)

Numerous movies are set in San Francisco. In this 1936 image, William Powell and Myrna Loy enjoy the view from the base of Coit Tower. This impressive film duo is taking a break from filming Metro-Goldwyn-Mayer's *After the Thin Man*. The base of Coit Tower is portrayed as the Charles's home and Pioneer Park as their garden area. (SFHC.)

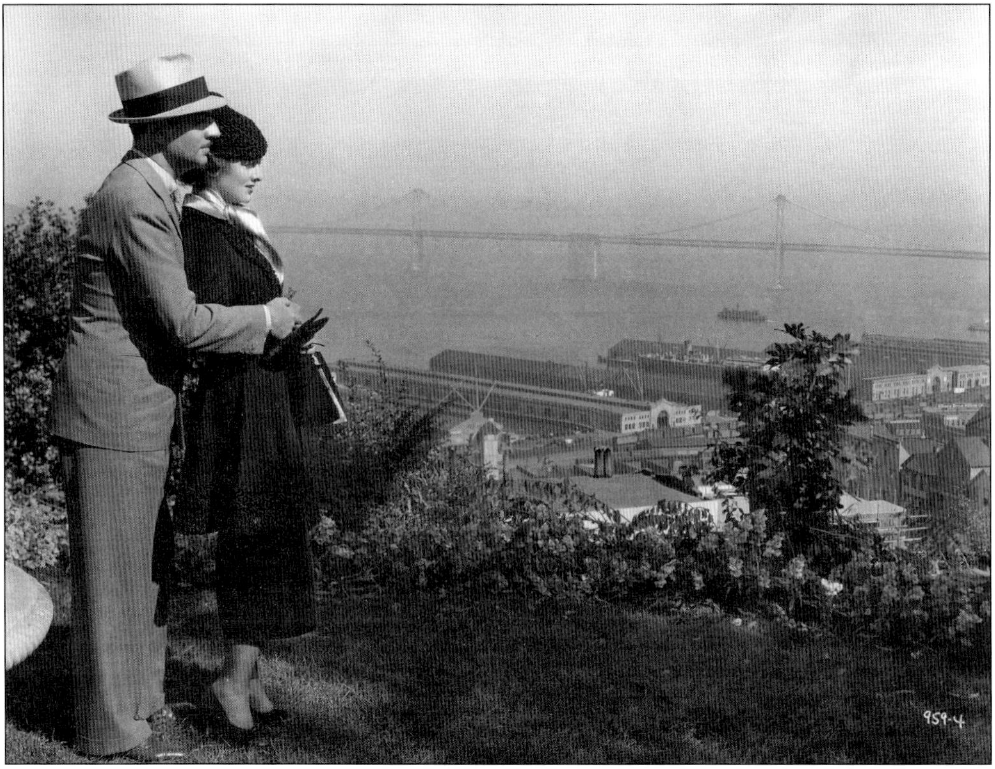

This is the door into the Coit Tower lobby. Pictured here are Shirley Staschon Triest and Julia Rogers, two of the Works Progress Administration project muralists posing on July 2, 1934. The opening of Coit Tower was delayed due to the perception, at the time, that some of the paintings portrayed controversial political items. Clifford Wight's mural contained a hammer and sickle, which was later removed. (SFHC.)

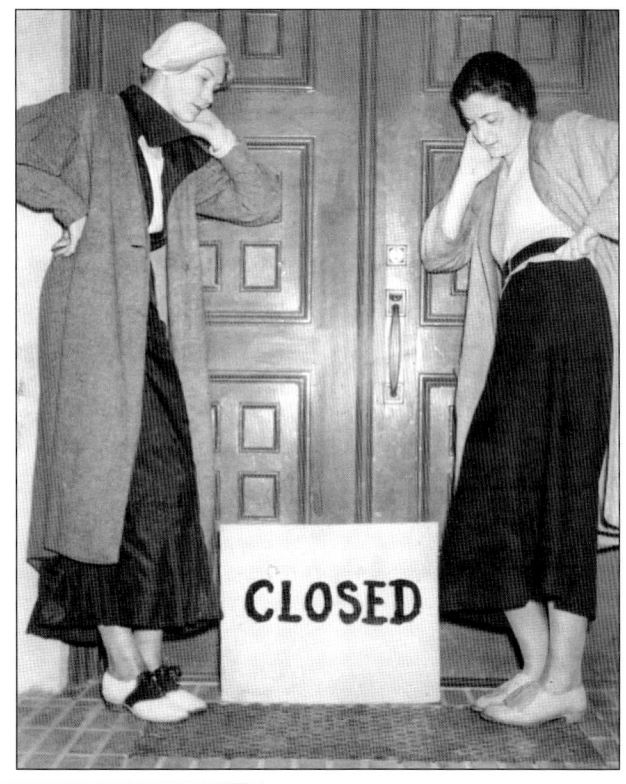

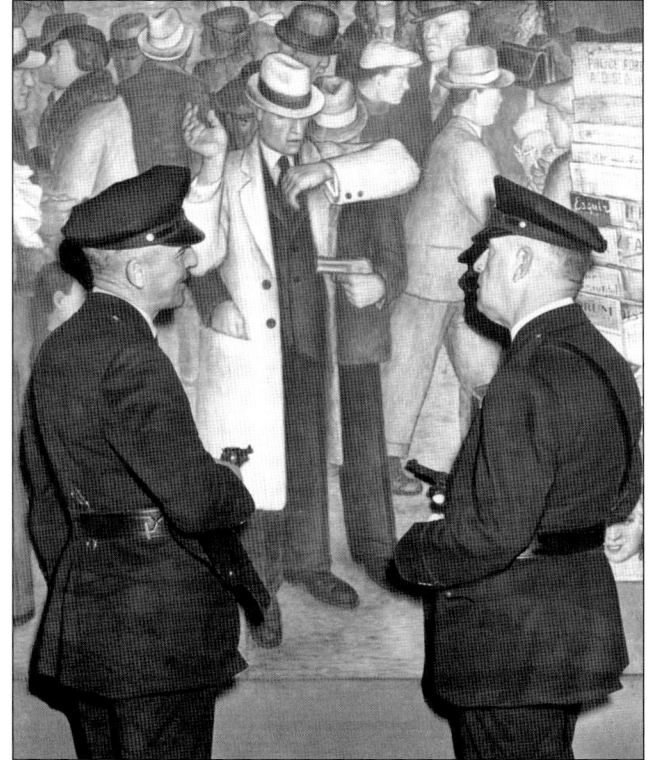

On October 12, 1934, two San Francisco police officers stood in front of a Coit Tower mural showing a robbery in progress at gunpoint. Visible here is a small portion of the mural *City Life*. It is one of the largest murals at Coit Tower, painted by Victor Mikhail Arnautoff, who was once assistant to Diego Rivera. (SFHC.)

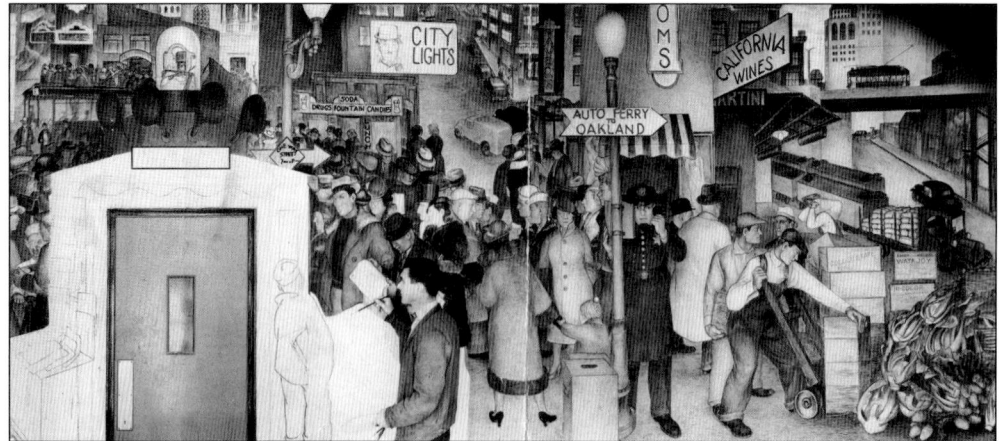

This is a photograph of artist Victor Arnautoff working on a portion of the *City Life* mural inside Coit Tower around 1934. Viewing these breathtaking works of art requires dedicated attention to detail. They are full of esoteric representations. On the far right, fruit crates are stacked up, one reading "Watajoy California Brand Bartlett Pears." (SFHC.)

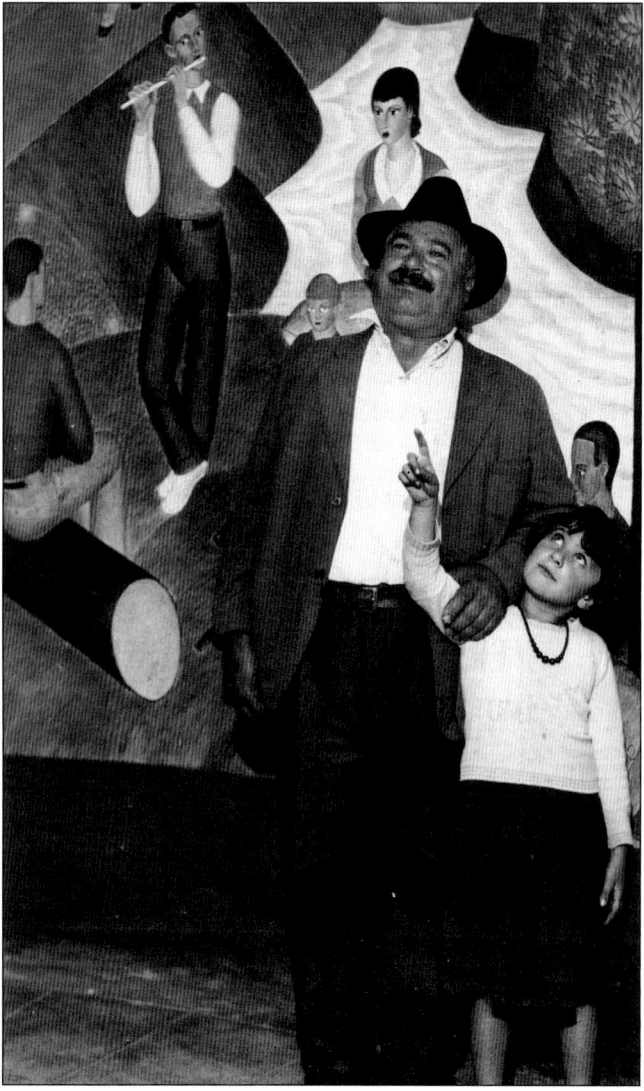

Most of the murals are family-friendly, as seen in the image at left. Louis Pasquale and his daughter Merceda are enjoying a turn around Coit Tower's mural lobby. Many of these Diego Rivera–inspired murals depict working-class Americans. Rivera had also recently finished two frescos in San Francisco between 1933 and 1934, with the assistance of several Coit Tower artists. (SFHC.)

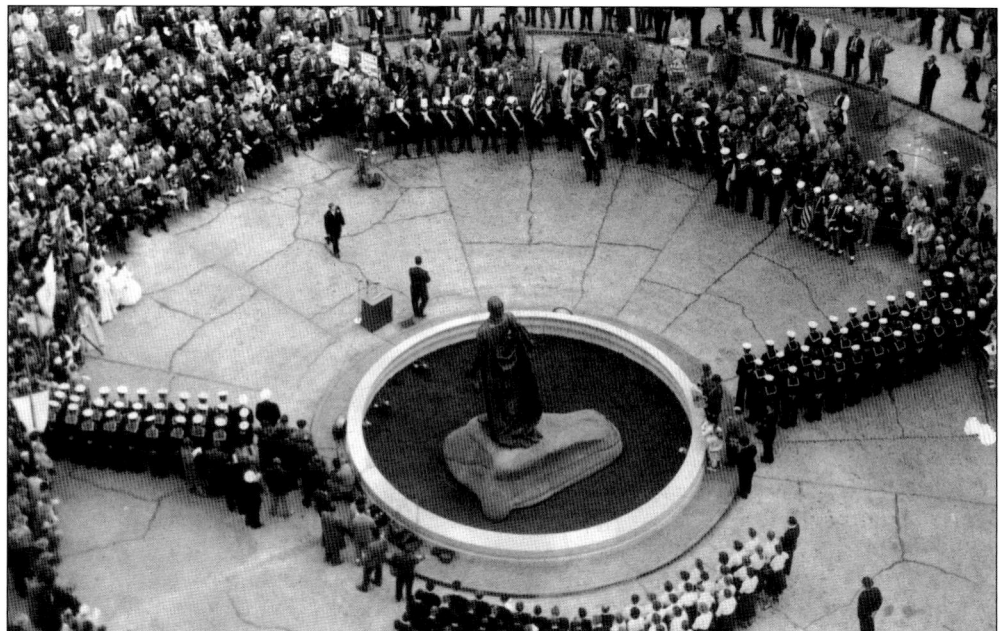

San Francisco citizens, particularly the Italian community, took October 12, 1957, very seriously. News copy of the day reads, "Singers, sailors from American and Italian navies, and spectators stand in reverent silence as 12-foot statue of Christopher Columbus is unveiled today on Telegraph Hill. The massive sculpture piece was the work of Italy's Vittorio de Colbertaldo. Columbus Day weekend will be highlighted here tomorrow with a parade." (SFHC.)

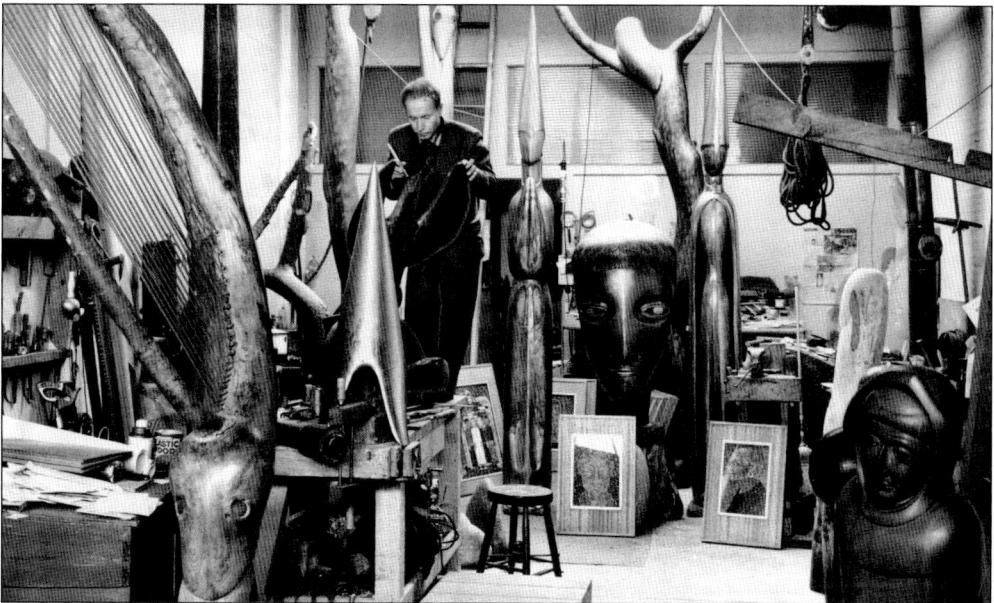

This is an image of Beniamino Bufano at work in his Greenwich Street studio on January 15, 1955. News copy of the day reads, "The artist's Greenwich Street studio contains nearly all the work he has done since fire destroyed another studio in 1931." Bufano maintained that the function of art is to create a universal culture that will guide the future course of world destiny to a better way of living. (SFHC.)

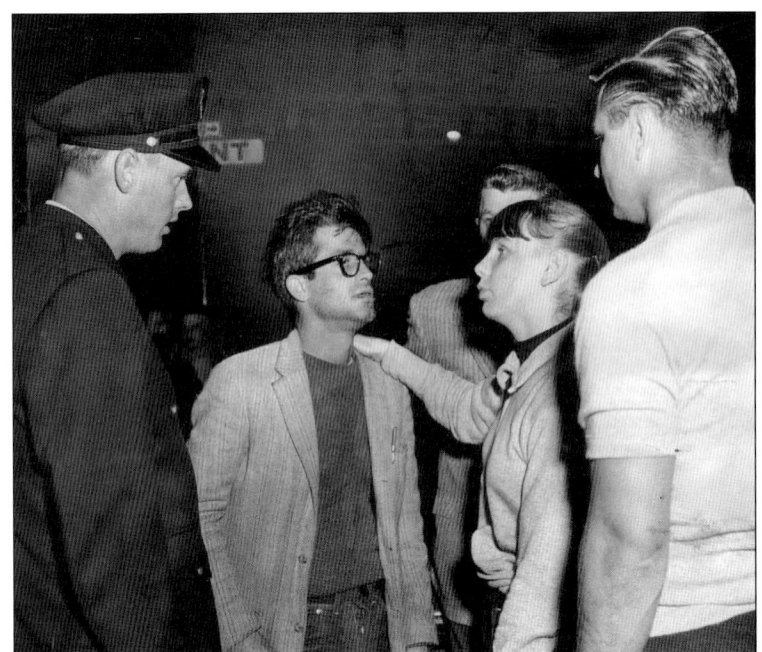

Pictured here on August 11, 1958, are several beatniks assembled for a march to protest their having become a tourist attraction. They called their assembly the Squareville Tour. Although New York City is considered the beatnik birthplace, this generation grew to prominence in 1950s San Francisco, mainly in North Beach. (SFHC.)

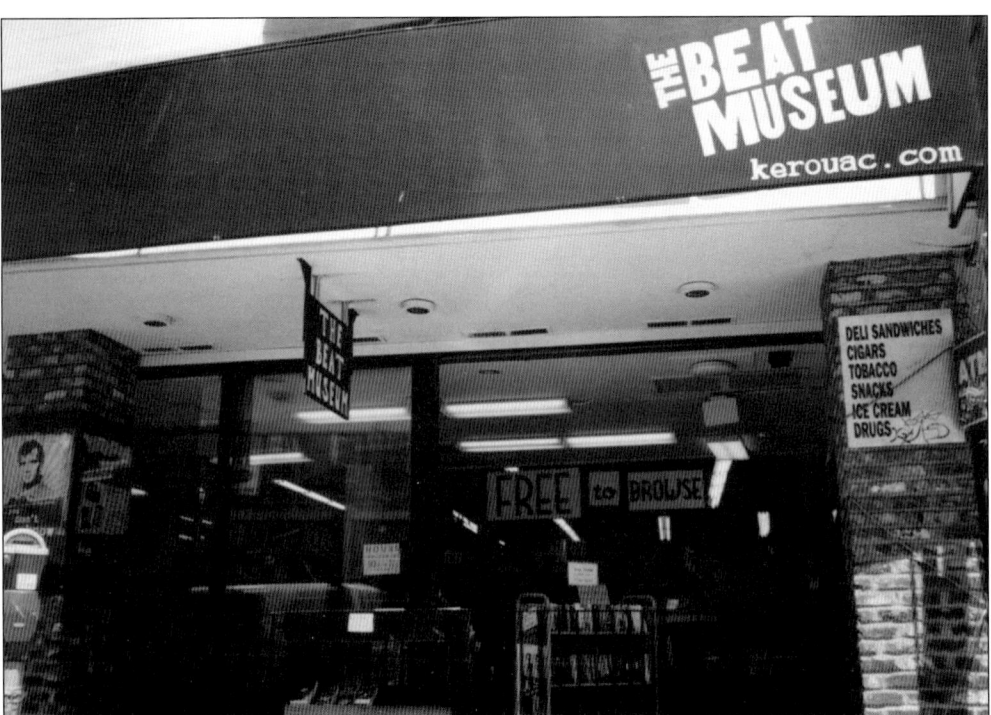

This is the Beat Museum located at 540 Broadway. It is filled with marvelous artwork, rare books, and photographs of the beatnik generation. Their Web site reads, "Where else but the home of The Beats: North Beach San Francisco!" (CAA.)

Mary Erckenbrack (left), Peter Macchiarini, and Judy Weld are standing with a street fair sign on June 22, 1956. Mary and Peter were artists, and Judy was Miss San Francisco 1956. The sign reads, "Upper Grant Avenue craftsmen present their third annual fair—exhibits, art in action." The fair continues to this day. At one time called the Grant Avenue Fair, now it is called the North Beach Festival. (SFHC.)

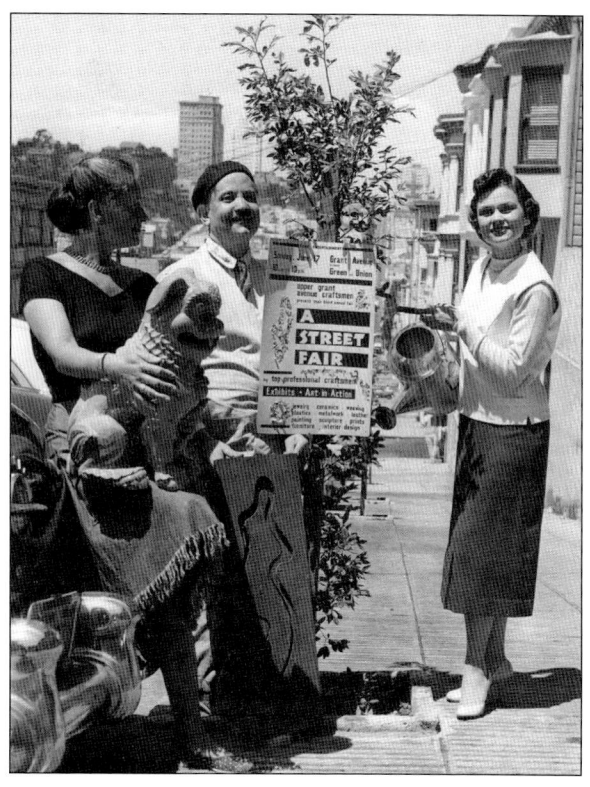

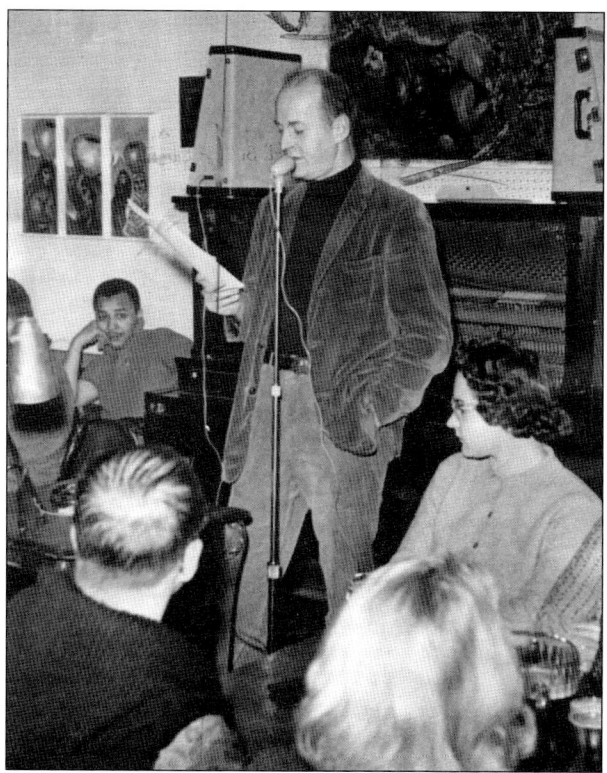

Lawrence Ferlinghetti reads his poem *Overpopulation* at the Coffee Gallery, 1353 Grant Avenue, on December 28, 1959. This was a longtime hangout offering beatnik music, art, comedy, poetry, and coffee. (SFHC.)

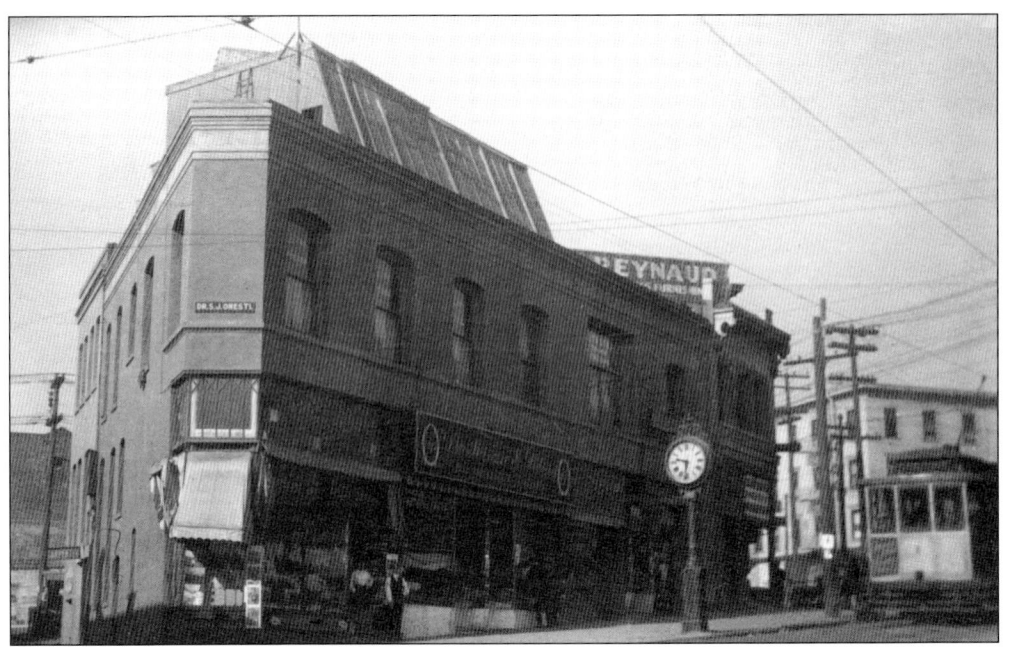

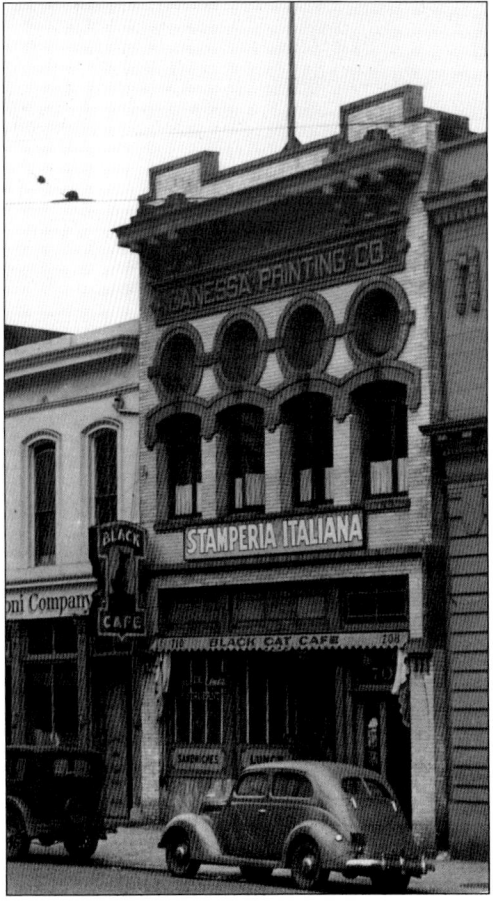

The Cavalli Bookstore location pictured would eventually become the location of the City Lights Bookstore. In 1907, after the 1906 earthquake and fire, brothers Emile and Jean Artigues commissioned Oliver Everett to design a new building in classical revival style. George Flavius Cavalli, an Italian Swiss immigrant, arrived in the United States in 1872. He opened a bookstore on Broadway and later one here on Columbus Avenue. (JBM.)

The original Black Cat Café was located on Mason Street. After the 1906 earthquake and fire, it was acquired by entrepreneur Charles Ridley in 1911, who turned it into a showplace for vaudeville-style acts, relocating the café here at 710 Montgomery. Eventually the café became a rendezvous for bohemians and later for the gay community. This colorful spot was in the Canessa Printing Company building; Canessa published *stamperia Italiana* (Italian printing). (SFHC.)

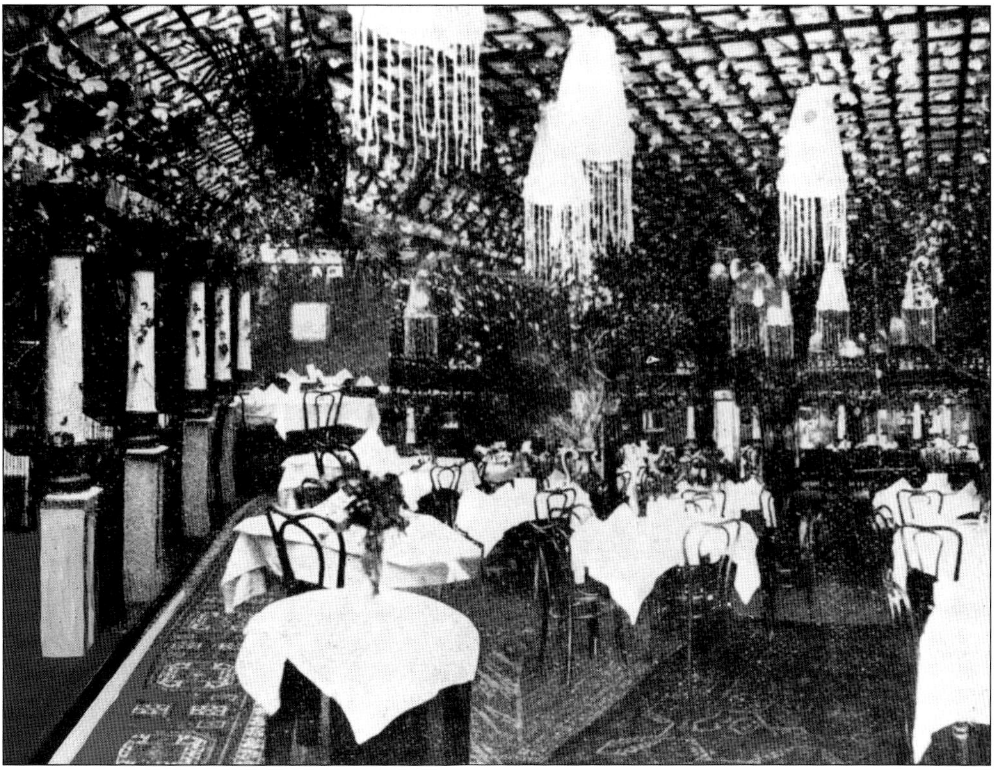

Here is the interior of the Black Cat Café. Sol Stoumen bought the bar in the 1940s, and it became the center for the bohemian and beatnik crowd. William Saroyan and John Steinbeck patronized the joint, as well as writers like Ernest Hemingway, Henry Miller, F. Scott Fitzgerald, and Gertrude Stein. Part of Jack Kerouac's beatnik novel *On the Road* is set in the bar. (SFHC.)

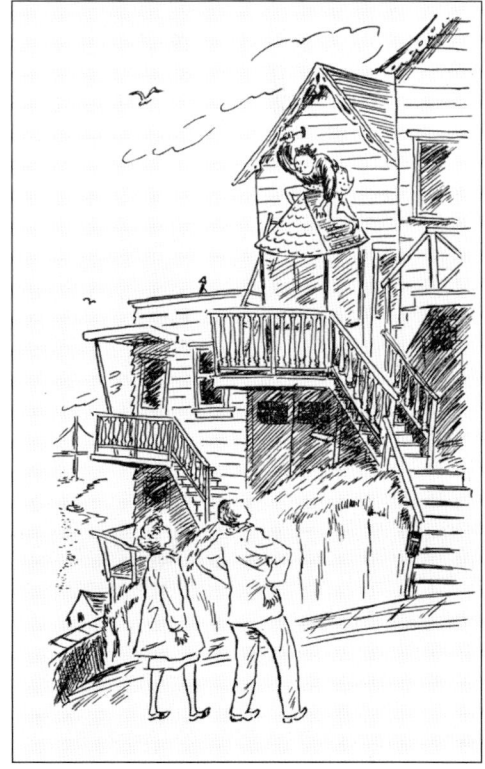

In 1945, Margaret Parton wrote a book called *Laughter on the Hill, A San Francisco Interlude*. It is a carefree account describing the adventures of a young woman's move to Telegraph Hill. Main character Margaret recounts: "The house in the middle had a pointed red roof, outlined with white gingerbread carving. A white-banistered flight of steps wound crazily to the porch, mainly occupied by a bay window." (CAA.)

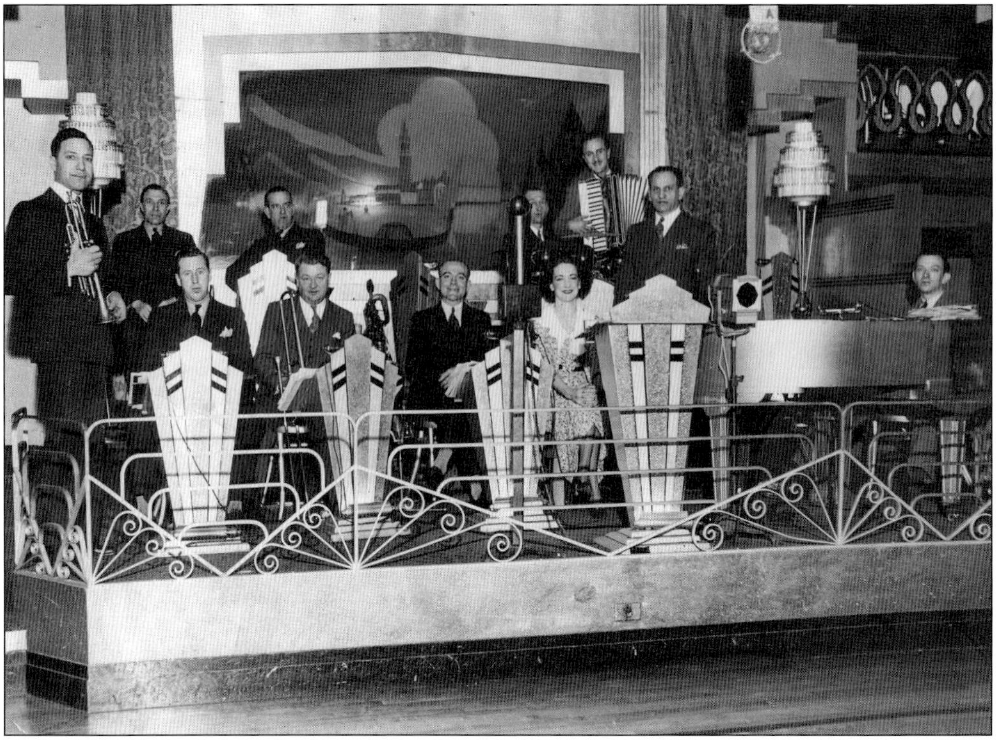

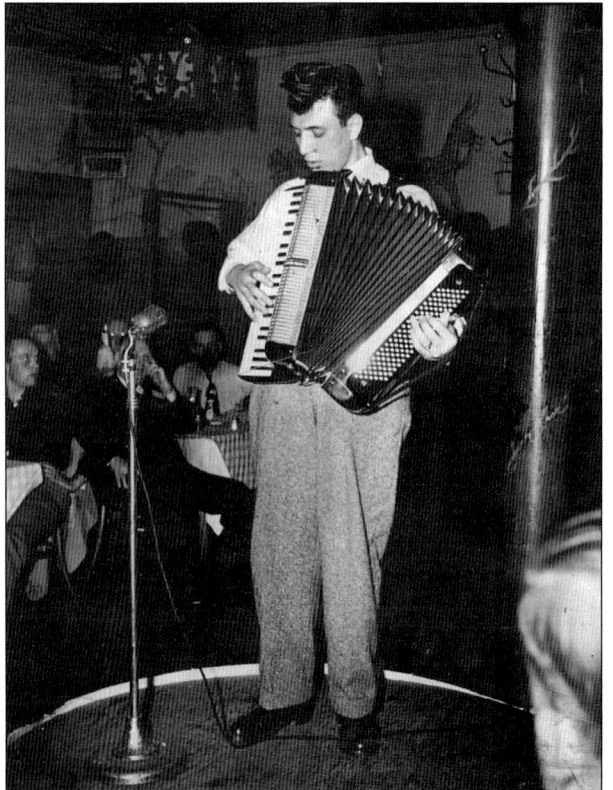

Music, and plenty of it, was often heard throughout North Beach. This image is of an orchestra at the Lido Café (also called Café Lido) on February 15, 1935. Lido Café was a favorite of nightlife aficionados, providing entertainment and good food. (SFHC.)

Accordions were quite the thing in the neighborhood. Here is a man playing his instrument in a North Beach restaurant. There were a number of master accordion craftsmen in the area. In the 1920s, the North Beach District was considered the center of accordion culture and a thriving accordion manufacturing industry. (SFHC.)

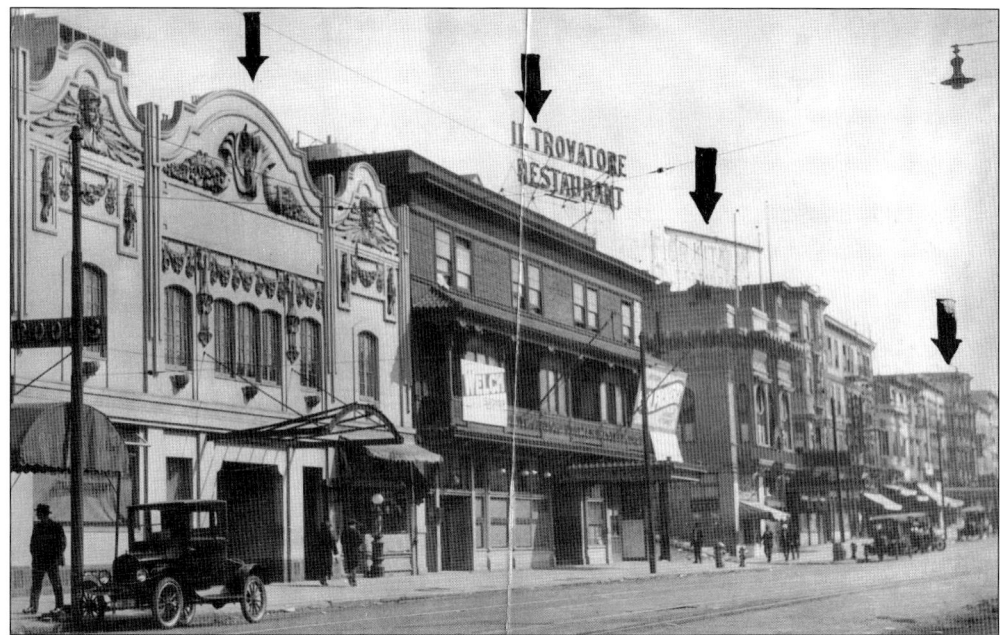

Il Trovatore Restaurant (center) is seen here in the early 1900s at 504 Broadway. It was owned by Archimedi Puccinelli, an early Italian pioneer who arrived in San Francisco from Lucca, Italy, at age 11. Historians report that there were 1,621 Italians in 1870 San Francisco. This is now the location of Enrico's Café. (SFHC.)

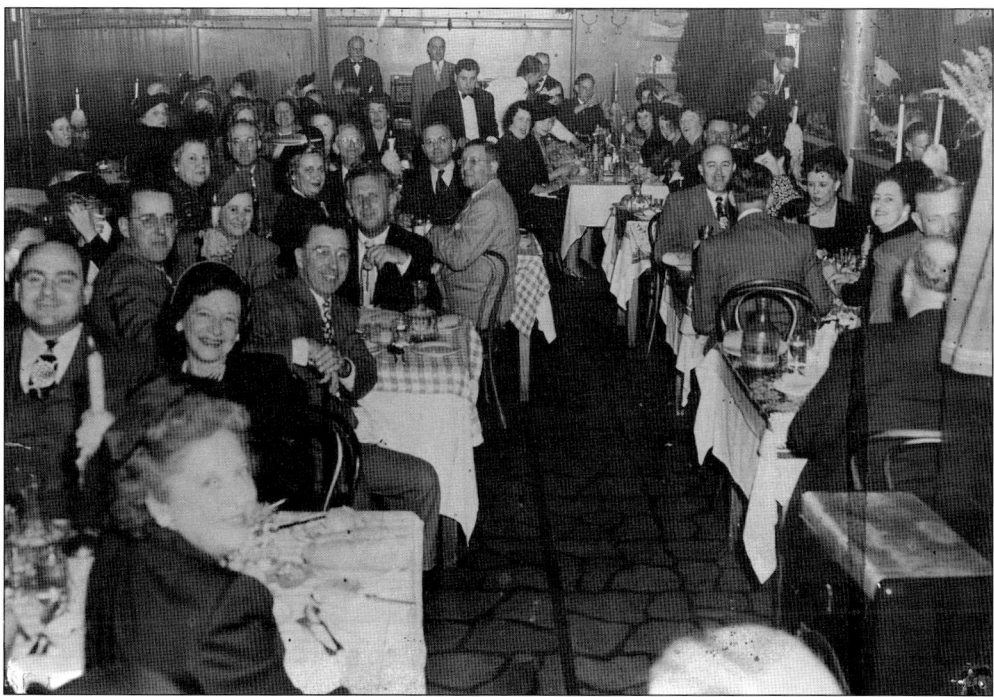

This is an undated image of the interior of an unidentified North Beach restaurant. It has been said that the secret of the decades-long success of North Beach is the appeal to the palate and taste buds. The phrases "*buon gusto*" and "*buon appetito*" were, and still are, expressed often. (SFHC.)

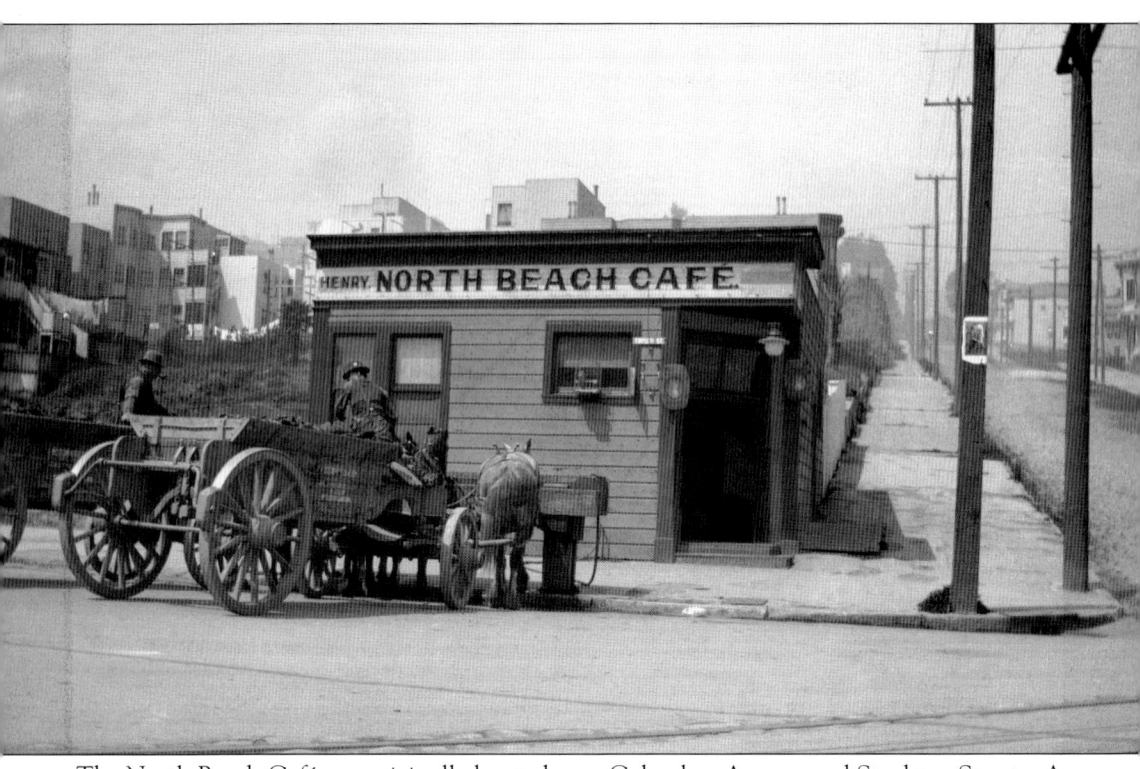

The North Beach Café was originally located near Columbus Avenue and Stockton Streets. A Mr. Rovero opened the café before Prohibition. In the late 1930s, Rovero opened the Columbus Café in what is now the Wells Fargo Bank building. This establishment continued until the mid-1940s, when it then moved to 562 Green Street. Note the bird in the cage watching the world go by from his perch at the window. Local establishments such as the North Beach Café were common in the neighborhood. They provided working-class citizens with a break from daily routine and a place to gather among friends to discuss the matters at hand. Unknowingly, they provided photographs like this, a historical image of North Beach. (JBM.)

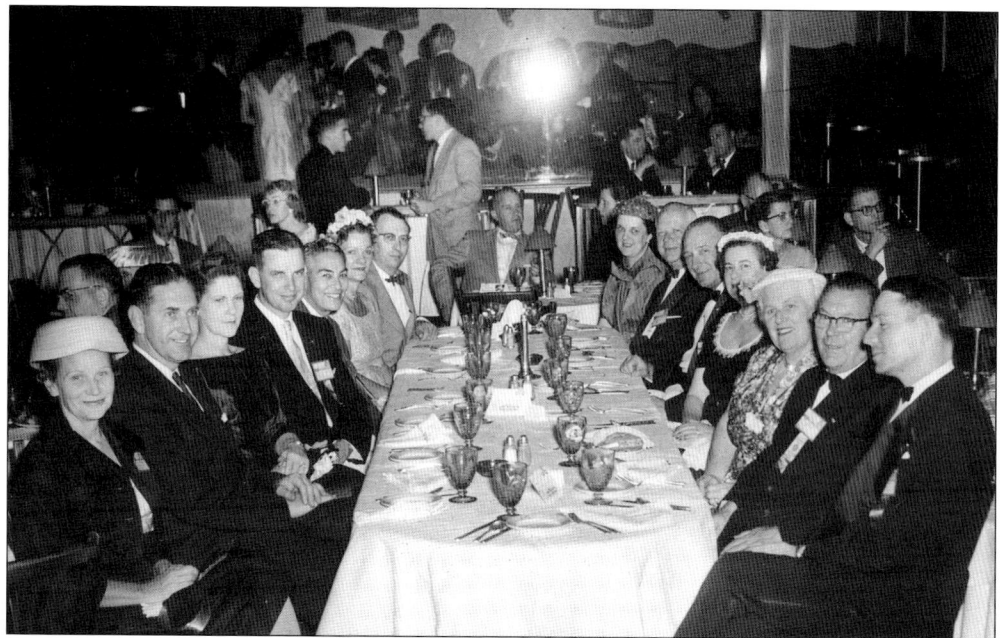

These folks are enjoying an evening at Bimbo's 365 nightclub. Agostino Giuntoli sailed to America in 1922 at the age of 19 from Tuscany, Italy. With a name difficult to pronounce, people called him Bimbo, the Italian word for boy. This boy opened a club at 365 Market Street, and years later in 1951, moved it to 1025 Columbus Avenue. (SFHC.)

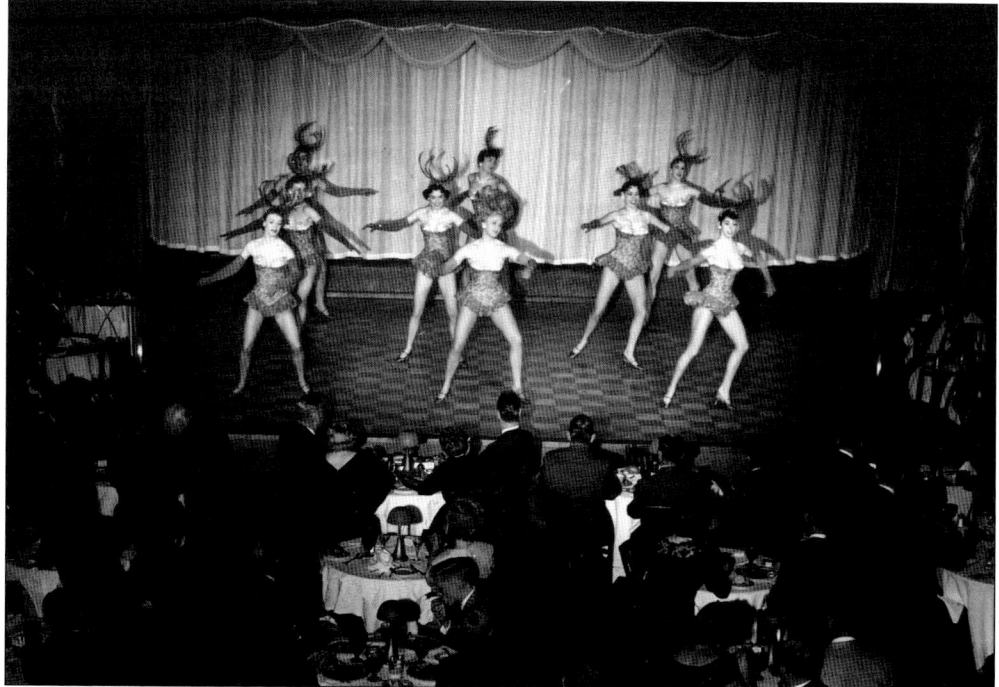

This is a lavish revue at Bimbo's. The club is famous for Dolfina, "the girl in a fishbowl," who appears to be swimming nude in a fish tank behind the bar. Clubs acts have included Chris Isaak, The Raconteurs, Robin Williams, and Jill Scott. (SFHC.)

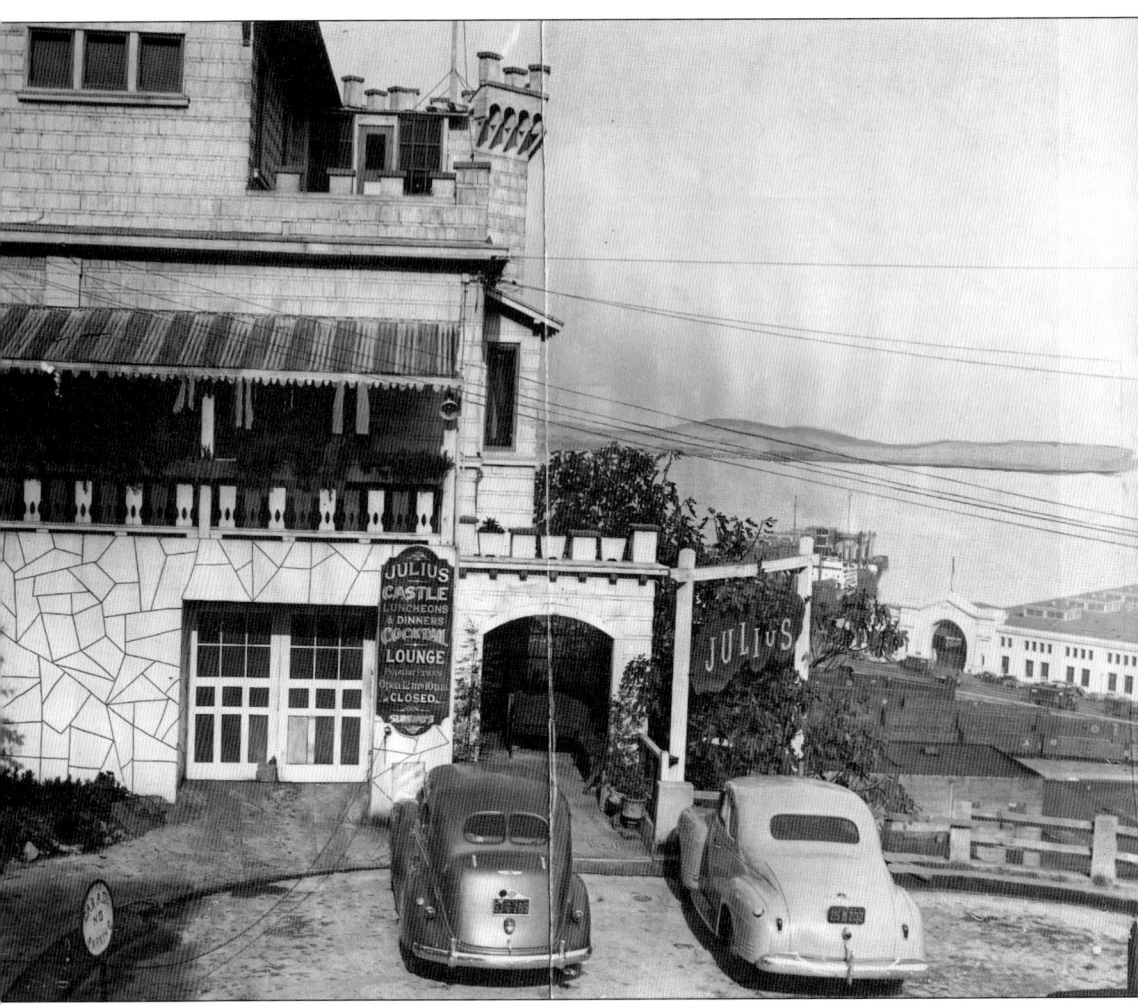

Julius' Castle restaurant is pictured as it was on November 26, 1941. Nestled at the base of Coit Tower near the Filbert steps, this one-of-a-kind establishment was a favorite of both longtime residents and tourists. Rarely does one find a castle in the center of an urban area. While technically not a castle in the true sense of the word, the name came about when Italian immigrant Julius Roz, envisioned a castle on the hill. Roz commissioned Italian architect Louis Mastropasqua to design the edifice, which opened in 1922. Interior wood paneling was reputedly purchased by Roz from the city's 1915 Panama Pacific Exposition. The words "Julius' Castle," on redwood on the front, were added by Julius in 1928. It was designated a landmark in 1980. Julius' Castle has been popular with politicians and visiting celebrities, such as Huey Lewis, Robert Redford, Sean Connery, and Ginger Rogers. (SFHC.)

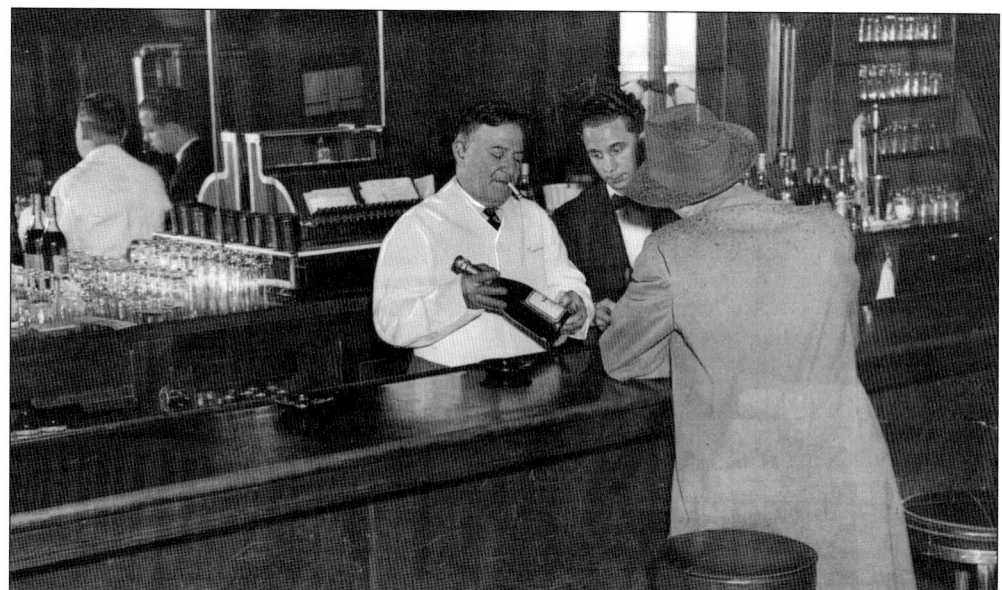

The interior of Ciccio's bar is seen on January 14, 1942. News copy of the day reads, "Here it is, says Frank Ciccio La Picolo, genial host at Ciccio's, as a customer asks for a particular brand of beverage. For seven years in the same spot at 1709 Powell Street, Ciccio's offers not only the finest in drinks but Italian food par excellence." (SFHC.)

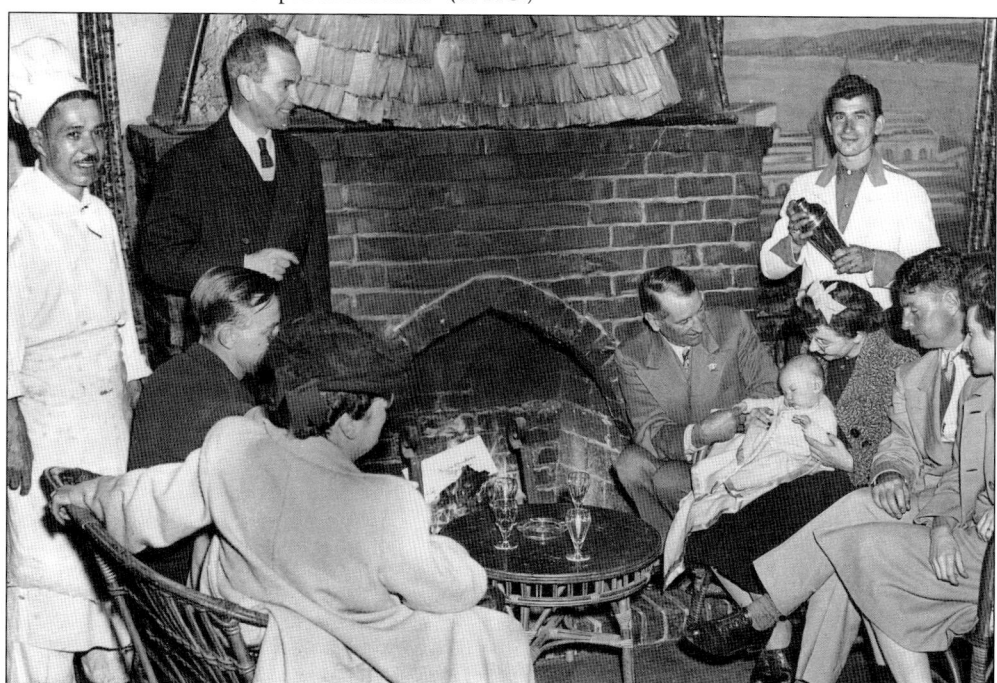

The interior of Lucca's Restaurant is pictured on May 5, 1943. News copy of the day reads, "Dal Toso and some of his capable staff peek in on the pre-dinner cocktailing of one of Lucca's oldest customers, W. Gaston Domerque, who holds the tiny had of one of this famous restaurants youngest customers." Pierino Gavello opened Lucca's with a plan to serve large portions of good cooking for only 50¢. (SFHC.)

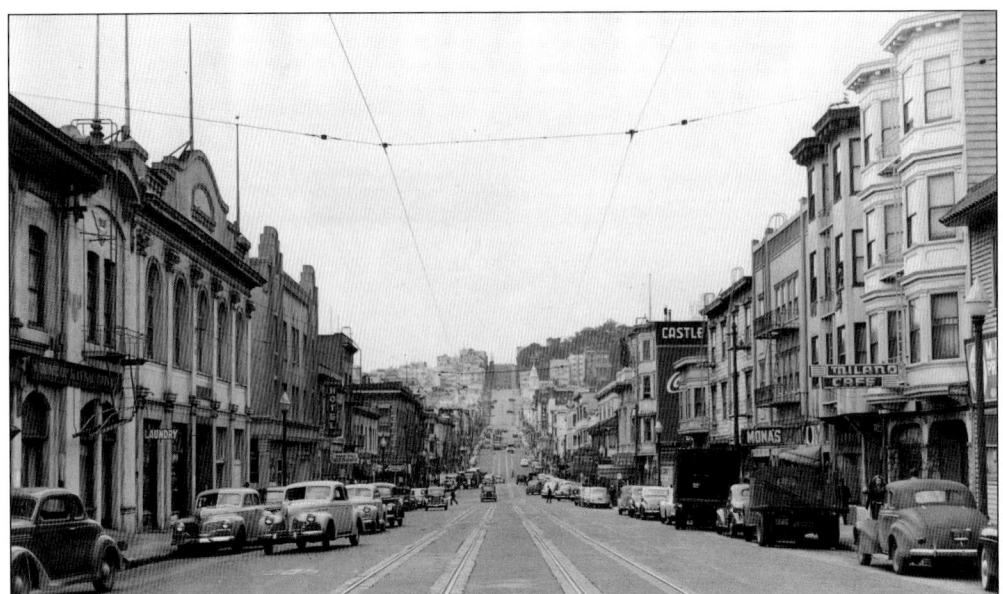

Broadway looked like this on April 29, 1944. Down the street on the right is the Verdi Theatre sign. It opened in 1909 as the Royal Palace, was renamed in 1914, and for 40 years offered third-run Hollywood films, bingo, and Italian films. Just down the street was Finocchio's, which was opened in 1936 by Joe Finocchio and his wife, Eva. A nightspot upstairs from the Fior, it featured female impersonators until its closure in 1999. (SFHC.)

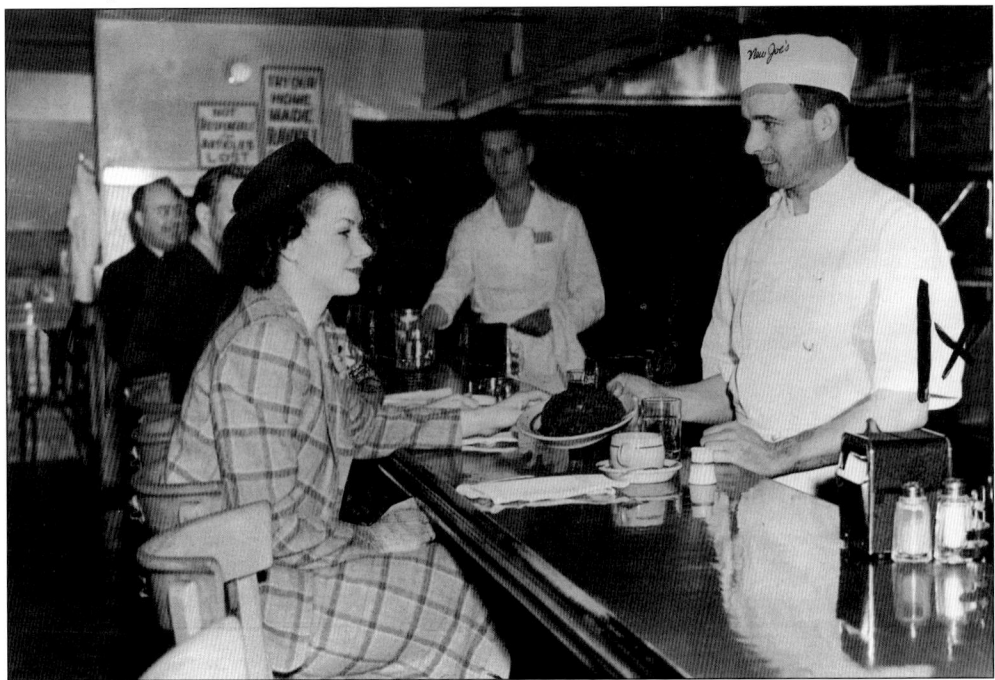

Here is Marino Biagi serving Marion Hall a plate of spaghetti at New Joe's restaurant on May 14, 1941. New Joe's became the first restaurant in San Francisco to do exhibition cooking, where food was prepared in full view of the customers. It was also the restaurant where the "Joe's Special" was created. (SFHC.)

The cellar at the Backyard Restaurant was located at 1020 Kearny Street. It looked like this on January 16, 1945. An advertisement of the day describes this place as "the most unique place in San Francisco." Years later, it would become the Cho-Cho Restaurant, a favorite hangout of American novelist and poet Richard Brautigan. (SFHC.)

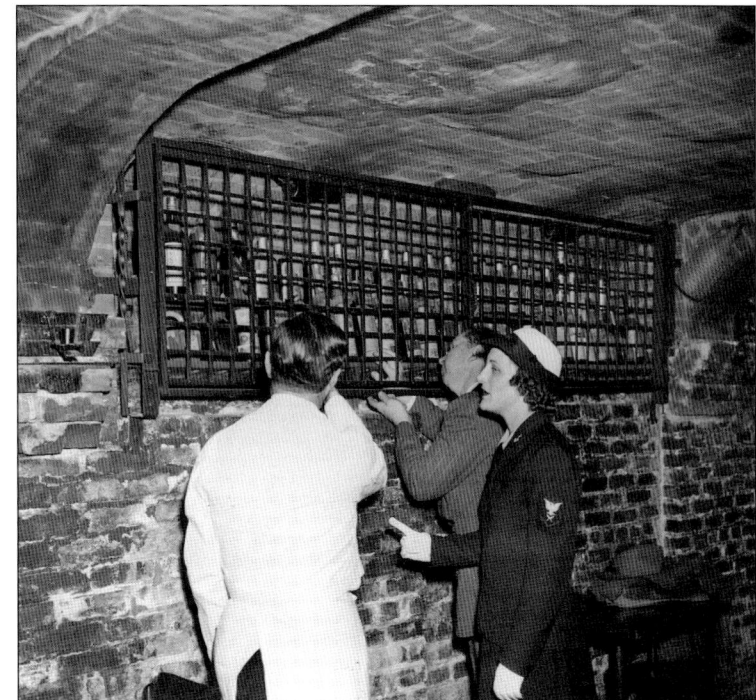

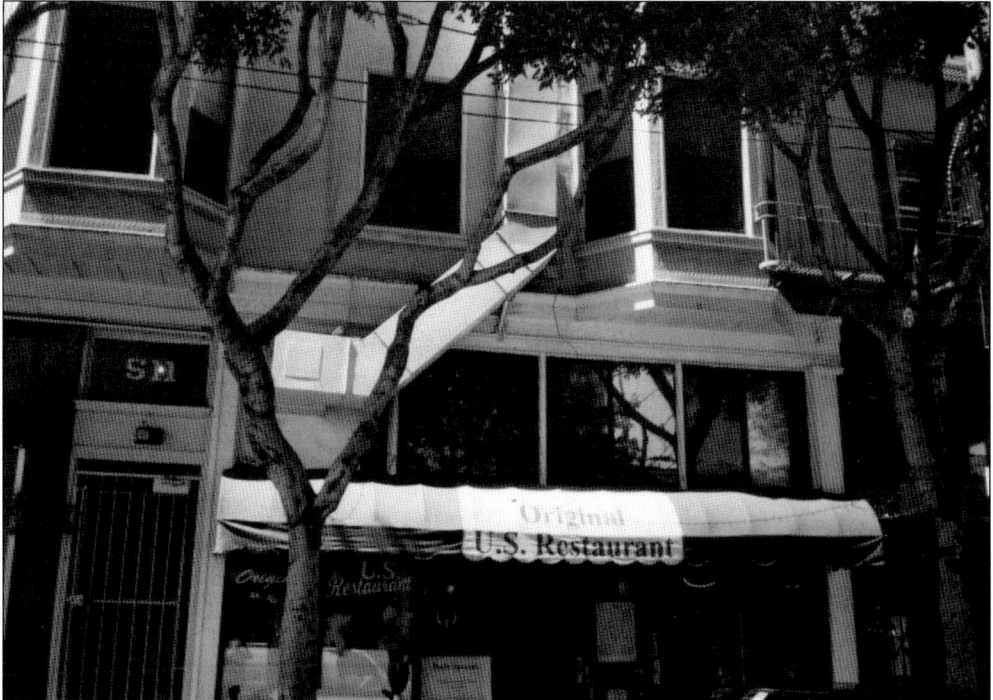

For over 50 years, the U.S. Restaurant served delicious Italian food at the corner of Columbus Avenue and Stockton Street. The "U.S." stands for Unione Sportivo, which means sport union or club, although it has always been a restaurant and family-owned for over 50 years. In 2001, the restaurant moved to a new location at 515 Columbus Avenue near Green Street. (CAA.)

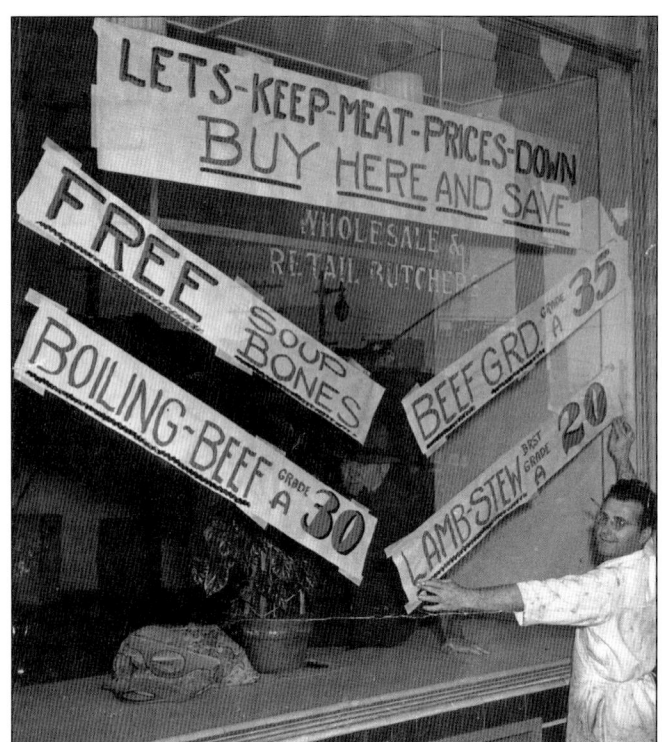

Food has always been at the heart of North Beach culture. Restaurants, cafés, and groceries all contributed to the beloved ambiance of one of San Francisco's most popular districts. Here on October 30, 1946, Louis Ranierei puts up signs advertising low meat prices in the window of the Panelli Meat Company shop at 801 Columbus Avenue. They advertised ground beef at 35¢, lamb stew at 20¢, and soup bones for free. (SFHC.)

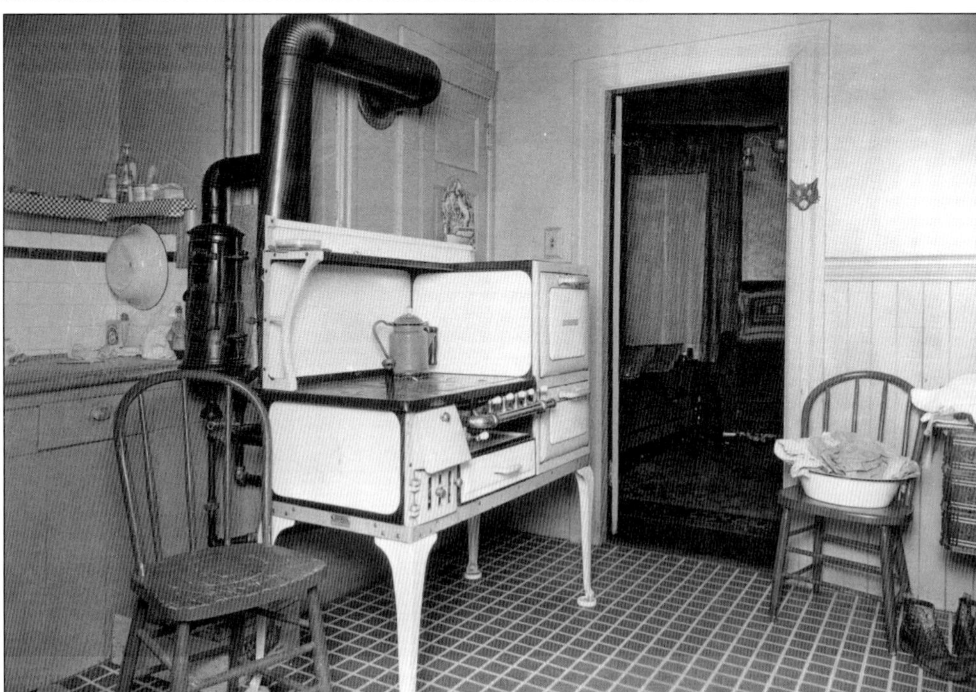

Here is a photograph of the kitchen at 429 Greenwich Street in 1932. By all accounts, this would have been a typical room for a working-class family at that time. Beyond this kitchen with a gas stove is a modest sitting room. This apartment was nestled at the base of Telegraph Hill. (SFHC.)

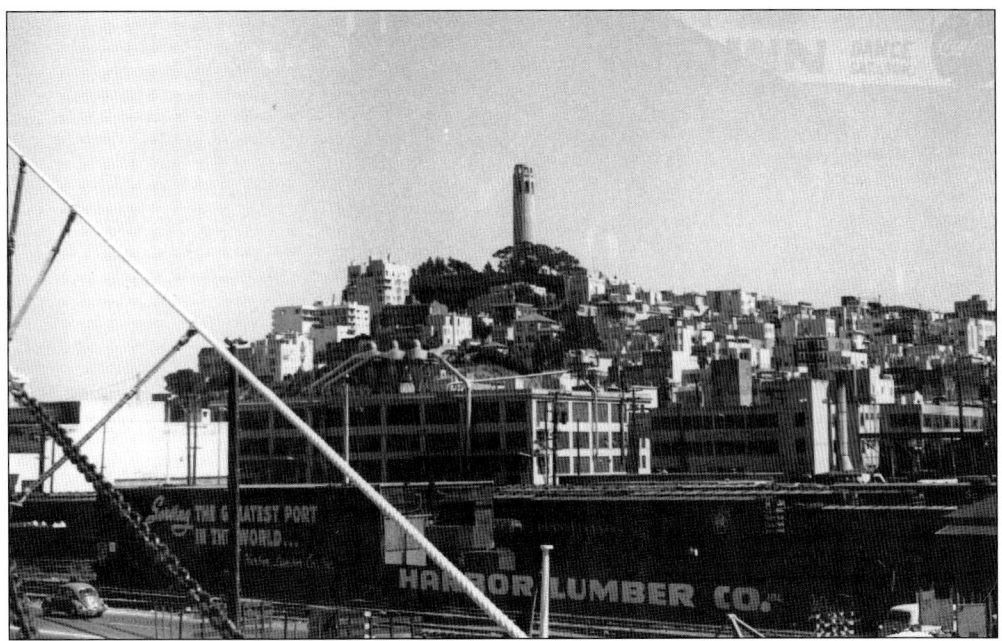

A view of Telegraph Hill and Coit Tower from the Embarcadero. In the middle of the hill was the Roma Macaroni Factory, making pasta around the clock during World War II for people serving in the U.S. armed forces. Roma Macaroni was located at 413 Francisco Street. The author's mother worked there in the 1940s. Also in this image is the Simmons Company, manufacturers of the famous Simmons Beautyrest mattresses. The author's father worked there from the 1940s to the early 1960s. (SFHC.)

In the center of this advertisement page is the Roma Macaroni advertisement, which reads, "Roma products excel for over 60 years—quality since 1875—The house with a complete line." This page is from the official program for the Golden Gate Bridge Fiesta, May 27 to June 2, 1937. (CAA.)

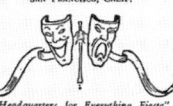

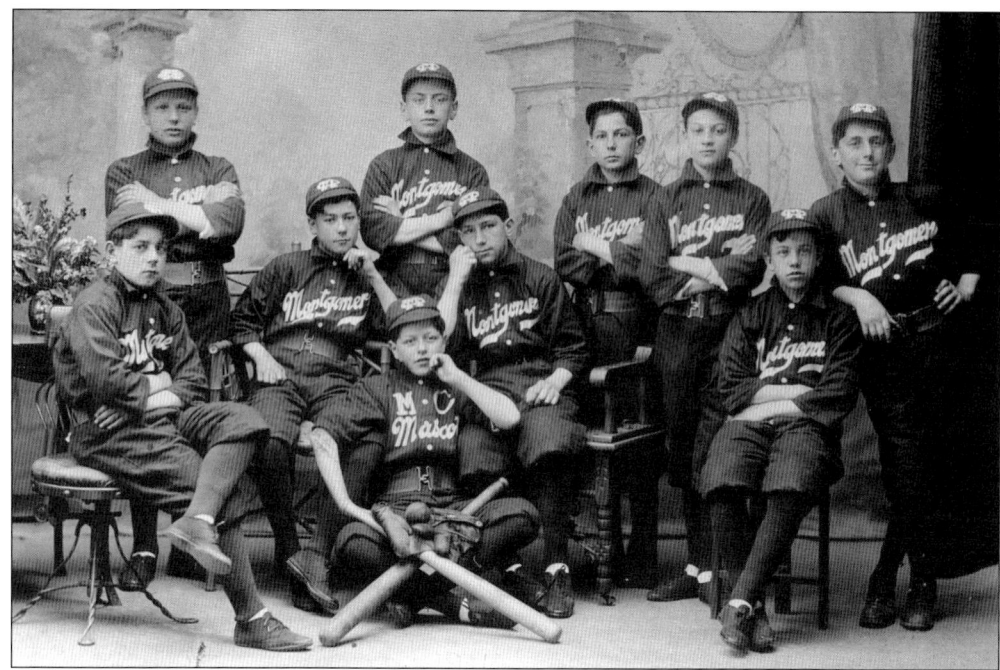

The Montgomery baseball team may have played in the area around the North Beach playground, now the Joe DiMaggio Playground. DiMaggio, who grew up in North Beach, became one of baseball's most famous and beloved athletes. He is quoted as saying: "Baseball to me in those days was merely an excuse to get away from the house and away from the chores of fishing." (JBM.)

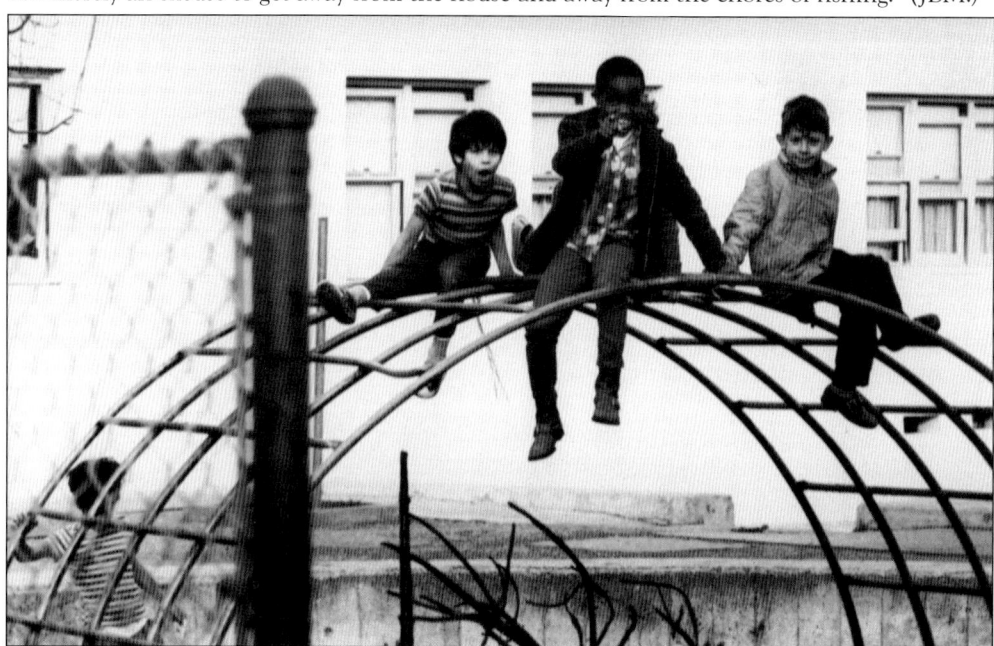

These children are playing in the North Beach playground at Lombard and Powell Streets around 1970. The playground is part of the recreation and park department financed by a bond issue approved by the voters in September 1903. The site has been renamed the Joe DiMaggio Playground and is undergoing renovation. (CAA.)

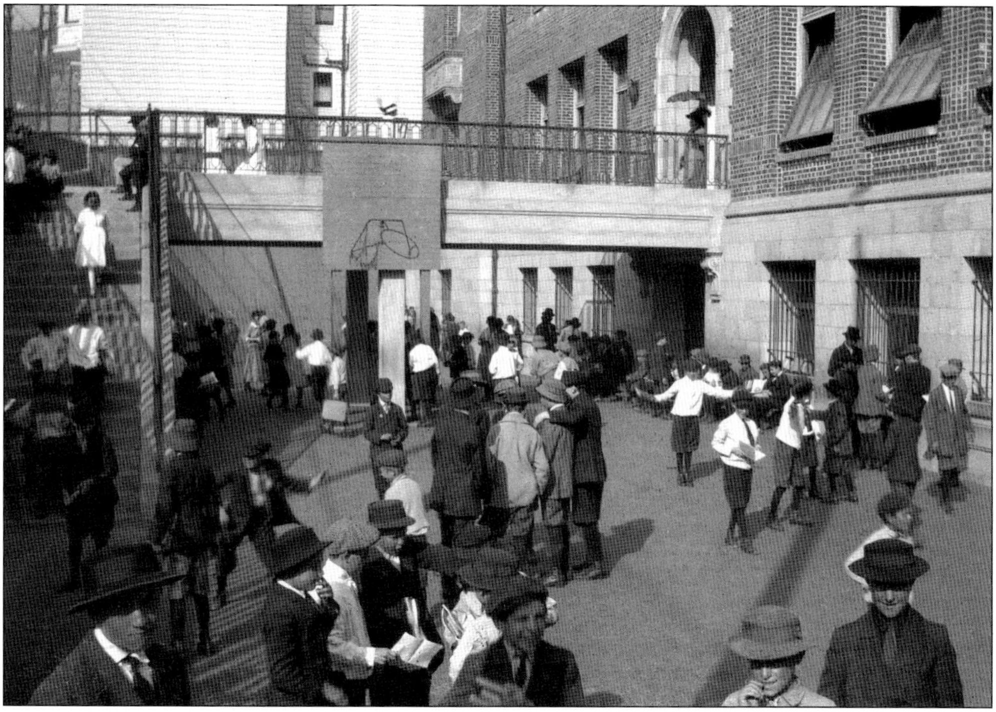

Here is the 1912 graduation at the Hancock School. Although the school was just outside the official boundaries of what is considered North Beach, many of the students were from the area. It was located at Filbert near Taylor. (JBM.)

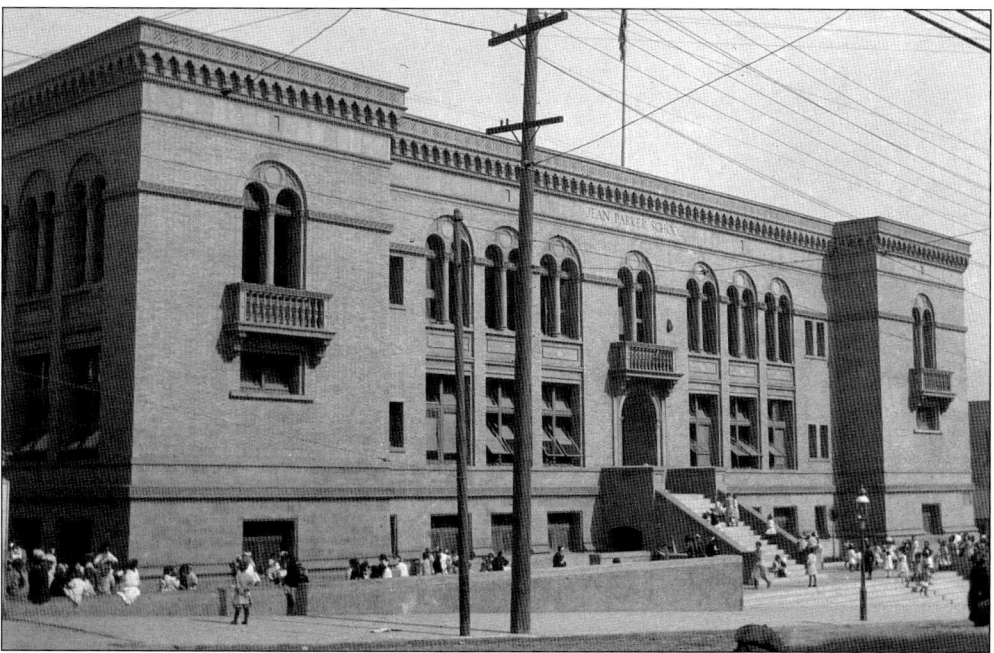

The Jean Parker School was one of two schools on Broadway. Located near Powell Street, this school dates back to 1861. Originally called the Broadway Grammar School, the name was changed in 1903 to honor Jean Parker, a former principal. (JBM.)

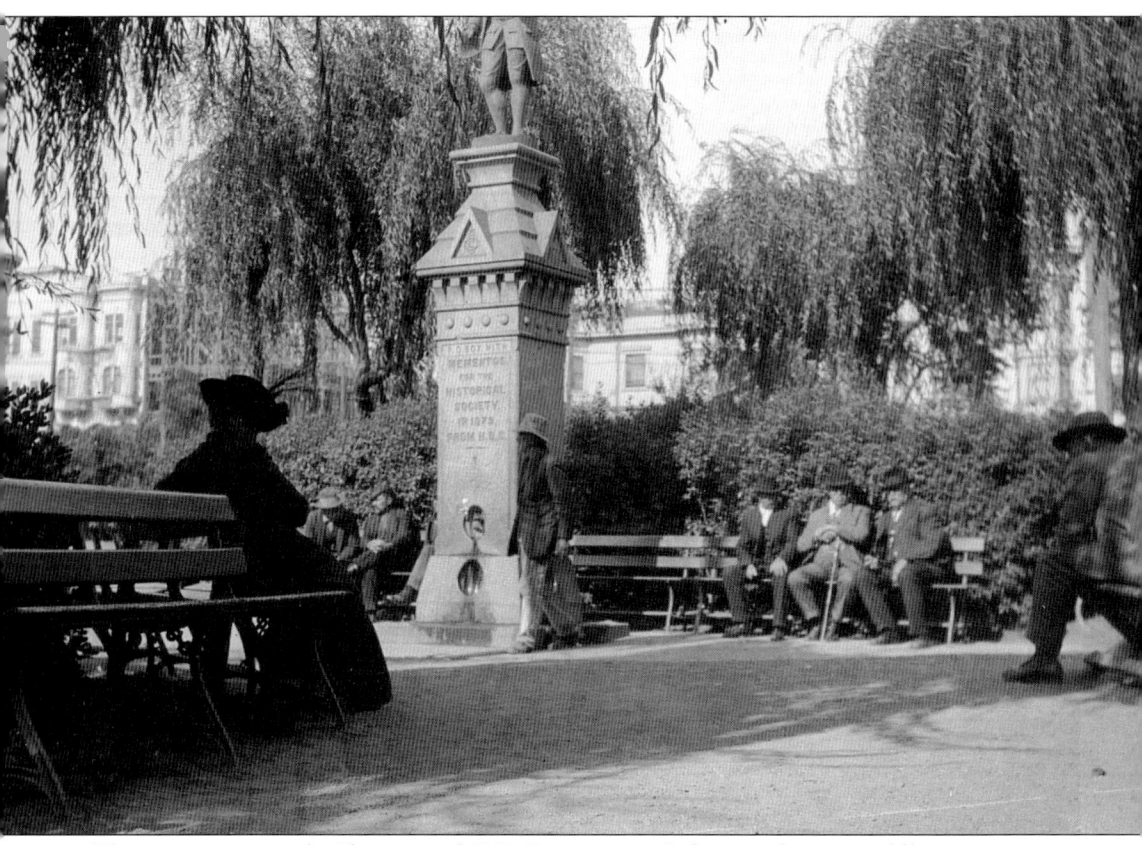

These are *paesani* in the Plaza around 1900. Paesani is an Italian word meaning fellow countrymen. These paesani would gather here on their usual bench most every day to discuss life. The men are seated next to a statue of Benjamin Franklin, the base of which reads, "P.O. box with momentos for the Historical Society in 1979 from H.D.C." H. D. C. stands for Henry Daniel Cogswell, a dentist who donated the funds for this statue. (JBM.)

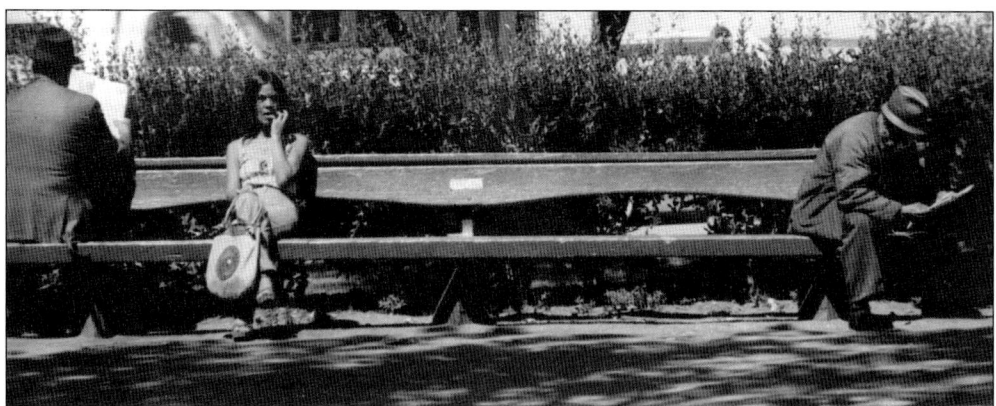

Above is another bench in Washington Square around 1980. This is a typical scene: two older men from the neighborhood, in their hats of course, reading their newspapers. The young woman rests for a moment as if to balance the bench for the young and old. (CAA.)

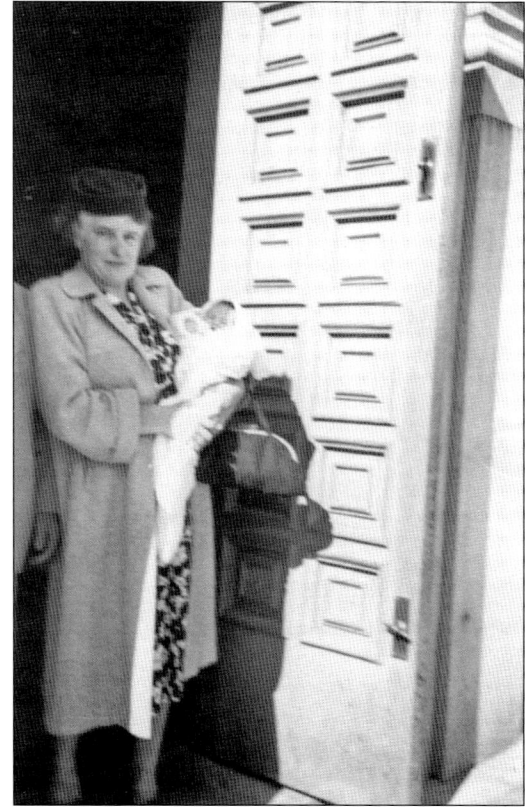

This is a photograph of the author, Catherine Accardi, held by her aunt Desolina Lippi at the doors of SS. Peter and Paul Church. This was the day of Catherine's baptism at 8 weeks old. The church is a favorite of San Francisco Catholics for weddings and baptisms. This is the same spot where, in 1954, Marilyn Monroe and Joe DiMaggio stood for photographs after their civil marriage ceremony at city hall. (Photograph by Albert Lippi.)

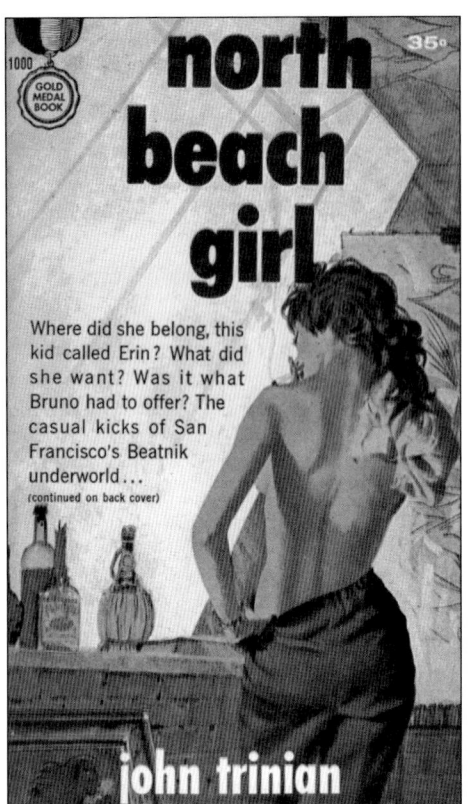

The book *North Beach Girl* by John Trinian, was just one of the many stories set in the North Beach district of San Francisco. The cover text states, "This particular tale is about the casual kicks of San Francisco's Beatnik underworld." (© 1960 *North Beach Girl* by John Trinian, published by Gold Medal Books, a division of Random House, Inc.)

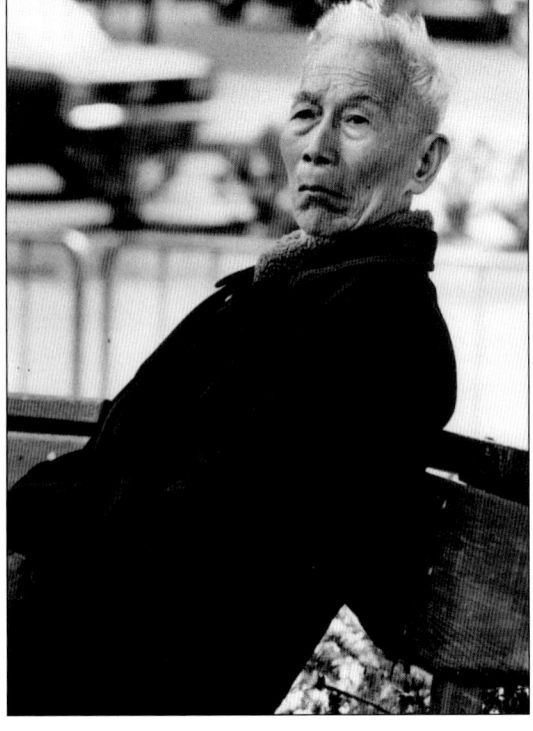

A resident of North Beach is pondering life as he sits on a bench in Washington Square around 1970. The area is, and originally was, primarily Italian, but as with San Francisco as a whole, ethnic and cultural diversity is welcomed and enjoyed by residents. (CAA.)

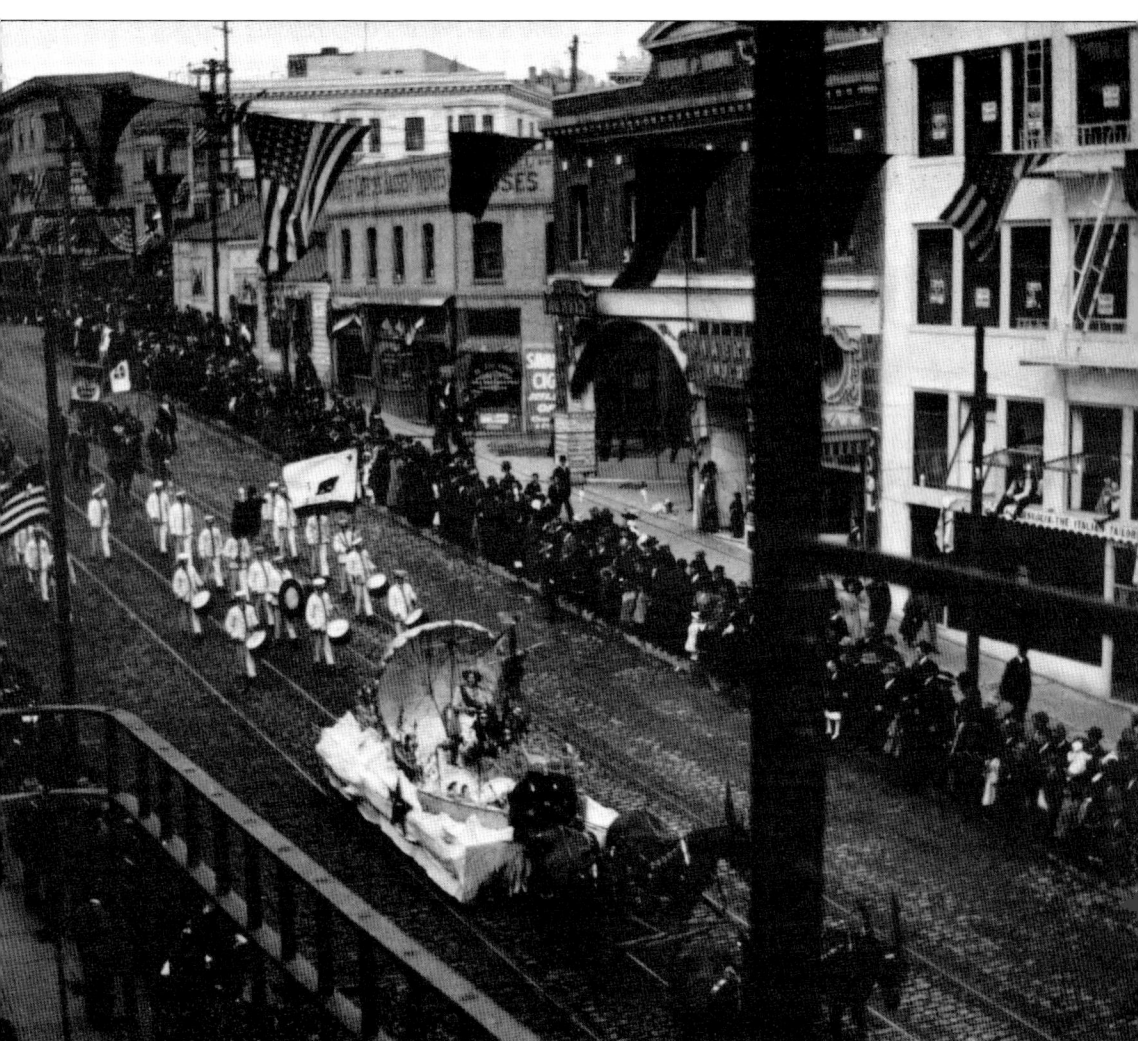

Pictured here is the Columbus Day Parade on Columbus Avenue just below Broadway. Columbus Day has been a unifying event in North Beach since 1869. Grand marshal A. D. Greenwood began the first 1869 procession, which included marching guards, bands, and many handsome horses. Floats included a car decorated with Italian, American, and Spanish flags, with a hemisphere symbolizing the New World. The Columbus Day Parade and Festival continues to this day. (JBM.)

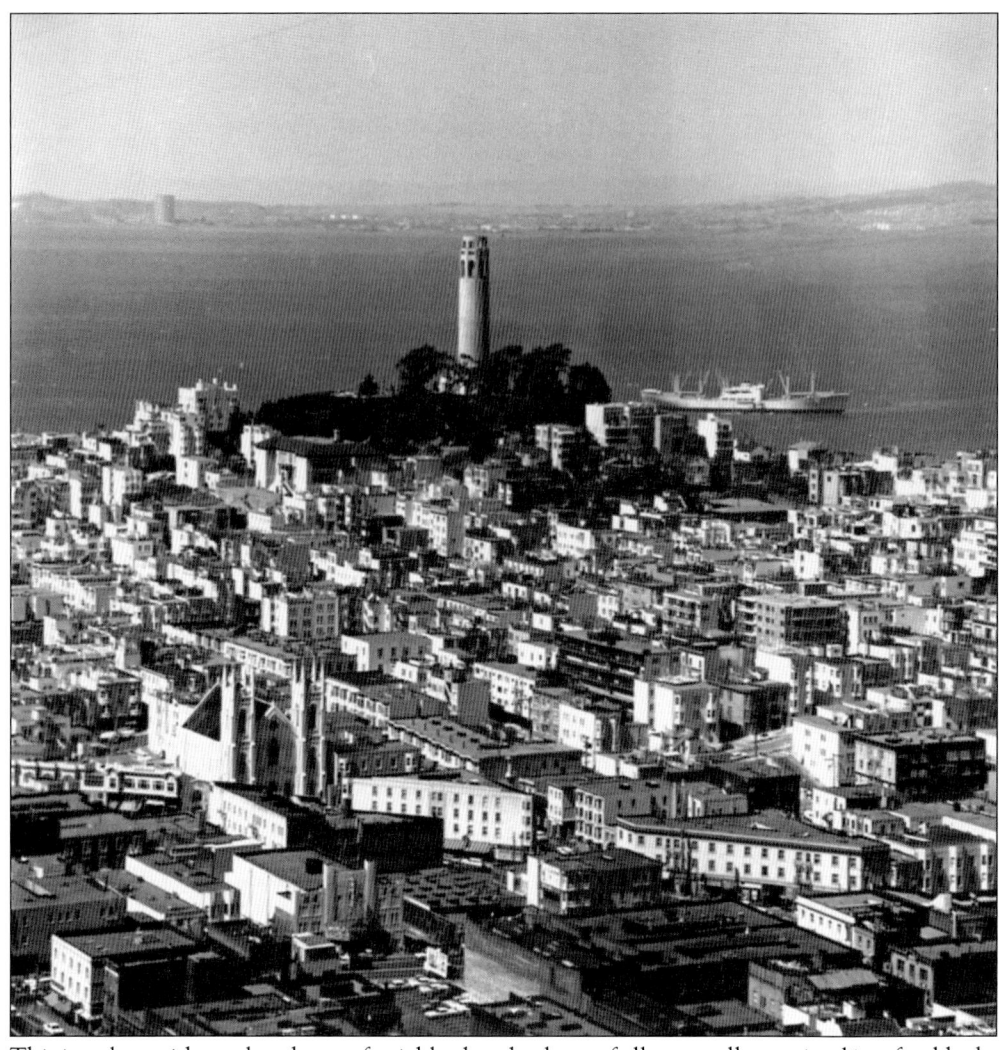

This is a place with an abundance of neighborhood culture of all types, all contained in a few blocks of extraordinary urban landscape. Columbus Avenue dramatically cuts through the neighborhood connecting San Francisco's Financial District with Fisherman's Wharf, as it has done for over 100 years. This amazing urban fabric is a result of decades, of layer upon layer of historical events, artists, writers, musicians, and everyday people's lives. These streets entice residents and visitors alike to experience the rich cultural treasure that is North Beach and Telegraph Hill. (SFHC.)

Four
PEOPLE AND PLACES

Chapter four focuses on the people and places that were the foundation of North Beach. Without the resourceful, energetic citizens and their families, North Beach would not have the fascinating atmosphere and historical sites that exist today. Some of the key people and places are represented in rare historical images. Certainly, numerous towns in America can rightfully say their people and places were the foundation and the glue that shaped their local history, but North Beach and Telegraph Hill may well be at the top of this list.

The Spanish and Mexican inhabitants called the hill Loma Alta, which translates to "high hill." At its western base, Juana Briones had a potato patch and dairy ranch near the intersection of Powell and Filbert Streets. Between 1848 and 1852, the settlement grew from 1,000 to 35,000 inhabitants. By the 1880s, quarrying on the eastern side of the hill by the Gray Brothers and other companies changed the scene forever.

Frederick O. Layman built his folly, called the German Castle, at the top of the hill in 1884. In 1931, a bequest from Lillie Hitchcock Coit funded the construction of Coit Tower on this same Loma Alta. Photographer and respected local resident J. B. Monaco captured life before, during, and after the 1906 disaster. The devastation of 1906 did bring major changes to the North Beach area. Prominent resident Amadeo Peter Giannini and his Bank of Italy (later Bank of America) were instrumental in providing banking services after the earthquake and fire. Redevelopment came quickly. In 1930, Pasquale Gogna built his romantic tower dwelling overlooking Broadway. Years later, Enrico Banducci was one of the people who brought the entertainment scene to the Broadway area. El Matator, the Hungry i, and Purple Onion made nightlife history. From its beginnings, Native American tribes, Spaniards, and European immigrants were the people of North Beach.

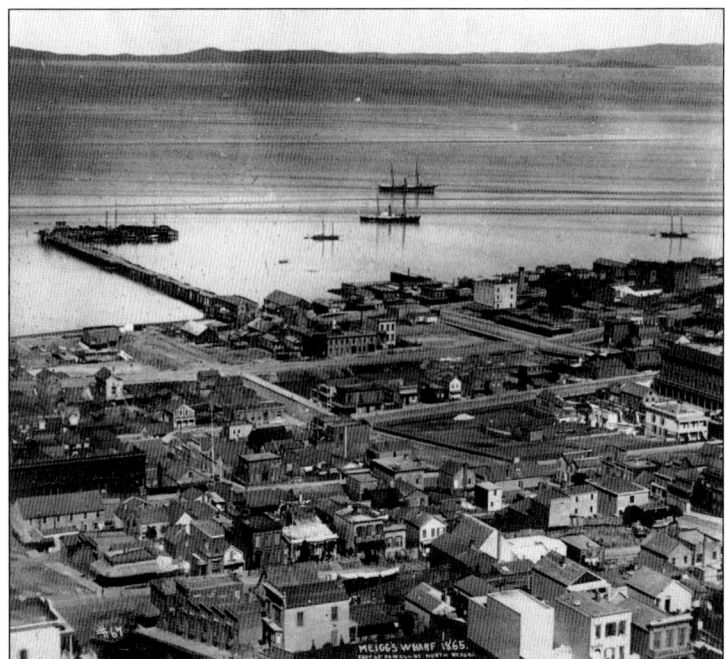

Looking north in the distance in 1865 is Meiggs' Wharf at the foot of Powell Street. Meiggs, often called the father of North Beach, arrived in 1850. He was responsible for construction of the approximately 1,600-foot-long wharf in 1853. The first ferry terminal for the Sausalito ferry was at Meiggs' Wharf. Originally, most vessels entering the Golden Gate anchored at Yerba Buena cover at the foot of Washington and Jackson Streets. (SFHC.)

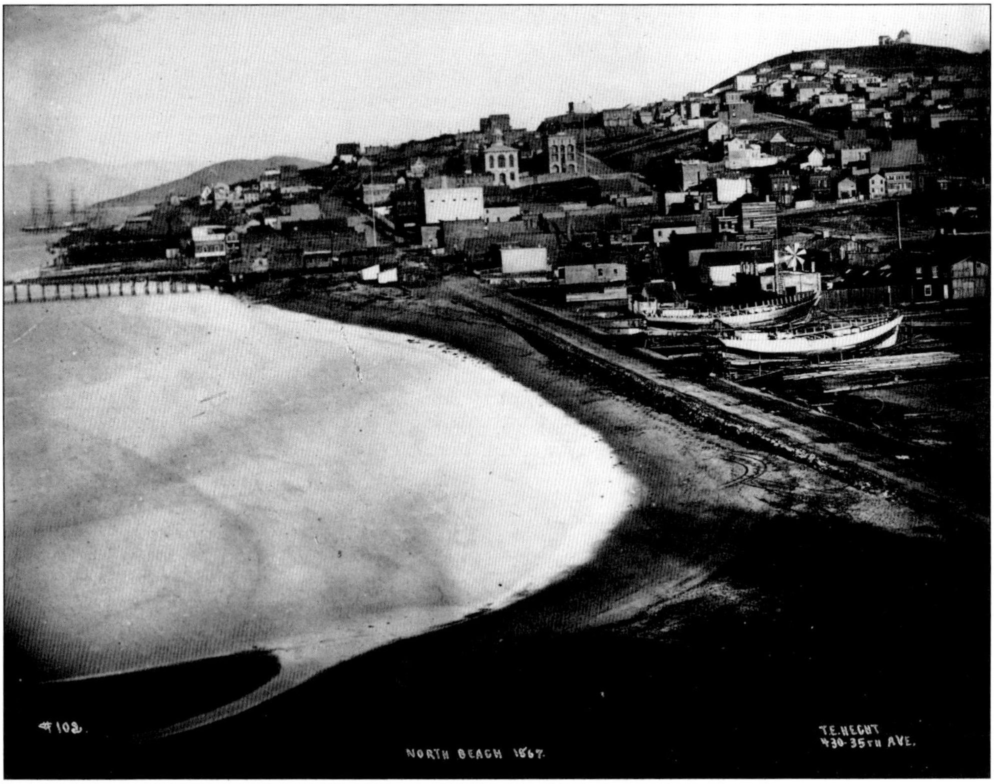

This is a closer look at Meiggs Wharf in 1867. A bit of beach is still visible in North Beach. The wharf was always a spot for the fishing fleet, swimmers, and sunbathers—some even claiming the style and character of Fisherman's Wharf can be traced to Henry Meiggs. (SFHC.)

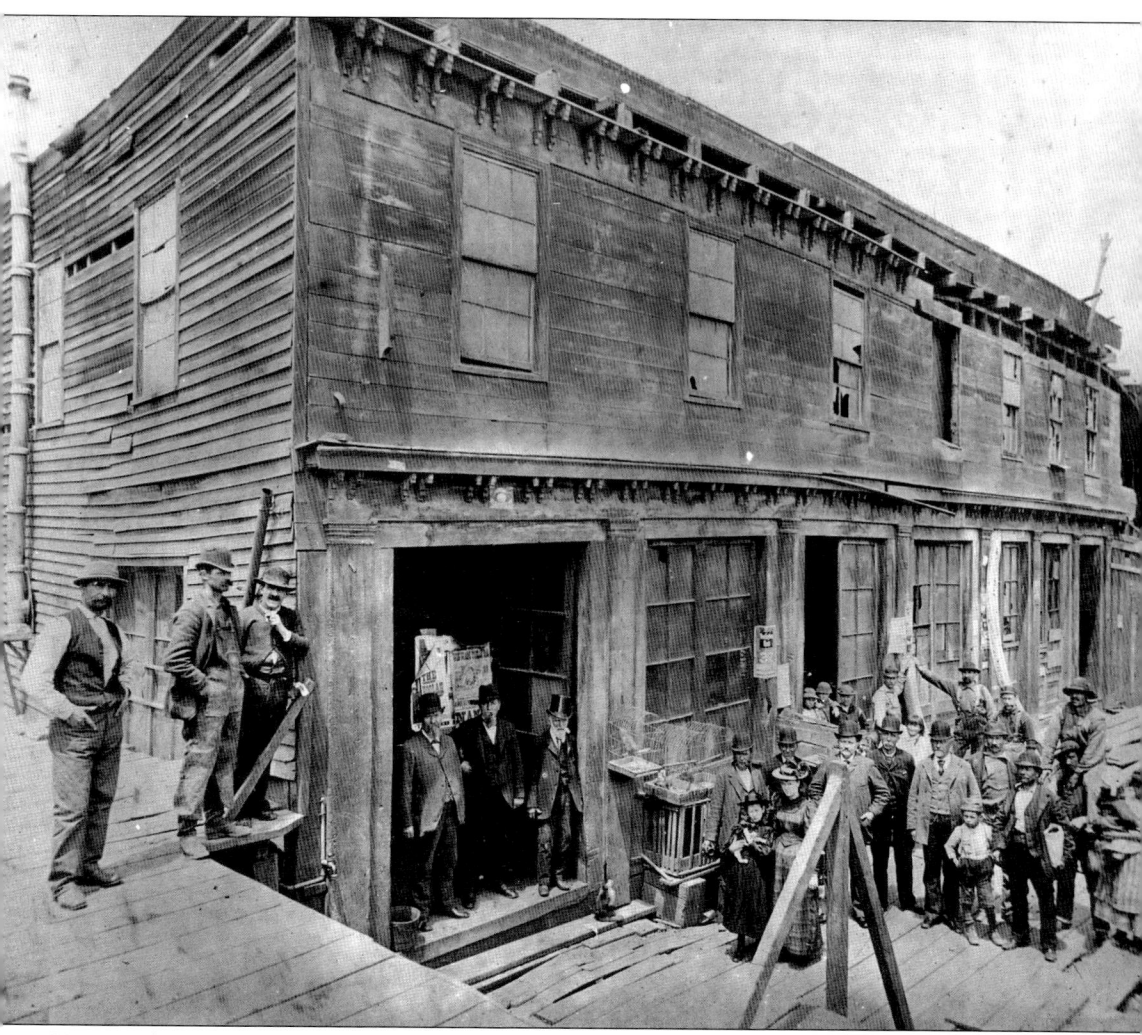

Here is Abe Warner's Cobweb Palace at Meigg's Wharf around 1902. This ramshackle structure was formerly a butcher shop. Quite an interesting gathering is posing for the camera, consisting of men, women, children, cats, several monkeys, and birds. One historical account of a visit to this place notes: "The strangest feature of that most strange hostelry was the amazing wealth of cobwebs that mantled it. Cobwebs as dense as crape waved in dusty rags from the ceiling; they veiled the pictures and festooned the picture-frames, that shone dimly through them. Not one of these cobwebs was ever molested." It is said that the unconstrained resident parrot had a taste for liquor and could curse in four languages. The drink of choice at the Cobweb was Abe's hot toddy, a mixture of cloves, whiskey, and gin. (SFHC.)

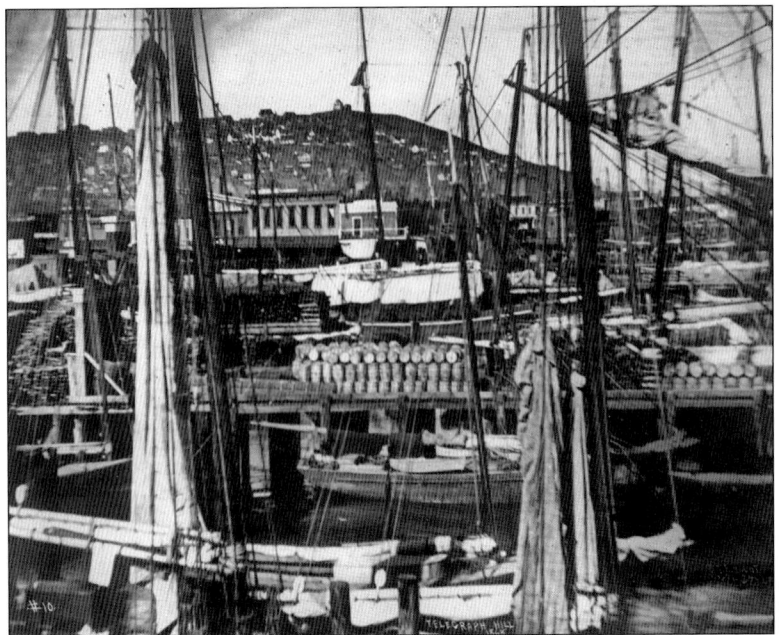

The famous San Francisco waterfront is pictured again in 1868. In the background is Telegraph Hill, through a maze of ships masts, boats, and cargo. Author Howard Pease wrote the marvelous book *Foghorn's* about a young man's adventures as a sailor at the port of San Francisco. (SFHC.)

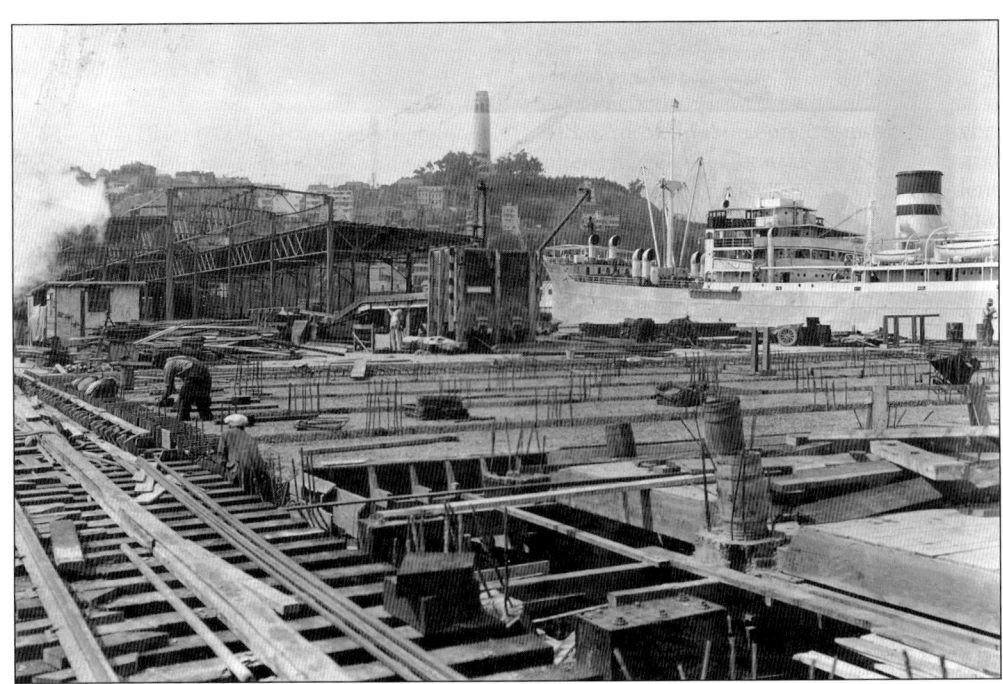

This photograph, taken on August 5, 1938, is of a pier under construction with Coit Tower visible in the background. News copy of the day reads, "Workmen laying concrete flooring for new pier on the Embarcadero. When completed it will cost $750,000, will add 129,732 feet of storage space to the waterfront's capacity." (SFHC.)

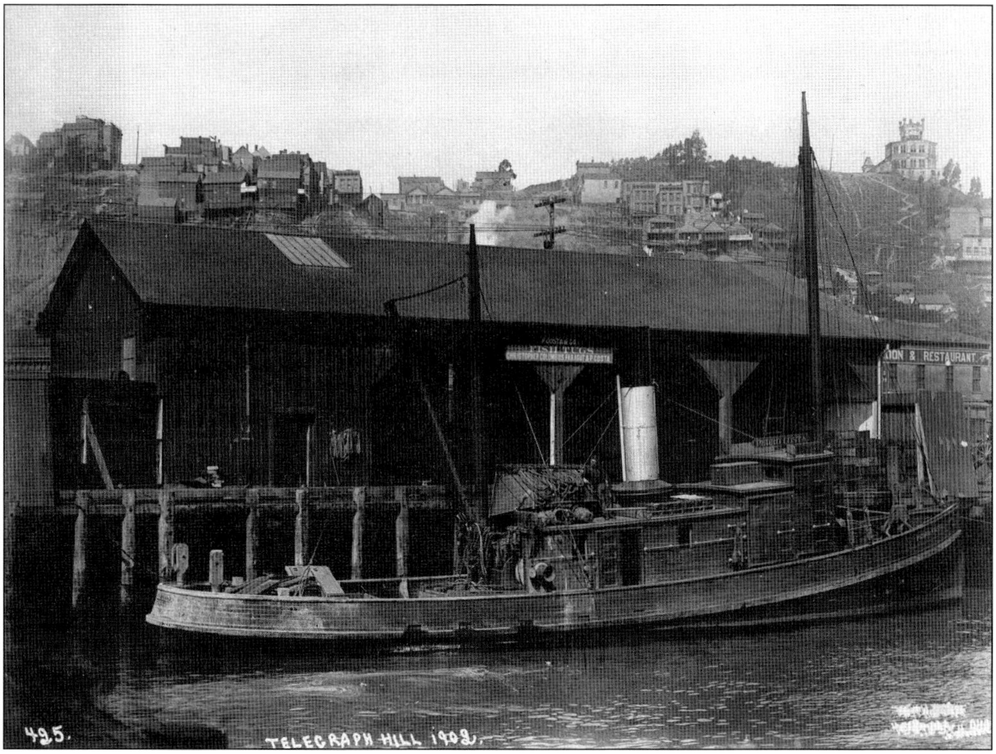

Another location at the waterfront, a rustic wooden shack, is home to a fisherman's boat. The sign reads, "P. Costa & Co.—Fish Tugs—Christopher Columbus Faragut, and P. Costa." (SFHC.)

San Francisco's early maritime industry was centered around the base of Telegraph Hill, seen here in this *c. 1864* image. The large structure in the center has a sign that reads, "Northpoint Dock Warehouse." It was built around 1853 and soon became the favorite berth for such famous clipper ships as the giant *Great Republic*. (SFHC.)

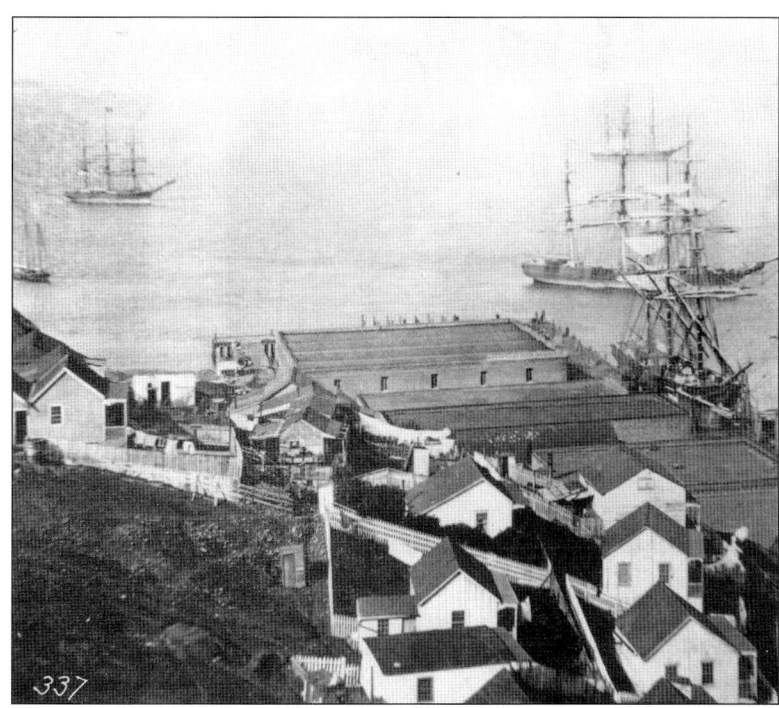

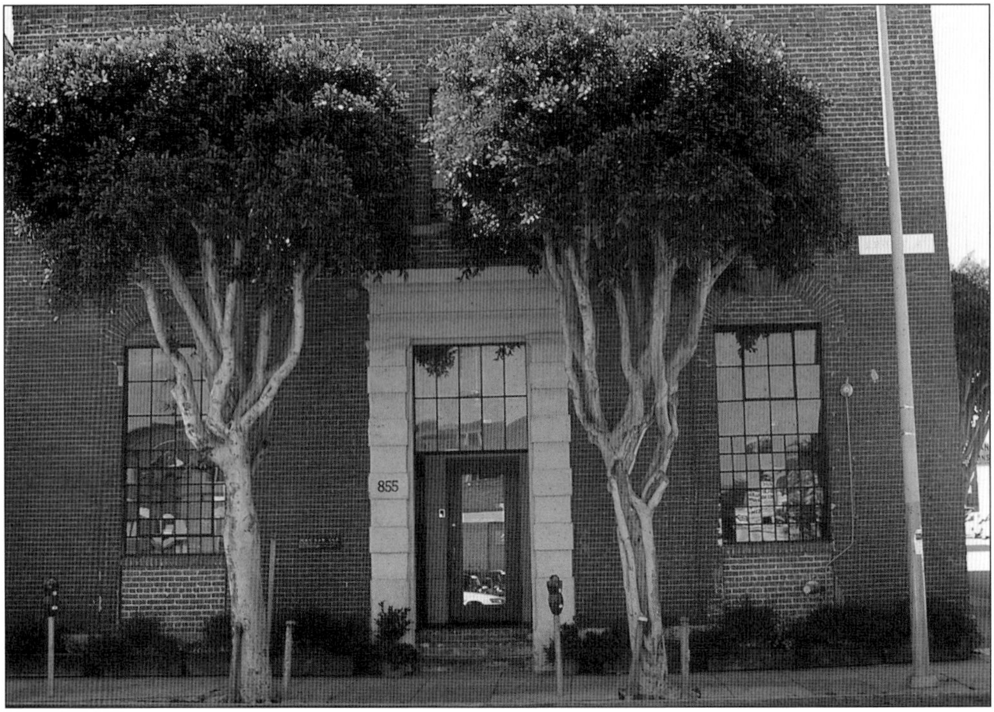

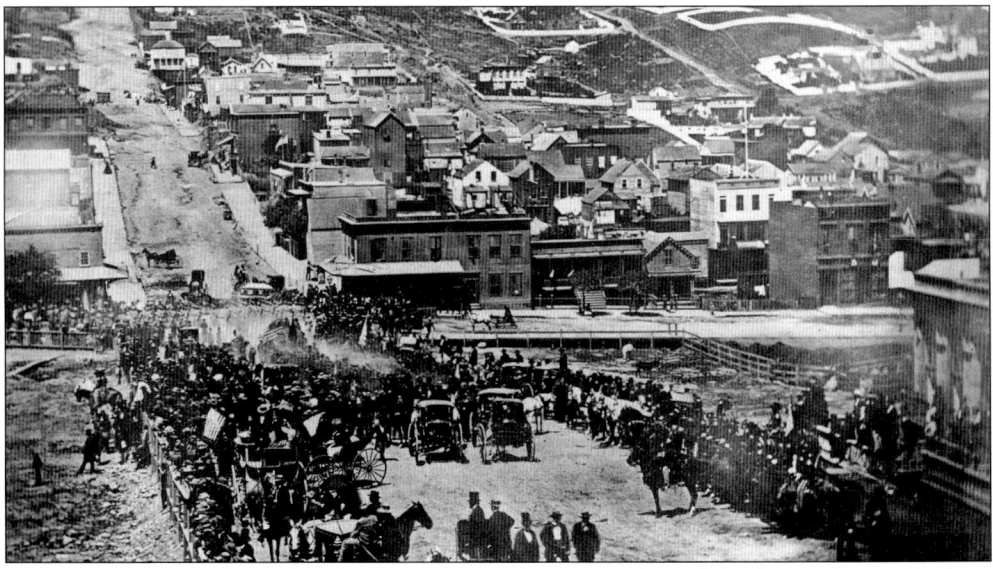

A glorious example of a Gold Rush warehouse at the base of Telegraph Hill is this structure, on the National Register of Historic Places and San Francisco Landmark No. 91 under the name Trinidad Bean and Elevator Company. Originally it was the Daniel Gibb and Company warehouse at 855 Front at Vallejo Street. Located at what was Clark's Point, two Gibb warehouses were constructed in 1855 on landfill. The original shoreline of San Francisco was across the street. (CAA.)

Historical accounts indicate that this is an image of the memorial march for deceased Pres. Abraham Lincoln in what is now Washington Square. The year was 1865. One account reads, "April 19. The funeral obsequies of President Lincoln, in a point of extent and grandeur, surpassed anything ever before seen on the Pacific coast, the procession being some miles in length." (SFHC.)

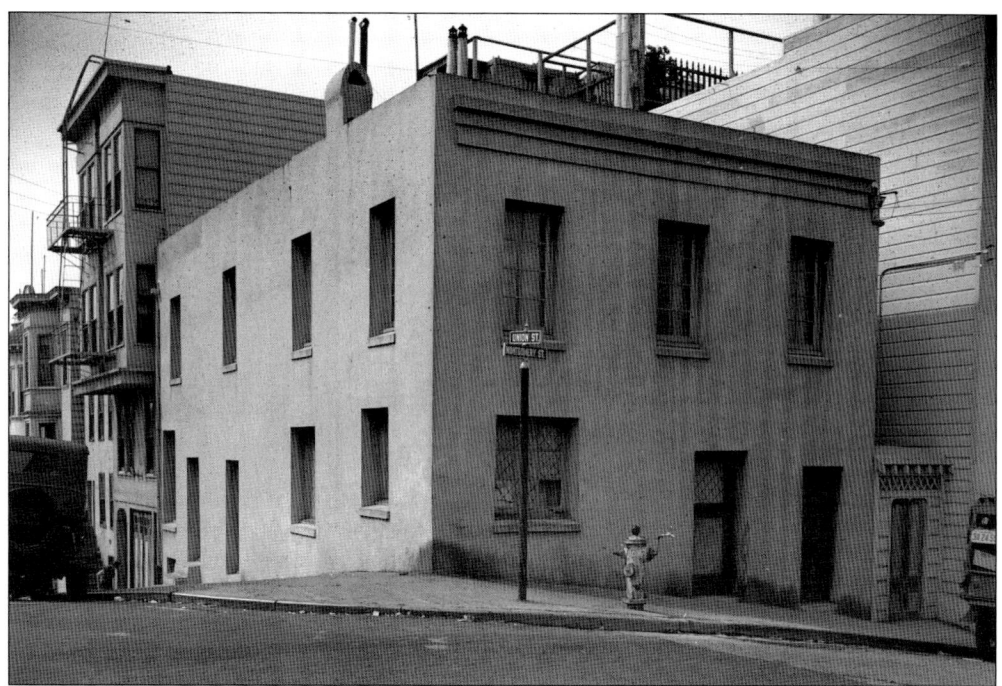

The building at 1301 Montgomery Street in 1940 is hardly recognizable from the structure at the same location in 1850. Under the plaster is one of the oldest brick buildings in San Francisco. The property belonged to German immigrant Herman A. Meisel. At one time or other over the years, it was a poolroom, a grocery store, and apartments. (LOC.)

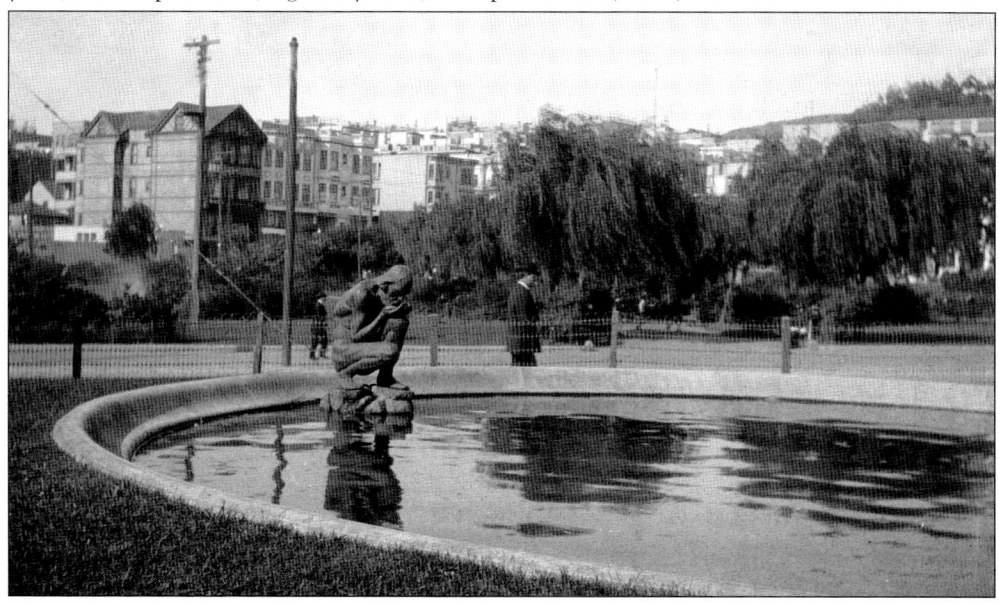

Above is a view of the Marini pond looking towards Washington Plaza across Montgomery Street. This image includes the Cummings statue in the pond. The bronze statue of a man drinking from a pool was created by Melvin E. Cummings in 1902. He used the same model for this bronze man as Aubuste Rodin did for his St. John the Baptist. Cummings donated his statue to the city of San Francisco in 1905. (JBM.)

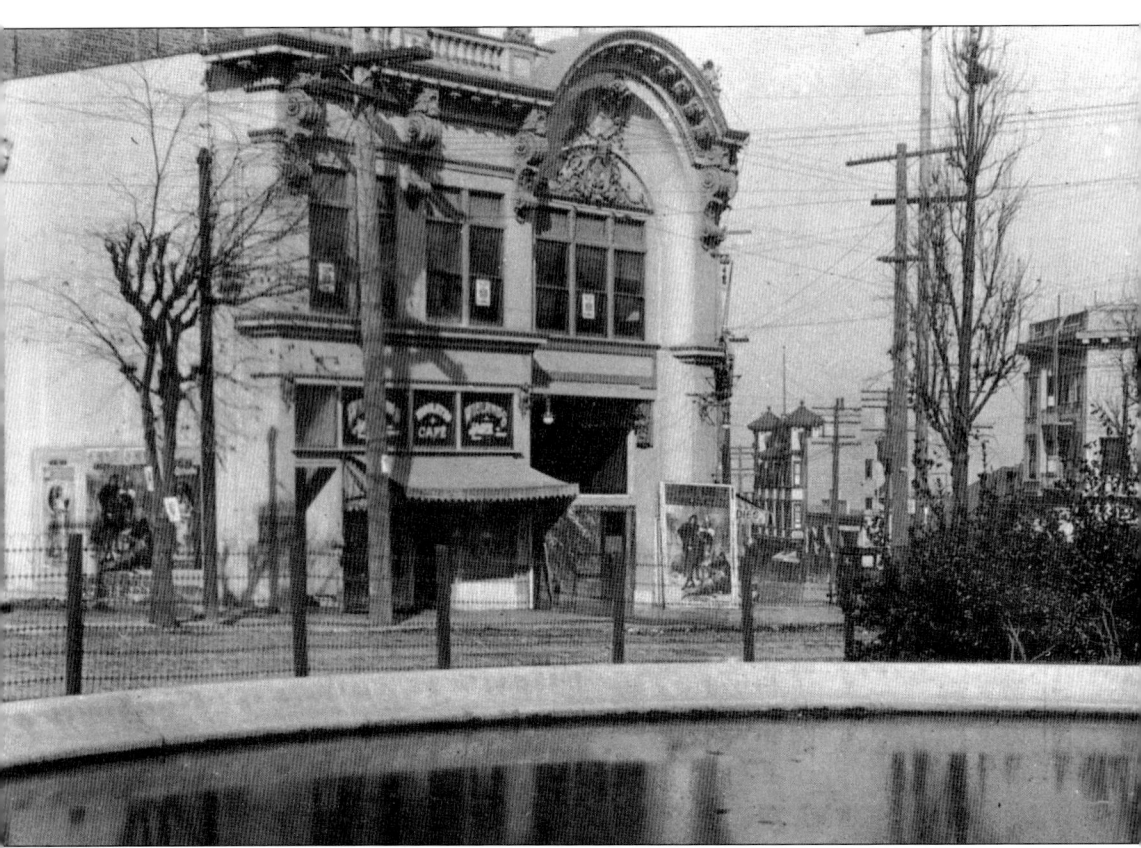

Here is the Marini pond at the corner of Powell Street and Columbus Avenue. Beyond is the Milano Theatre (later the Palace movie theater) and former site of the Russian church. The theater opened as the Washington Square Theatre on April 10, 1909, with 1,000 seats at 5¢ or 10¢ per seat. The opening as an Italian theater was a great event in the community. Cesare, the *capo comico* of the Compagnia Comica-Draramatlca Italiana announced that the repertoire for the forthcoming season would include drama, comedy, farce, *bozzettl* (sketches), *romanze* (ballads), and *pezzi d'opera* (operatic numbers). Operating as such until the 1930s, it was sold and renamed the Milano, only to be extensively remodeled in the late 1930s in the moderne style, reopening as the Palace on November 5, 1937. It was again renamed as the Pagoda on August 5, 1974, featuring Chinese films. Its last days as a film theater were in December 1994. During the 1930s and up until 1941, it featured English-language films during the day and Italian-language films and plays in the evenings. (JBM.)

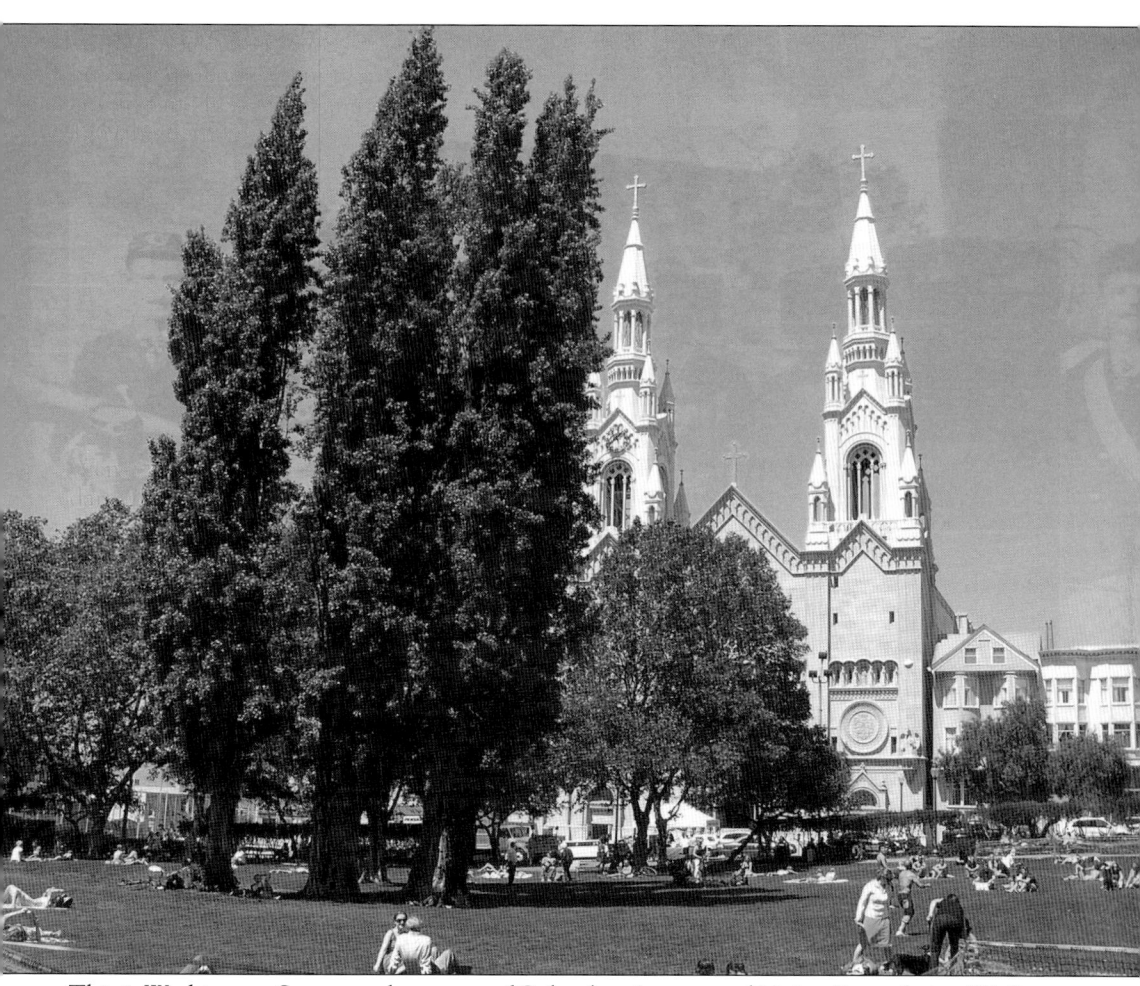

This is Washington Square at the corner of Columbus Avenue and Union Street facing SS. Peter and Paul Church. The church was originally located at Filbert Street and Grant Avenue, then called San Pietro, and was a wooden structure founded by Rev. Carlo Franchi. Construction began in 1912 and was completed in 1924. Cecil B. DeMille filmed the workers and used the scene to show the building of the Temple of Jerusalem in his 1923 film *The Ten Commandments*. Director Don Siegel features the church in scenes from the movie *Dirty Harry*. Called *cattedrale d'Italia ovest*, or "the Italian cathedral of the west," Charles Fantoni and John Porporato's neo-Gothic design is ornamented in Romanesque style and features twin spires soaring 191 feet high. (CAA.)

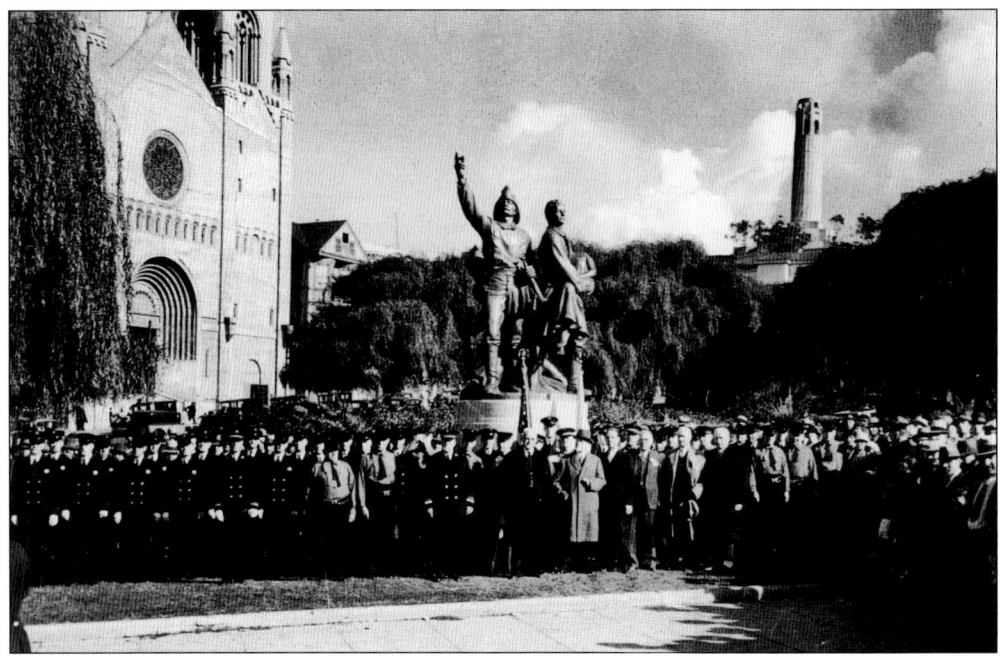

The December 3, 1933, dedication of a bronze statue commemorating the San Francisco Volunteer Fire Department is seen here. The statue was crafted by sculptor Haig Paigian. Dignitaries, members of the fire department, and proud citizens pose for this photograph on a fine sunny day. In the background is Coit Tower, also dedicated to the brave firefighters of the city. (SFHC.)

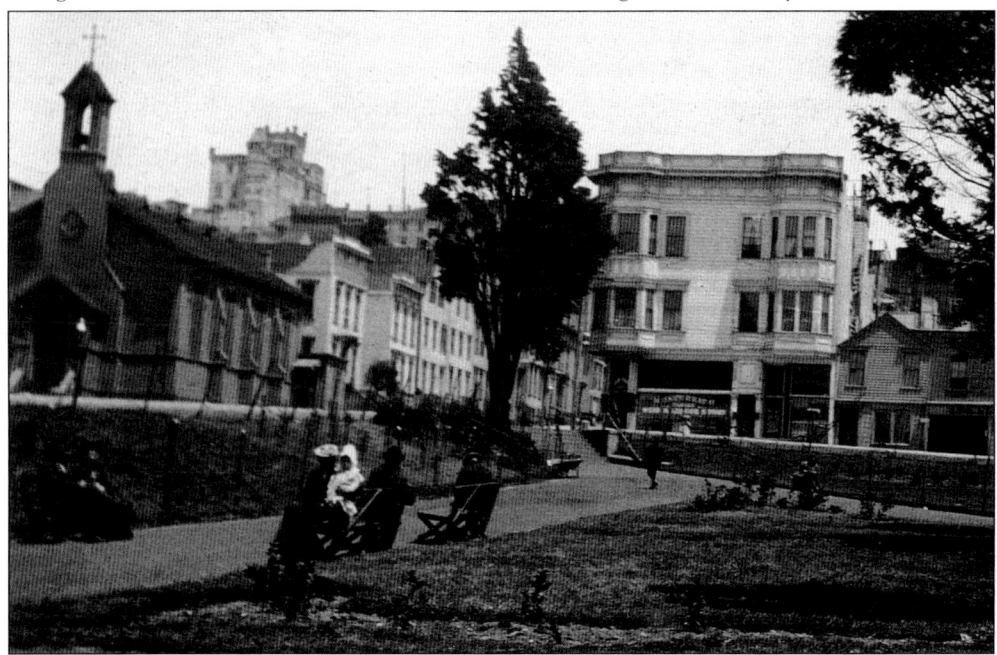

Here is Washington Square in the late 1800s. On the left is St. Peter's Episcopal Church at the northeast corner of Stockton and Filbert Streets. Seated on a bench in the center of this photograph is the young child, Dante Monaco, with his mother, Katherine, who was the wife of photographer J. B. Monaco. (JBM.)

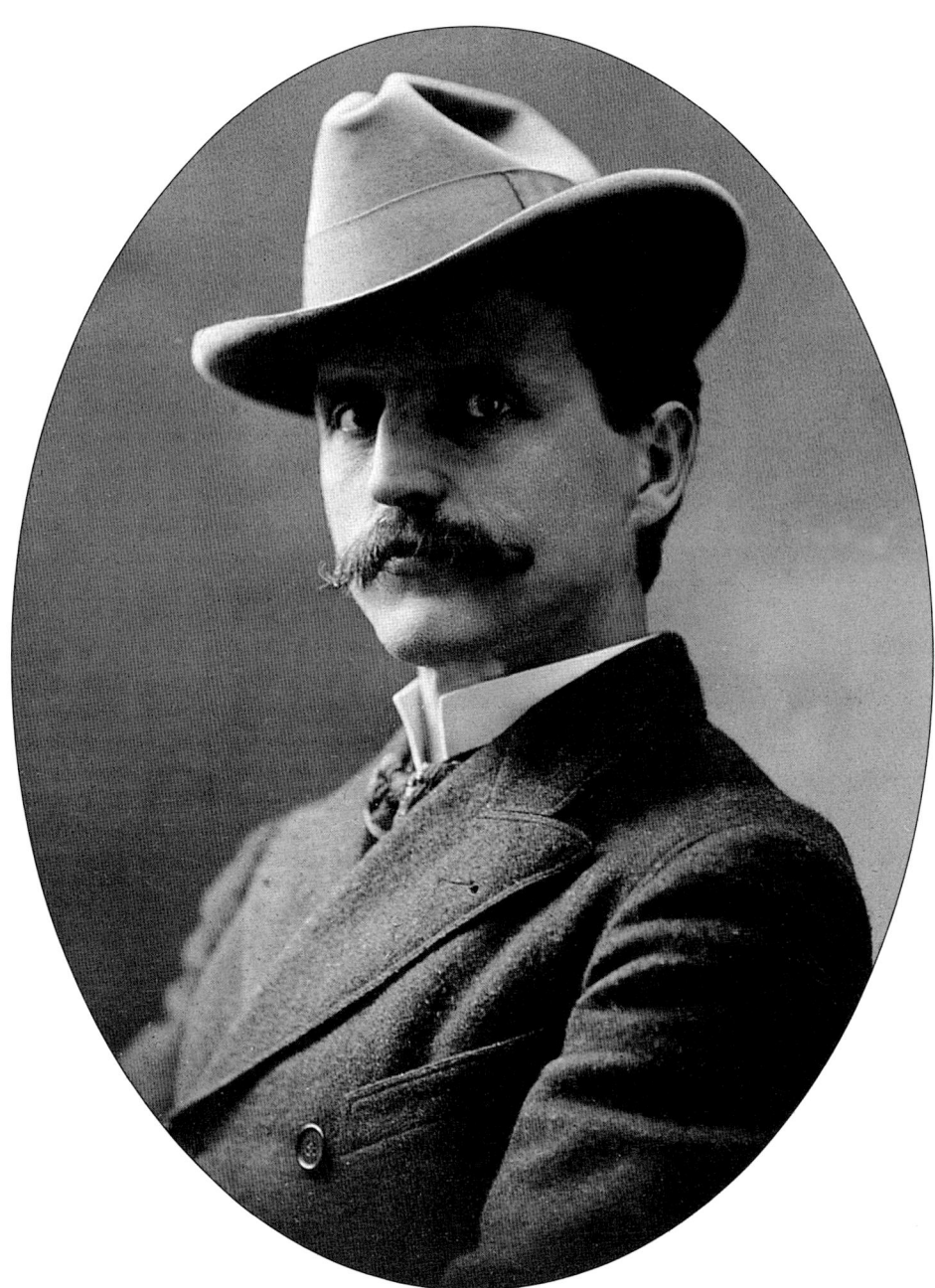

Among the many notable people important to North Beach was J. B. Monaco (Giovanni Battista), the photographer who took many of the images in this book. He came to the United States from his native Switzerland in 1875. He joined his brother Louis in Eureka, Nevada, then they moved to San Francisco is 1888. The original San Francisco location for their photography studio was 1228 Market Street, and later 702 Market Street. After Louis's passing in 1887, J. B. moved the photography business to North Beach, where he remained until his retirement in 1937. During his lifetime, J. B., considered the dean of North Beach photographers, left an impressive photographic collection spanning the years 1856 to 1938. This image was taken in 1908 when J. B. was 52. (JBM.)

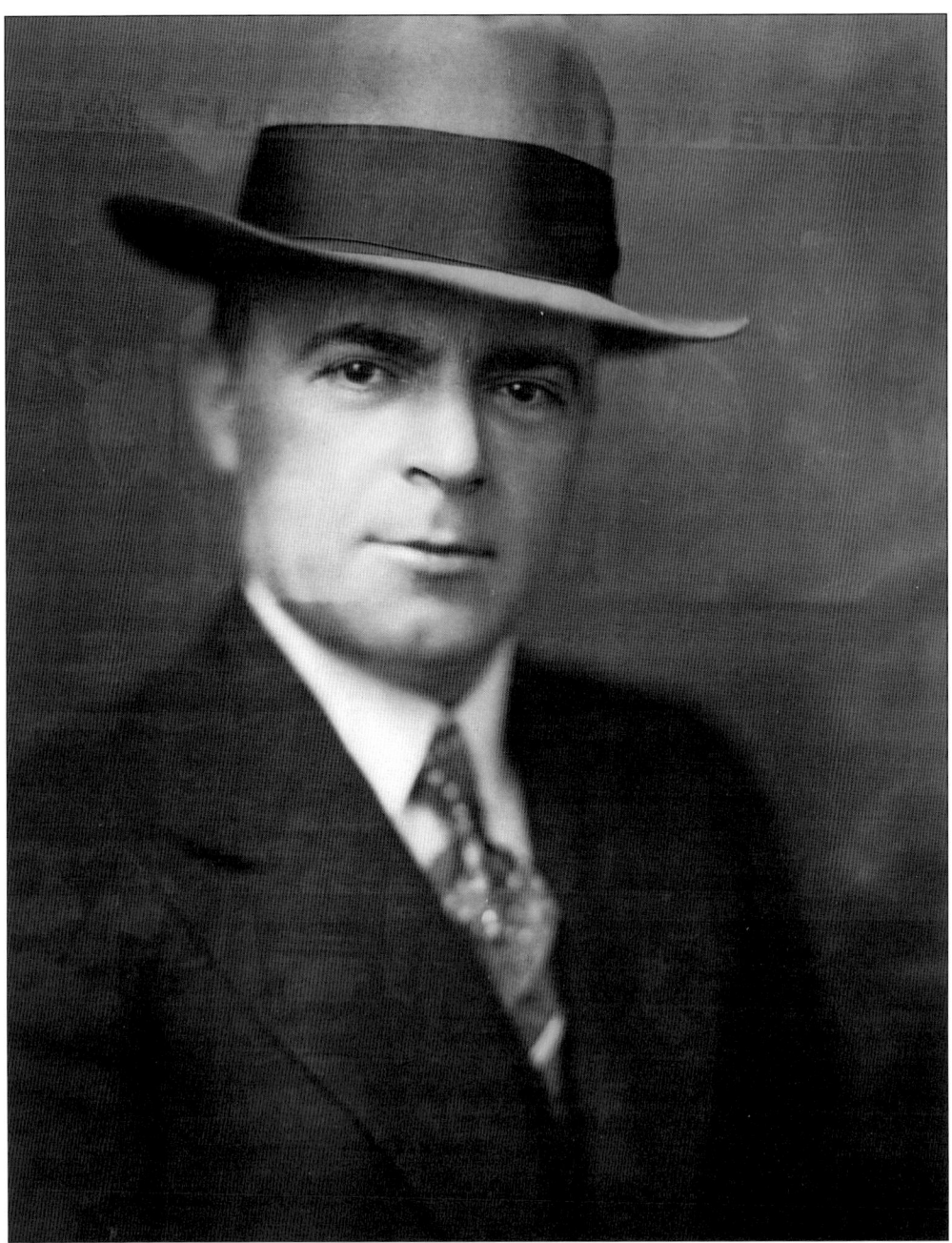

This is a portrait of Sylvester Andriano, San Francisco supervisor in the 1920s. He also served as chairman of the Columbus Day Celebration Committee. Sylvester Andriano arrived in San Francisco in 1901, a month before his 12th birthday, from his birthplace in Castelnuovo d'Asti, near Turin in the Piedmont region of Italy. He became a naturalized citizen while a student at Hastings College of the Law, graduating in 1915. Andriano's public career included both city politics and Catholic church activities. About 2,000 of the 60,000 Italian aliens in the United States were interned during the war. Several of these were important figures in North Beach, including Andriano. (SFHC.)

San Francisco mayor George Christopher (left) and artist Beniamino Bufano are pictured on June 16, 1958. News copy of the day read, "Sculptor Benny Bufano (center) and Mayor George Christopher, a surprise visitor, inspect some of the works of art at upper Grant Avenue Fair yesterday. The fair, which had to fight for its existence in the face of opposition from both police and fire departments, drew some 35,000 visitors. Works of some 70 artists were displayed." (SFHC.)

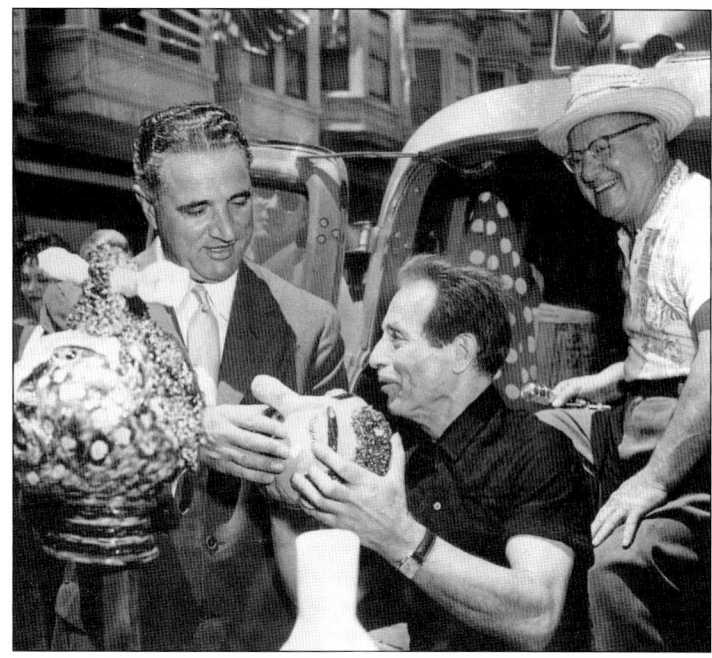

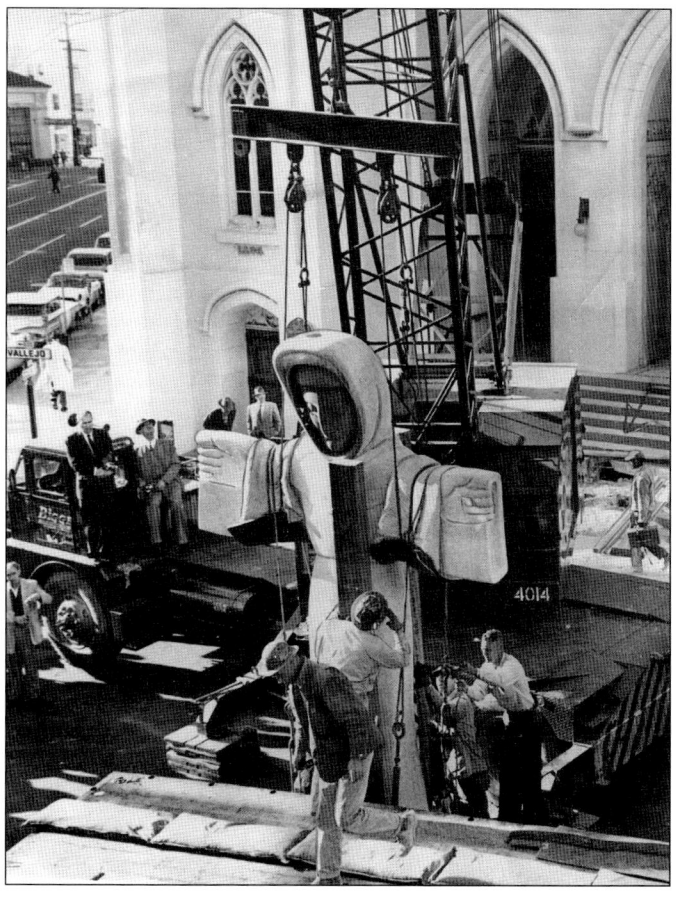

On March 16, 1961, workers remove the Bufano statue from the steps of St. Francis of Assisi Church on Vallejo Street. The statue was thought to be too big and heavy for the church steps and blocked wedding and funeral access to the church entrance. The statue was moved to Oakland for a time, and then Bufano had it moved back to San Francisco, to a spot at Fisherman's Wharf in front of the Longshoremen's Hall at Beach and Taylor Streets. (SFHC.)

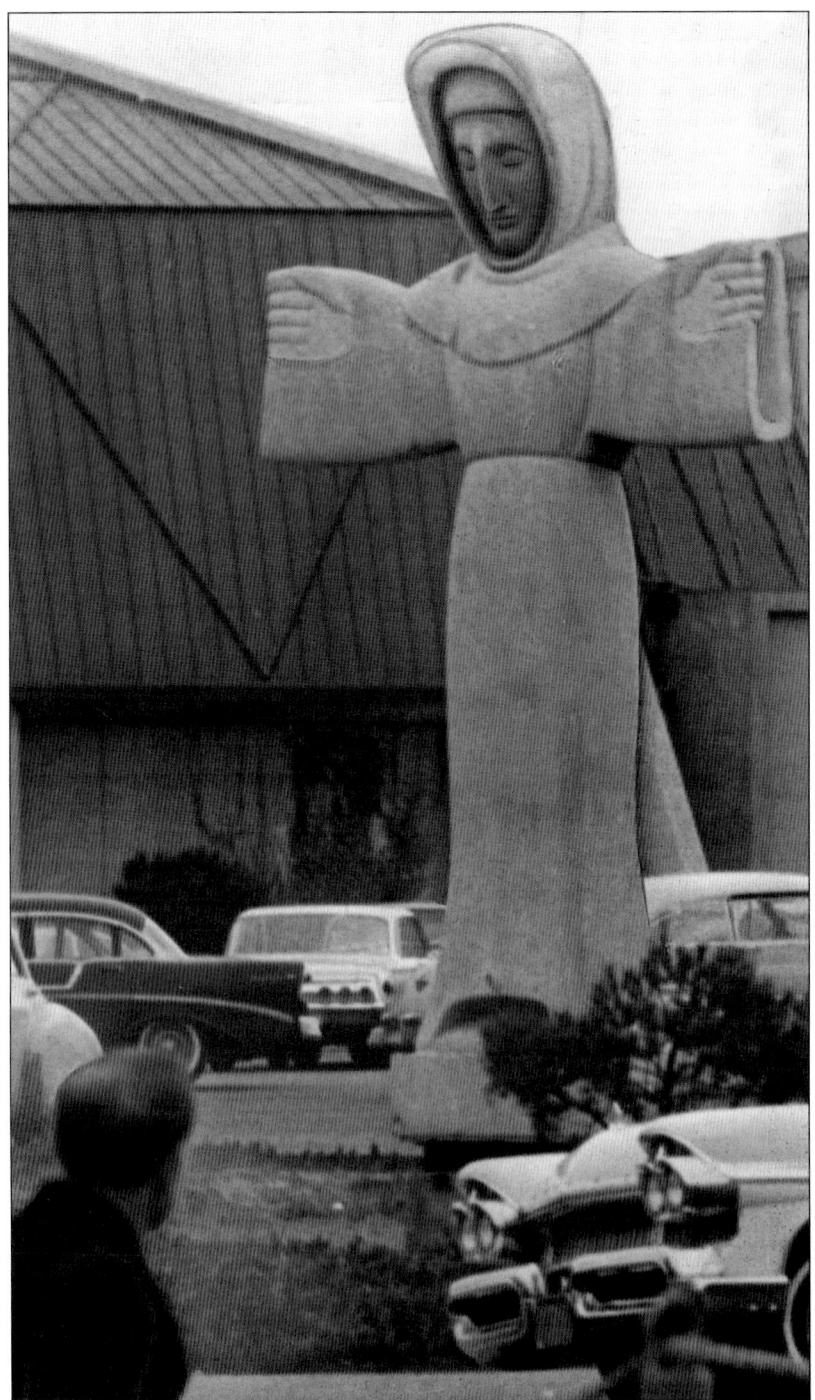

The Bufano statue of St. Francis of Assisi is pictured with the International Longshore and Warehouse Union Memorial Hall on Fisherman's Wharf behind it. Sculptor Beniamino Bufano sits gazing at his statue on December 31, 1962. He is quoted as saying, "No more to roam, I am glad it's the end of the divine comedy." The statue was in a Paris warehouse for 27 years before it was brought to San Francisco in 1956. (SFHC.)

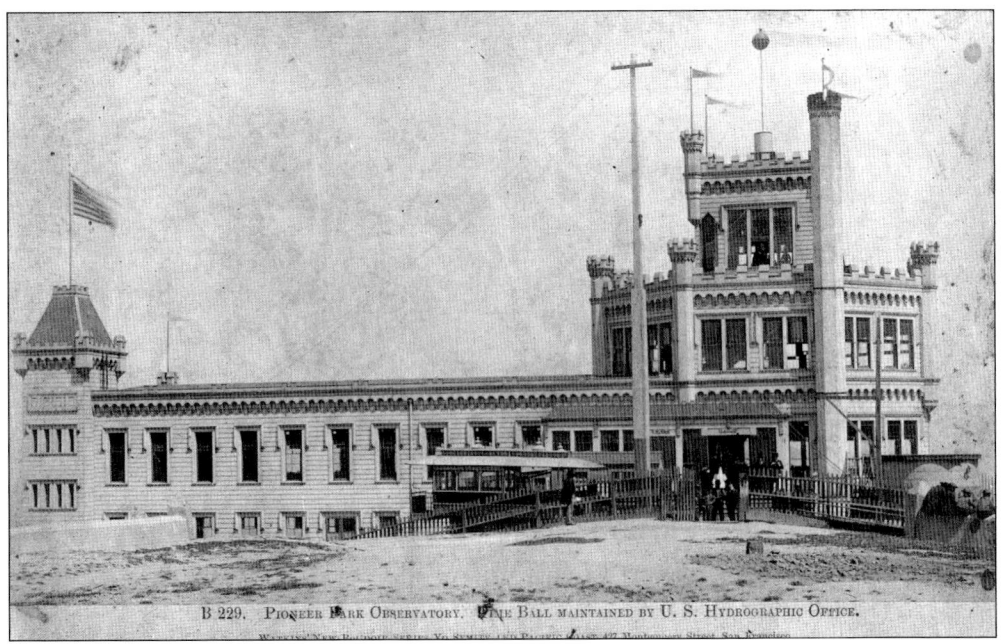

Here is what the top of Telegraph Hill looked like around 1884, before Coit Tower and the murals. This is the Pioneer Park observatory showing the time ball maintained by the U.S. Hydrographic Office. Frederick O. Layman built this observatory in a German baronial castle style of architecture. Opening in 1882, it had a restaurant, concert hall, and cable car service. After several years, interest in the whole enterprise appeared to wane and eventually failed, only to burn down in 1903. (SFHC.)

Before the castle on Telegraph Hill burned down in 1903, there were times that it drew very large crowds, such as pictured here on August 25, 1899. News copy of the day read: "That was a great day for San Francisco when the transport Sherman returned with California volunteers from the Philippines, August 25, 1899 . . . Some tens of thousands who witnessed the return are crowed around the Old Castle on Telegraph Hill." (SFHC.)

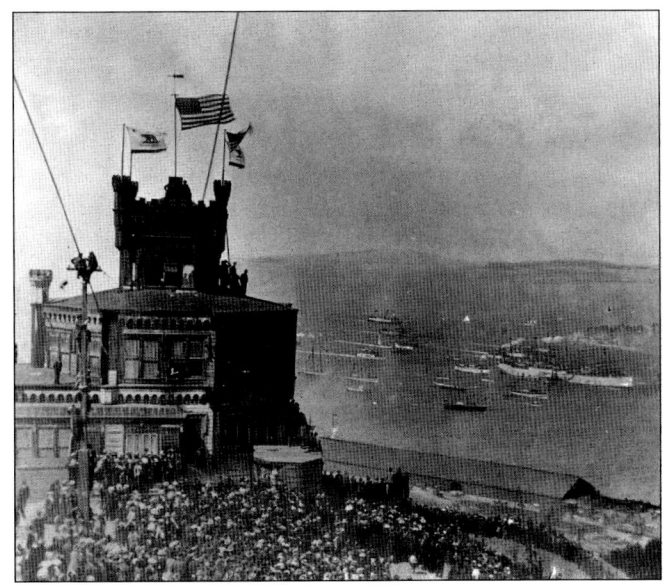

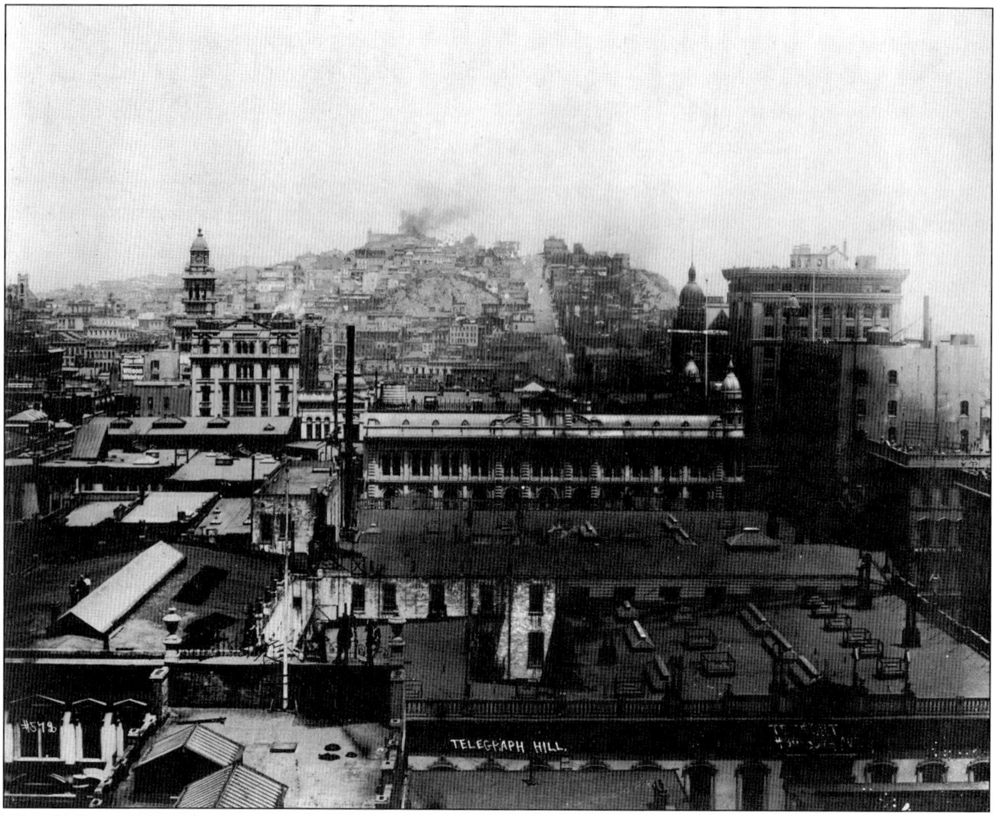

The Telegraph Hill observatory, also called the "Old German Castle," is on fire in the distance. The date was July 25, 1903, at 11:00 a.m. There are numerous people standing on rooftops in the foreground watching this scene. (SFHC.)

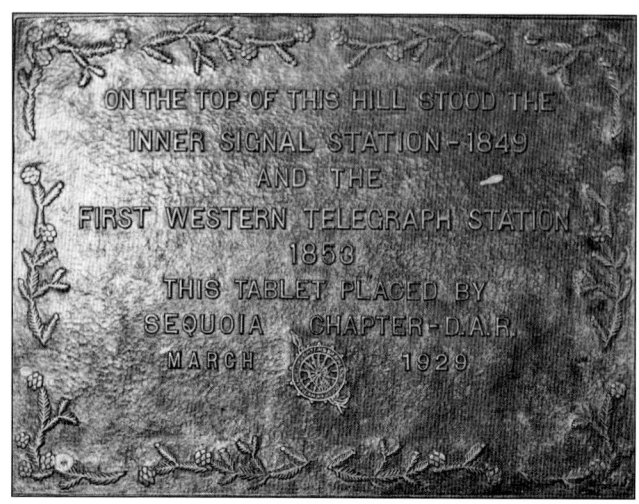

This plaque in Coit Tower reads, "On the top of the hill stood the inner signal station—1849, and the first western telegraph station—1853. This tablet placed by Sequoia Chapter-D.A.R. March 1929." The D.A.R. stands for Daughters of the American Revolution. This photograph of the plaque was taken on October 7, 1933. (SFHC.)

Here is the lobby of Coit Tower on August 8, 1934. One is greeted by these beautiful windows. They are surrounded by a fresco painted by Clifford Wight, controversial at the time because over the top of the window at the right is painted a Soviet hammer and sickle. (SFHC.)

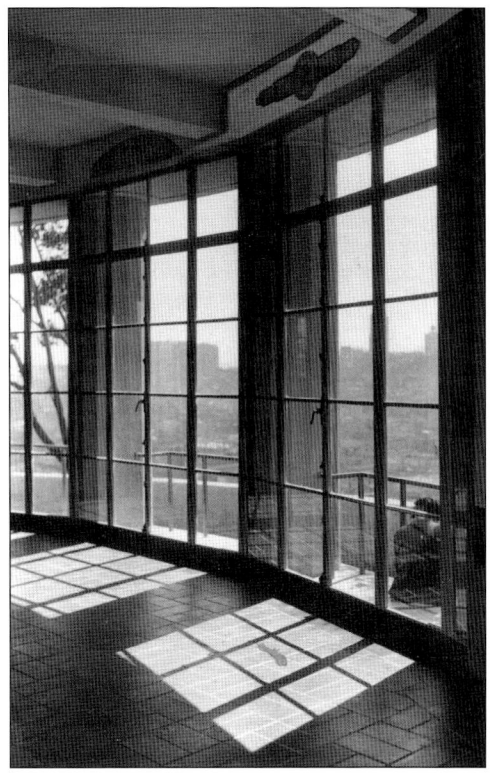

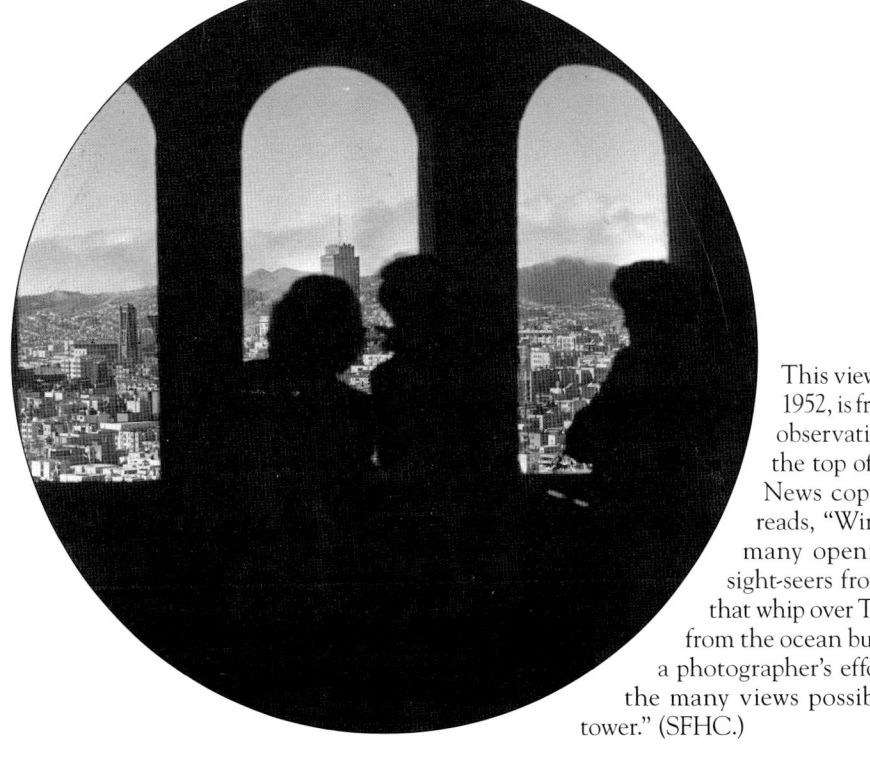

This view, on June 24, 1952, is from inside the observation gallery at the top of Coit Tower. News copy of the day reads, "Windows at the many openings protect sight-seers from the winds that whip over Telegraph Hill from the ocean but do not ruin a photographer's efforts to catch the many views possible from the tower." (SFHC.)

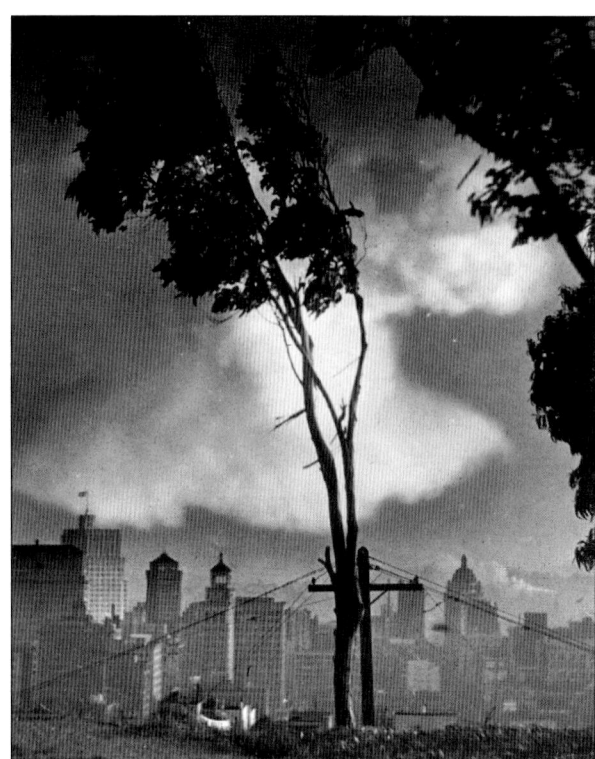

Here is the view outside the tower. Although this image was taken on November 13, 1930, vistas are just as spectacular now as they were then. Note the legendary San Francisco fog blowing in off the bay. (SFHC.)

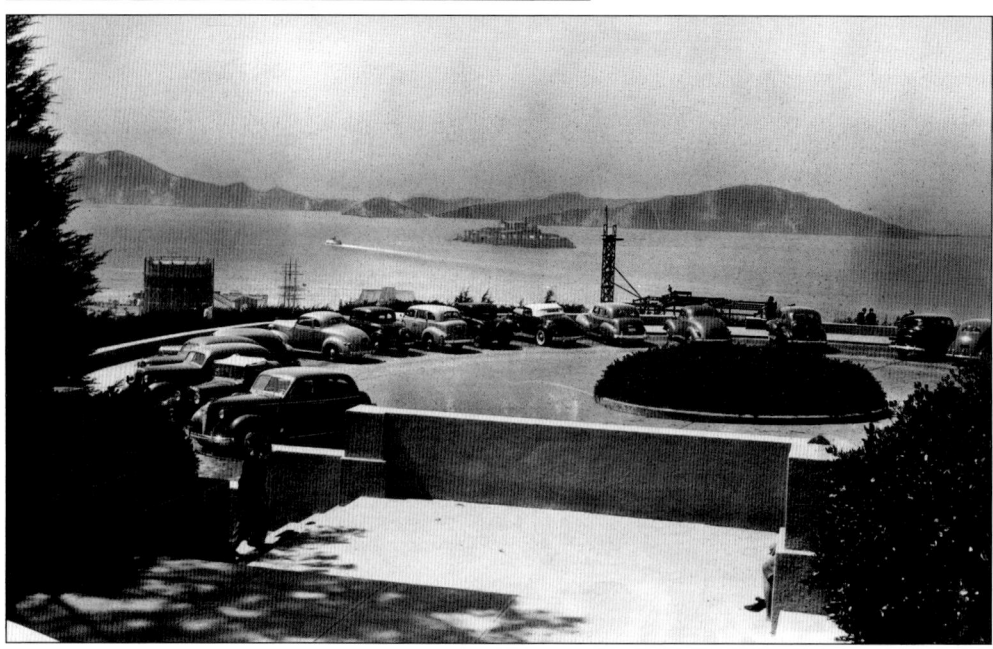

On July 3, 1940, ten years after the photograph above, the area looked like this. This view looks across the bay to the Marin hills, with Alcatraz Island at the center top of the image. News copy of the day reads, "People who come from all parts of the country are entranced by the scenic beauty here. The City's importance as a vacation spot grows each year, because of the many attractions it has." (SFHC.)

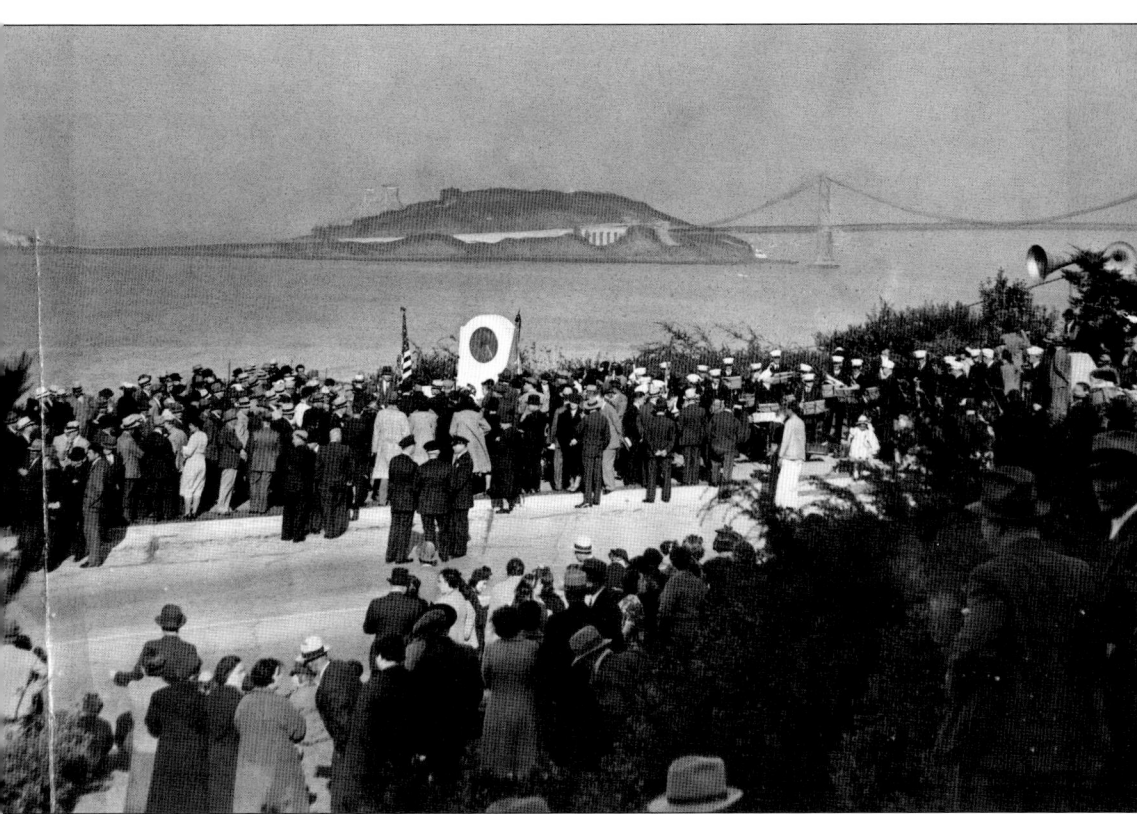

A crowd is assembled on Telegraph Hill for the unveiling of a bench dedicated to Guglielmo Marconi. The date is September 11, 1939. The stone bench pays tribute to the inventor of the wireless telegraph. An inscription in Latin on the monument reads, "Outstripping the lightning, the voice races through the empty sky." A group called the Marconi Memorial Foundation incorporated in the 1930s for the purpose of highlighting Marconi's achievements. The foundation collected public subscriptions from the supportive Italian–American community at the base of the hill, and on April 13, 1938, received permission from the U.S. Congress and Pres. Franklin Roosevelt to erect the memorial designed by sculptor Attilio Piccirilli. (SFHC.)

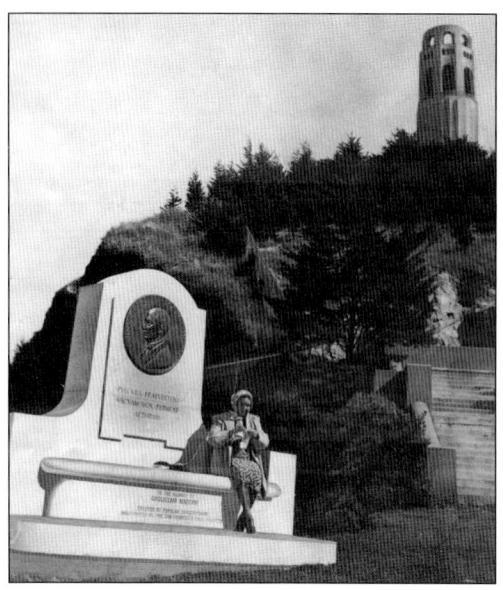

Here is a woman sitting on a bench with her knitting in hand. This is the monument dedicated to Guglielmo Marconi, who is credited with invention of the radio/telegraph system. The bench is located near 290 Lombard Street on Telegraph Hill. The bronze relief artwork was by artist Raimondo Puccinelli. News copy of the day reads, "A monument may be useful as well as ornate." (SFHC.)

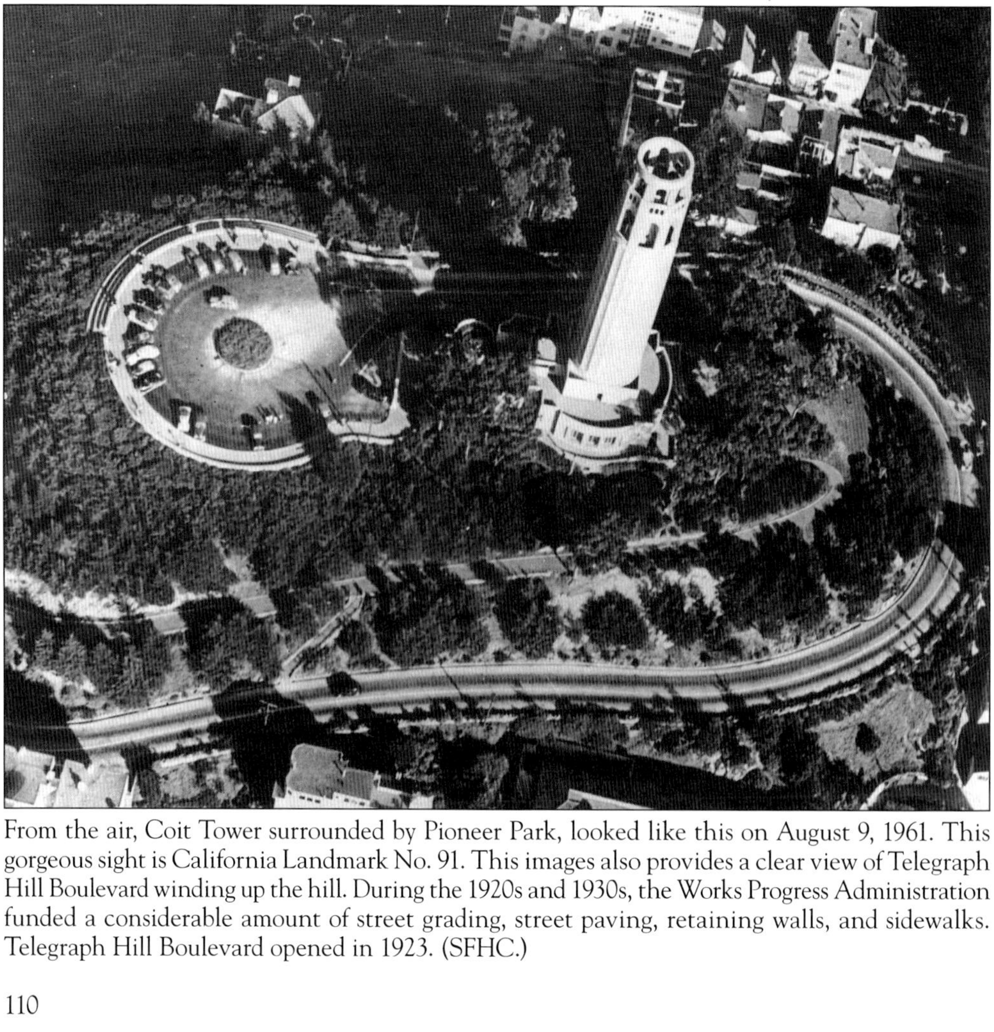

From the air, Coit Tower surrounded by Pioneer Park, looked like this on August 9, 1961. This gorgeous sight is California Landmark No. 91. This images also provides a clear view of Telegraph Hill Boulevard winding up the hill. During the 1920s and 1930s, the Works Progress Administration funded a considerable amount of street grading, street paving, retaining walls, and sidewalks. Telegraph Hill Boulevard opened in 1923. (SFHC.)

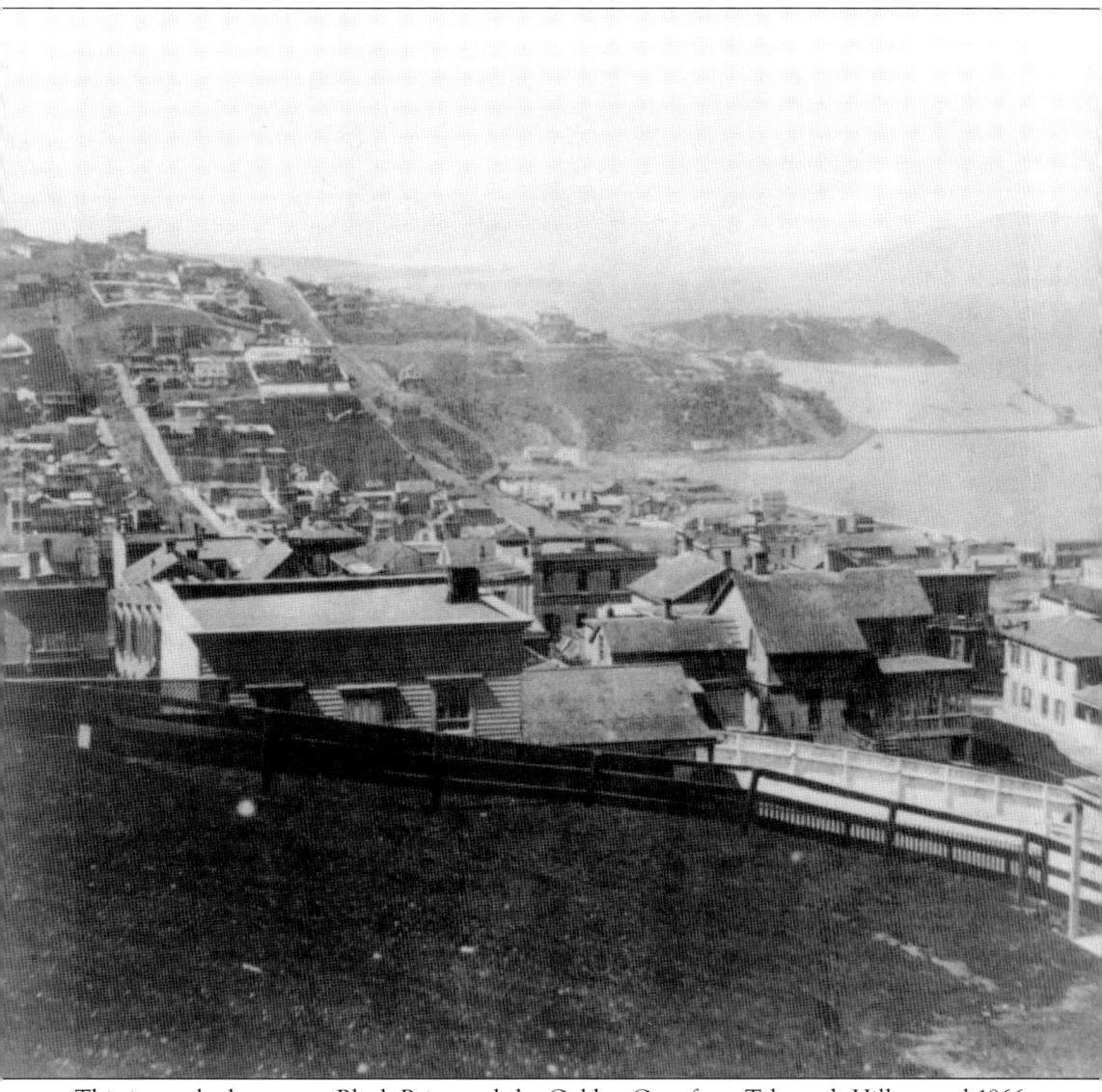

This image looks west at Black Point and the Golden Gate from Telegraph Hill around 1866. Black Point garnered the name due to the dark vegetation in the area. During the Civil War, Black Point was taken over by the military for defense purposes and renamed Fort Mason. Between the photographer and Black Point lies a working class neighborhood. Along the water line, area fishing shacks and a well-placed dock jutting out into the bay. Forty years after the 1906 earthquake, tents of earthquake refugees would be located where Fort Mason's Great Meadow is now. While the city collapsed and burned, thousands of hungry and homeless people received care at Fort Mason, which served as the headquarters for army relief field operations. (LOC)

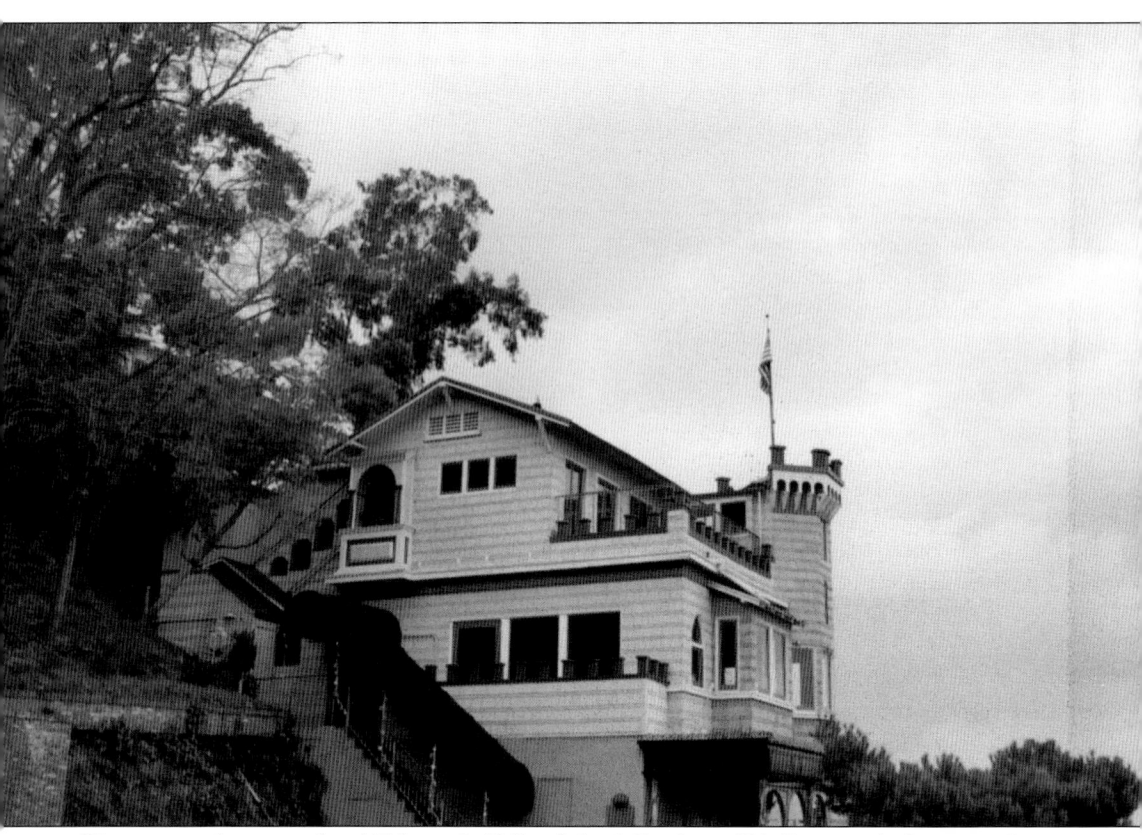

Clinging to the east side of Telegraph Hill is Julius' Castle at 302 Greenwich Street at Grant Avenue. The civil engineer and architect Louis Mastropasqua designed this amazing and unusual structure in 1923 for Julius Roz, a local restaurateur and fellow Italian who immigrated to San Francisco in 1902. When Roz died in 1943, the property passed through several owners, though it has always retained its name. One of the most quaint, picturesque spots in San Francisco, the restaurant rests at the edge of a precipice here on November 26, 1941. According to film archives, Twentieth Century Fox used the front of the castle in the film *House on Telegraph Hill.* Creative changes to the image of the structure were made so that it would look like the entrance to a stately home. Scenes were also shot in the driveway and at the base of Coit Tower's back garden area. (SFHC.)

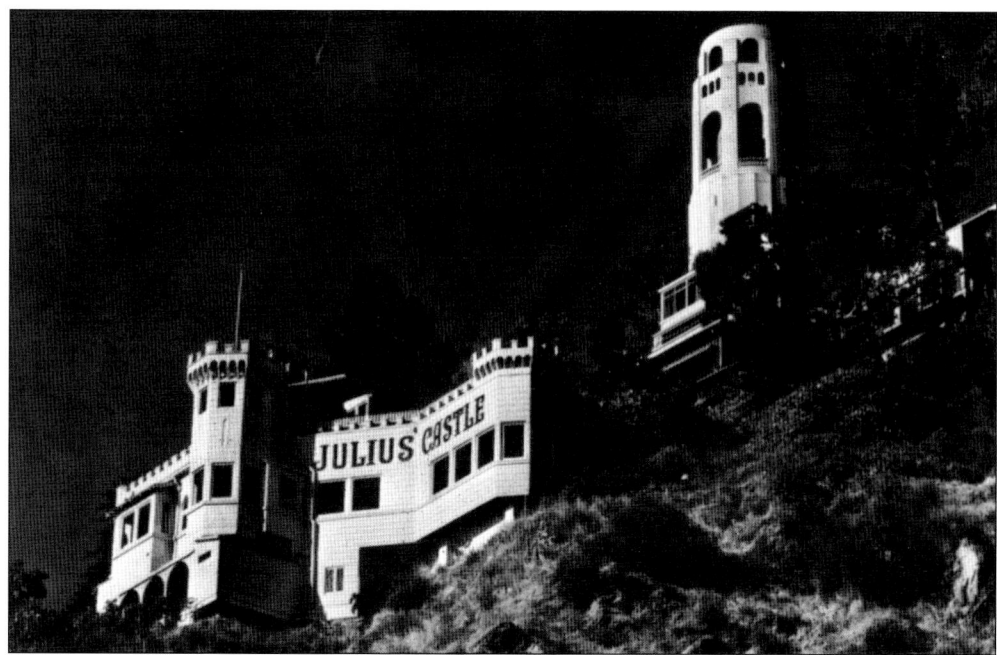

Julius' Castle is really not a castle. It has been a leading San Francisco restaurant for over 87 years. The castle is city landmark No. 121. It has been a popular celebrity hangout for politicians; musicians like Huey Lewis; Hollywood actors Robert Redford, Sean Connery, and Ginger Rogers; and even famed Mount Everest climber Sir Edmund Hillary. (SFHC.)

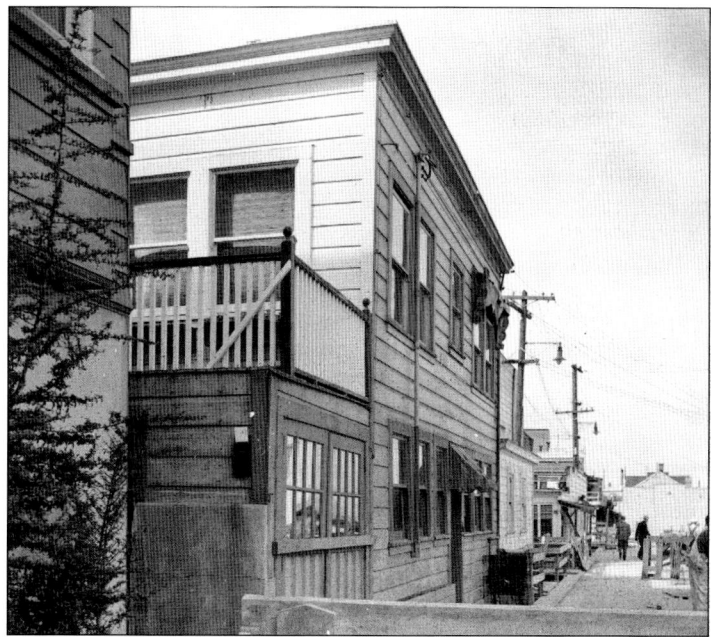

According to Library of Congress records, the building in the center is the Edwin Booth house at 35 Calhoun Street. Several Booth brothers lived here at one time or other. They were American actors in the mid-1800s. The brothers included Edwin, Junius, and John Wilkes Booth, the assassin of President Lincoln. Calhoun Street was sometimes called Calhoun Terrace because there is an upper and lower level. (LOC.)

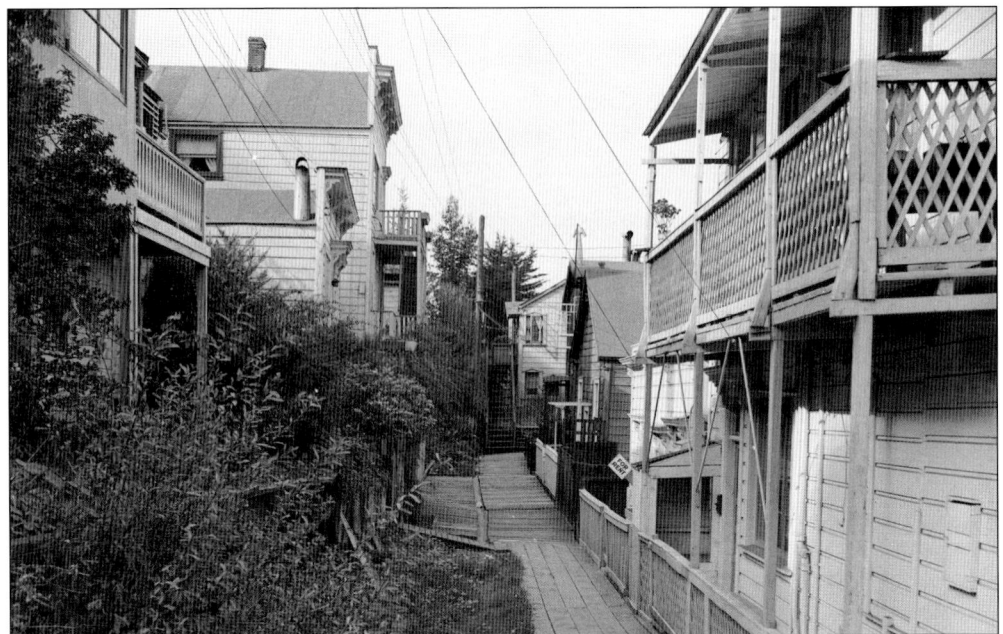

The bibliographic information on this image reads, "Built in the 1850s and 1860s, this enclave of wooden houses is a remnant of pre-1900 San Francisco, untouched by the Great Fire. Occupying a narrow lane on the steep eastern slope of Telegraph Hill, the row preserves a type of modest 1 and 2, and occasionally 3-story residences of frame and siding with few period details. Some modifications—including removal of verandas, etc." (LOC.)

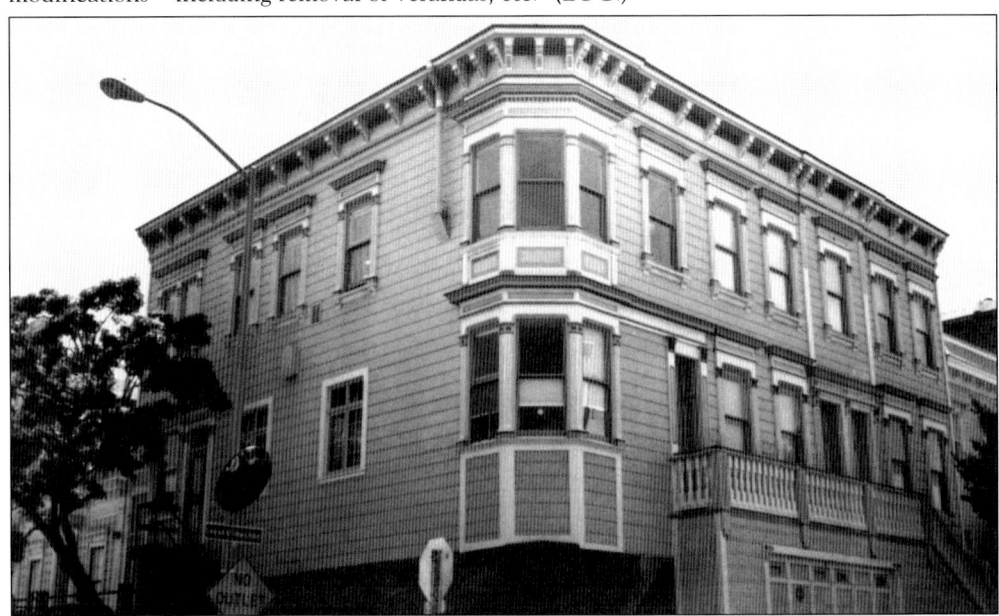

Located at 1254–1262 Montgomery Street, this building is a survivor of the 1906 fire and was placed on the National Register of Historic Places in 1979. A neighborhood fire brigade doused the fire's flames with burlap sacks soaked in wine from casks in the basement. From 1850 to 1861, the site was home to Hudson's Windmill. In 1865, a one-story building was constructed, a second story was added in the 1890s, and a staircase was added in 1939. (CAA.)

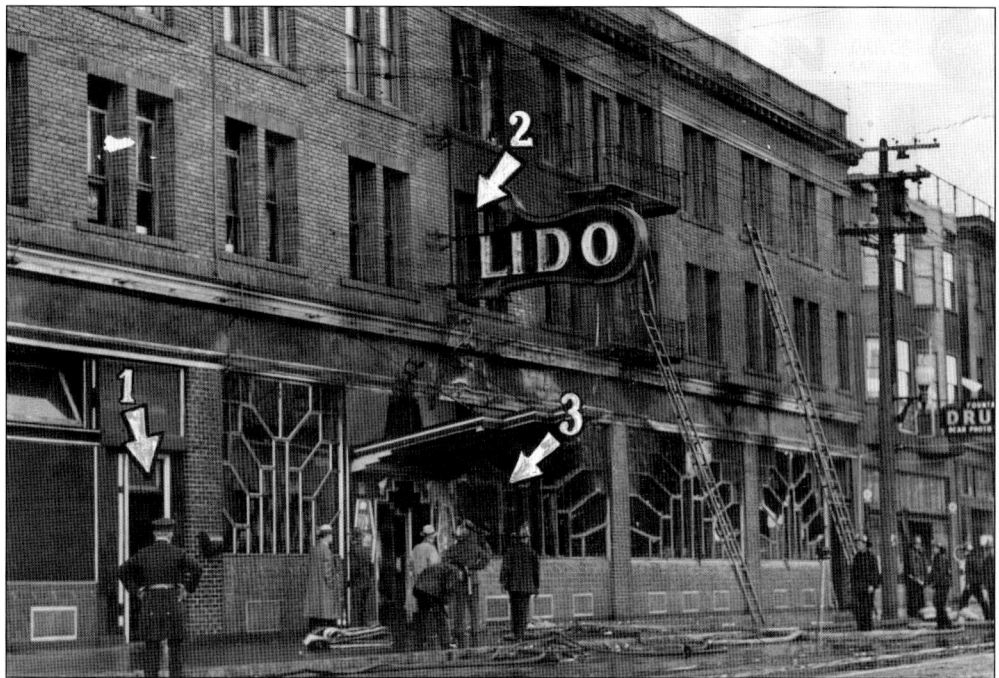

This edifice at 915 Columbus Avenue was built in 1923 as a nightclub and has remained so to this day. Here it is as the Lido Café and Lounge on February 10, 1933. It catered to San Francisco's politicos and society elite of the late 1920s and 1930s, and also housed several other nightclubs, including the Italian Village and Cobb's Comedy Club. (SFHC.)

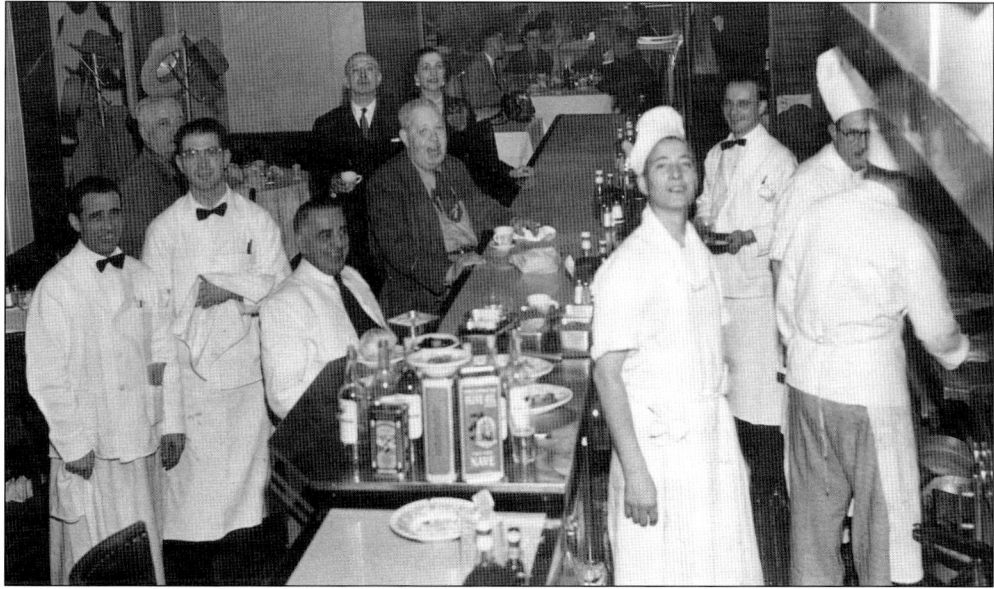

This is inside Vanessi's restaurant on December 26, 1952. Famous for its osso bucco and zabaglione, the restaurant was opened in 1936 by Joe Vanessi and Silvio Zorzi at 438 Broadway. One of the first exhibition kitchen eateries, customers could sit at the counter and watch chefs cook their favorite dishes, which included a number of Tuscan rabbit recipes. Vanessi's on Broadway closed its doors and relocated to Nob Hill in 1986. (SFHC.)

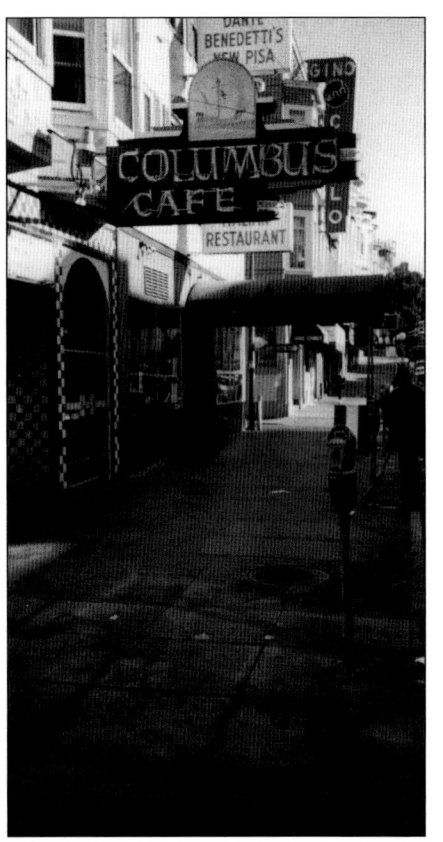

The original Columbus Café was at 562 Green Street, established in 1936 to serve the waterfront's longshoremen. Just down the street is the New Pisa. Dating back to 1927, it was one of the original Italian restaurants owned and operated by the Benedetti family. Benedetti the elder immigrated from northern Italy in 1911, worked hard, saving every penny, and eventually bought his own restaurant. His son, Dante, was born in Jasper Alley just behind the New Pisa. (CAA.)

The original U.S. Restaurant was located at the corner of Columbus Avenue and Stockton Street. Family-operated for over 50 years, the "U.S." stands for Unione Sportiva, a popular soccer team from Palermo, Sicily. After losing their original location, the Cipollina family moved to 515 Columbus Avenue. This postcard was sent to longtime customers to advertise the new location. (CAA.)

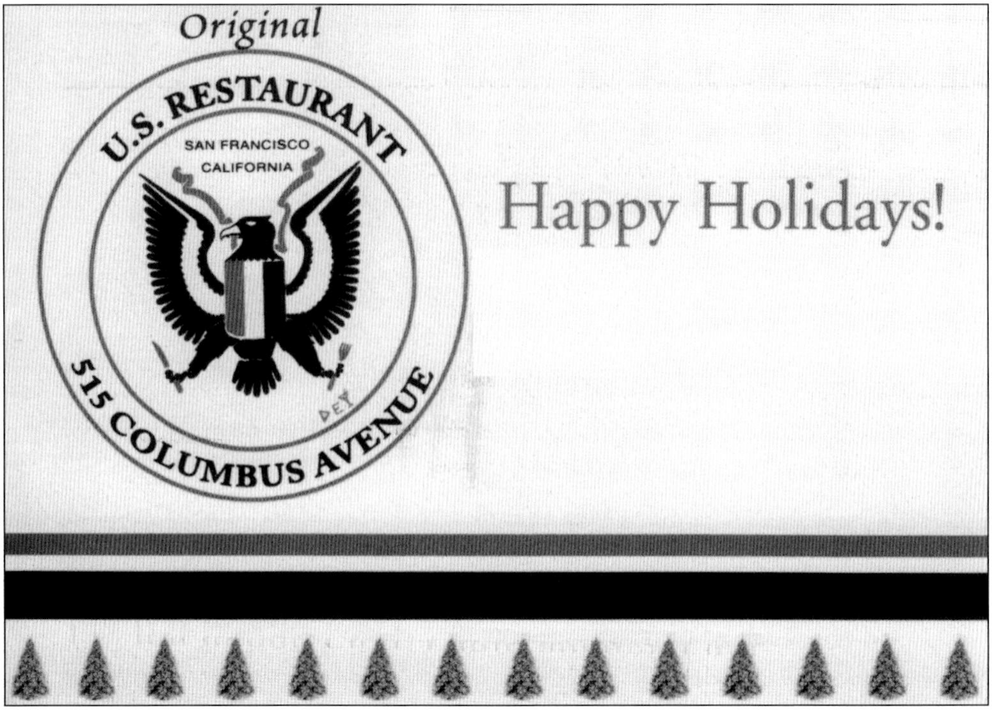

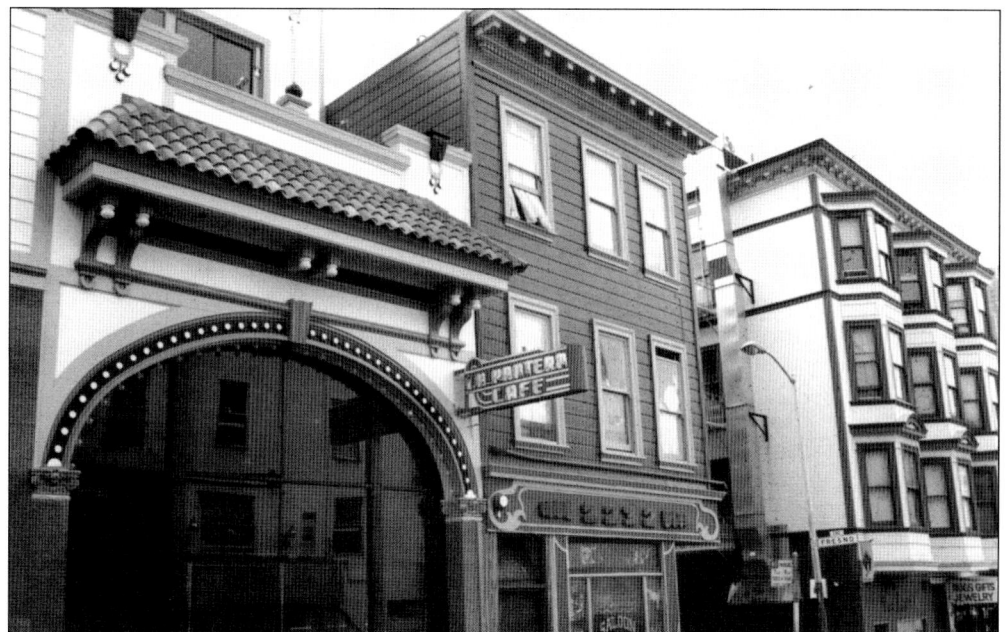

La Pantera, next door to The Saloon at Fresno Alley, was near enough to the infamous Barbary Coast to attract a salty crowd back in the day. The Saloon was originally Wagner's Beer Hall, opened by Mr. Wagner back in 1861, shortly after he emigrated from Alsace, making it the oldest existing bar in the city. Historical accounts imply that the reason it survived the 1906 fire was due to local firemen's fondness for the brothel upstairs. (CAA.)

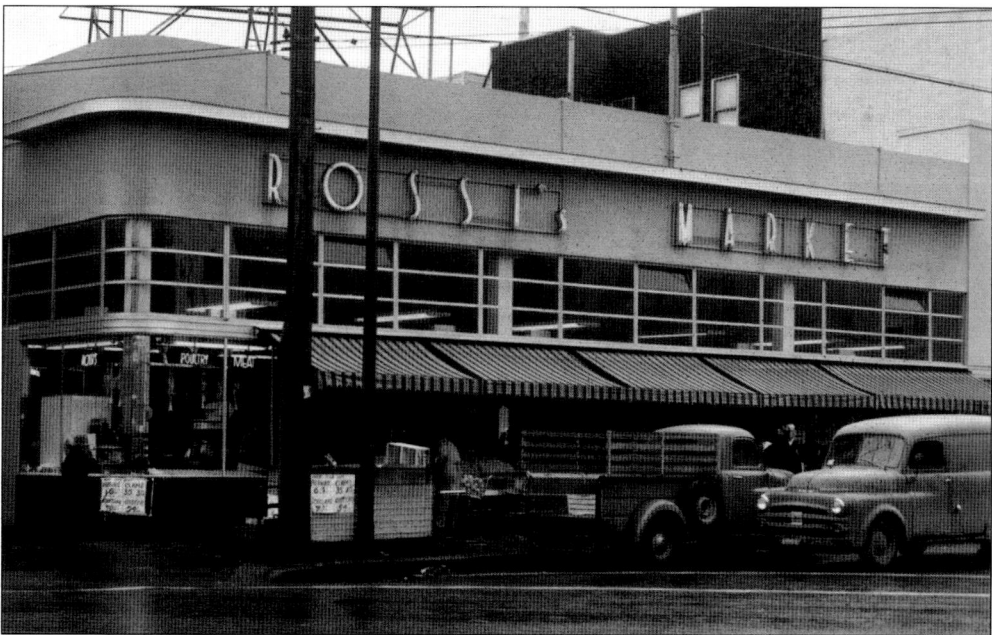

An Italian neighborhood be nothing without great grocery stores like Rossi's Market at 627 Vallejo Street on the corner of Columbus Avenue. Here is the market on January 18, 1955. This was a full-service market providing fresh fruit, vegetables, and a butcher. The signs in the windows offer prawns, scallops, oysters, and clams, all advertised by the pound. (SFHC.)

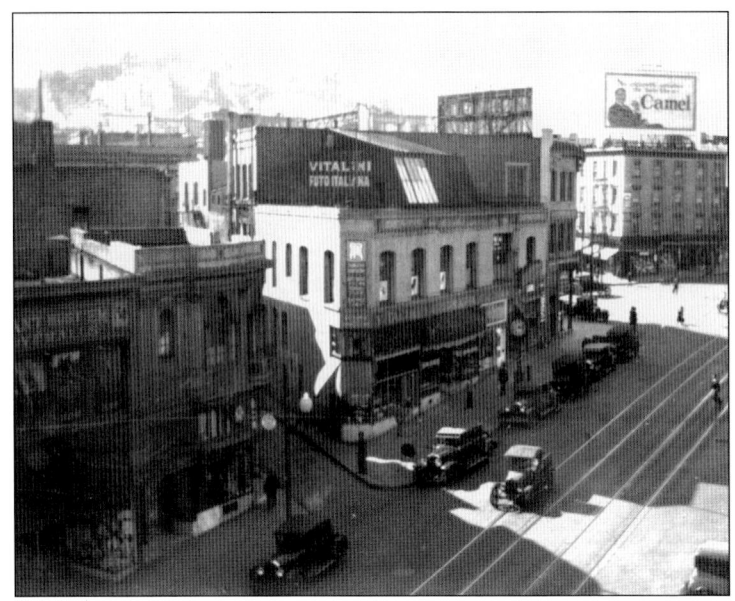

The Cavalli Bookstore became the location of the famous City Lights Bookstore. This image was taken in the mid-1920s. On the lower left, the 1913 Vesuvio building was designed by architect Italo Zanolini, who also built Club Fugazi, the North Beach home of the giddy, perennial "Beach Blanket Babylon" revue. (JBM.)

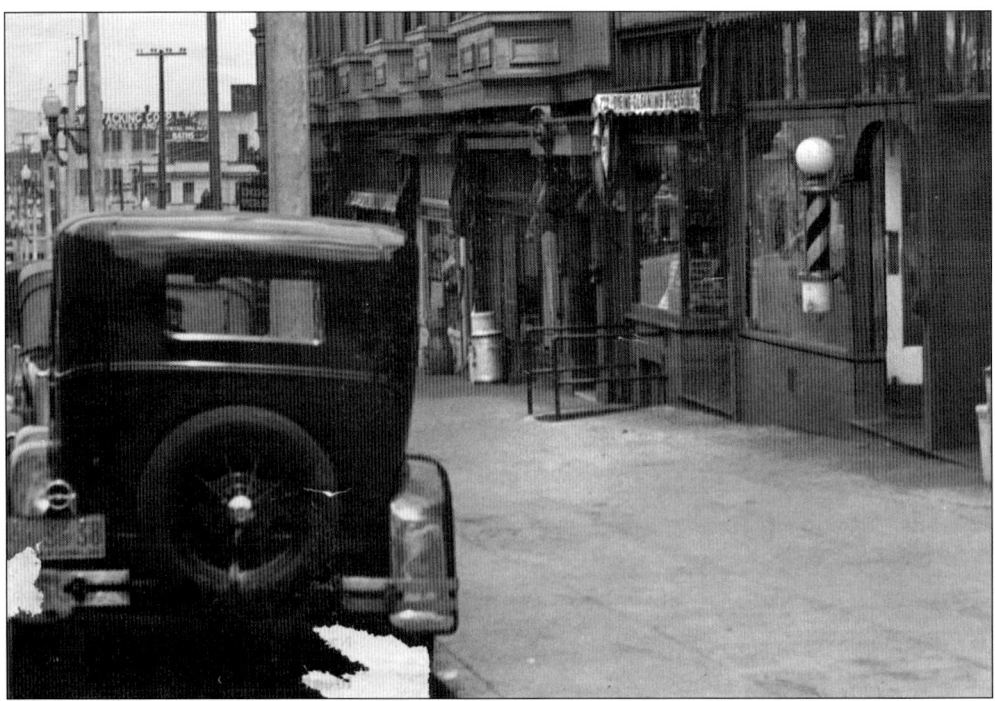

For the most part, North Beach was peaceable during Prohibition. However, as was the case in many U.S. cities, speakeasies could be found even in quaint North Beach. There were some unsavory characters, even into the 1930s. One unfortunate example was the slaying of Luigi Malvese on May 18, 1932, here in front of the Del Monte Barbershop at 720 Columbus Avenue. Malvese was reputed to have been a bootleg gangster. (SFHC.)

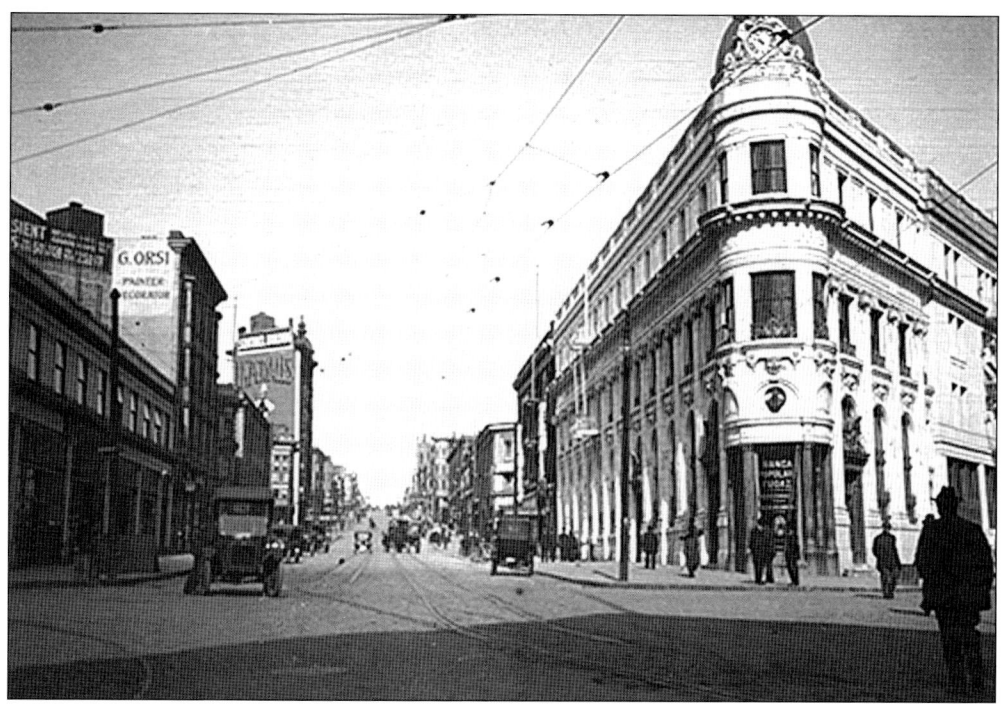

The majority of businesspersons were solid citizens. One fine example is A. P. Giannini, who was instrumental in providing North Beach residents loans in order to move on with their lives after the 1906 disaster. The structure is San Francisco Landmark No. 52, built in 1904 at 4 Columbus Avenue. A. P. Giannini was a member of the bank's board of directors before founding his Bank of Italy, eventually becoming his Transamerica Corporation headquarters. (SFHC.)

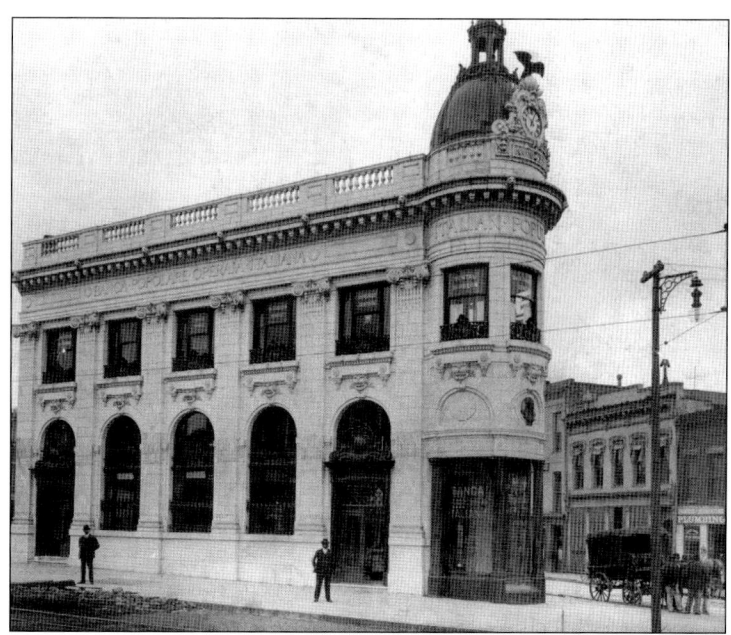

The original Transamerica building is a Beaux-Arts flatiron-shaped building covered in terra-cotta. Built for the Banco Populare Italiano Operaia Fugazi in 1909, it was originally a two-story building and gained a third floor in 1916. In 1928, Fugazi merged his bank with the Bank of America, which was founded by A. P. Giannini. (SFHC.)

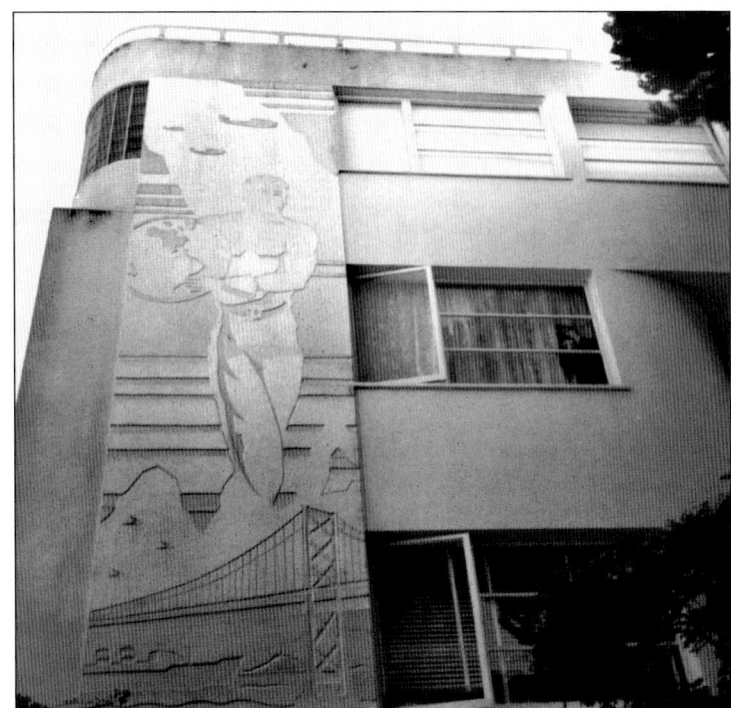

Several notable films were set on Telegraph Hill, including the film noir classic *Dark Passage* starring Humphrey Bogart and Lauren Bacall. This apartment building, at 1360 Montgomery Street, was designed in 1938 by architect Irvine Goldstine in streamline moderne style. It was here that Bacall's character, Irene Jansen, resided. Note the life-size image of Bogart in the second-floor window that was placed there by the current residents. (CAA.)

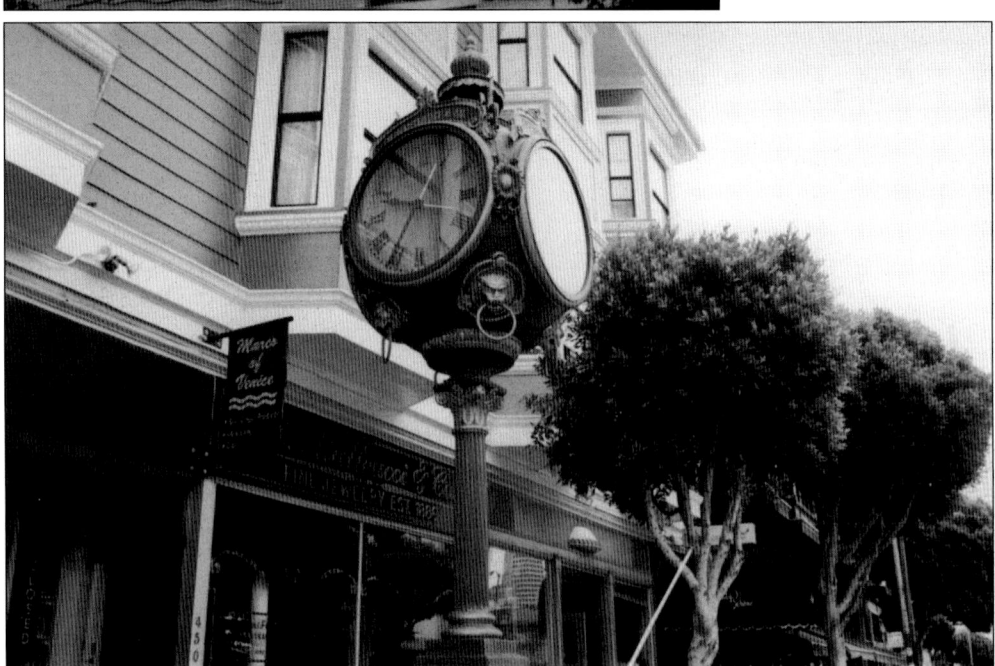

The R. Matteucci and Company jewelers date back to the start of the 20th century. They are well known for the beautiful clock the company placed in front of its shop. In 1999, a renegade truck struck this beloved symbol of North Beach, resulting in the following news copy: "A truck making deliveries was backing into a rare North Beach parking place at 8:30 or so, when the top of the truck hit the 93-year-old clock, knocking it from its perch in front of the R. Matteucci & Co. jewelry store on Columbus Avenue. It swayed for a moment, then crashed to the ground." (CAA.)

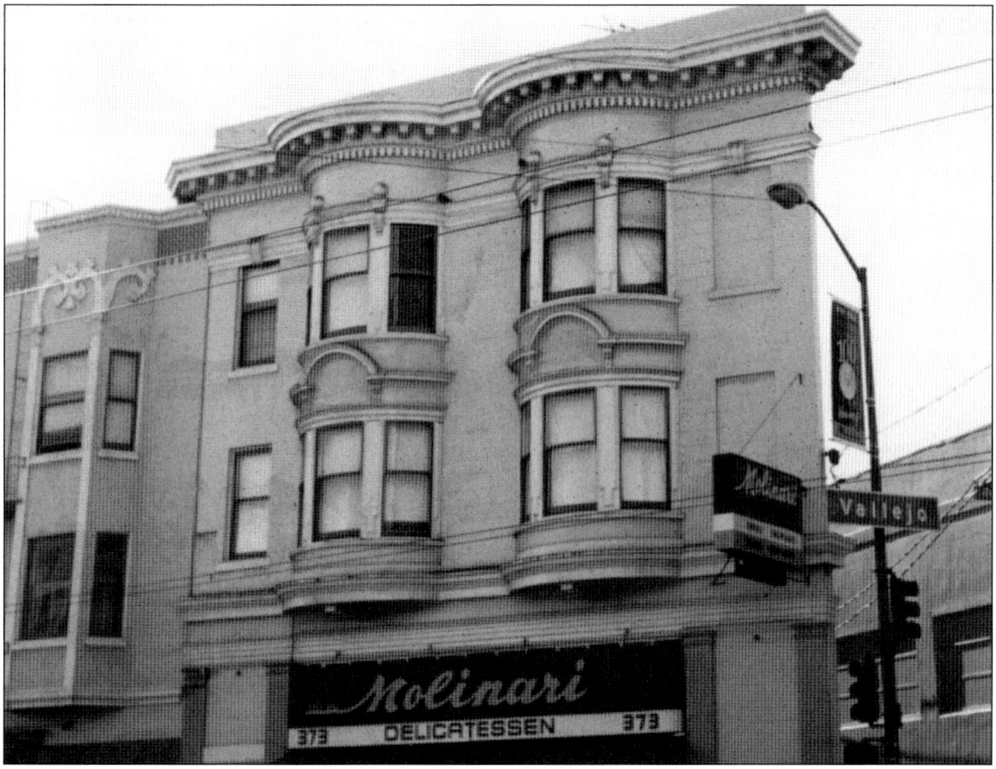

Molinari Delicatessen has been in San Francisco since 1896, when P. G. Molinari founded a salami factory at 433 Broadway. In 1912, he moved the business to 373 Columbus Avenue. Renowned for their salami, imported groceries, and lots of charm, their location on Columbus Avenue and Vallejo Street has drawn in loyal customers for well over 100 years. (CAA.)

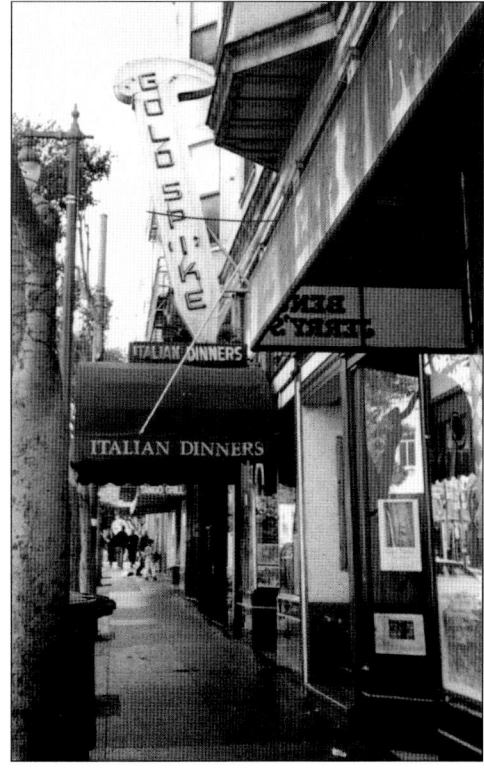

The Gold Spike was a longtime North Beach landmark restaurant. It boasts 86 years at the same location on Columbus Avenue. The Mechetti family immigrated from Italy's Tuscany region, opening their establishment in 1920 as the Columbus Candy Store and Soda Fountain. Years later, they turned it into a saloon and restaurant, serving five-course family-style meals. (CAA.)

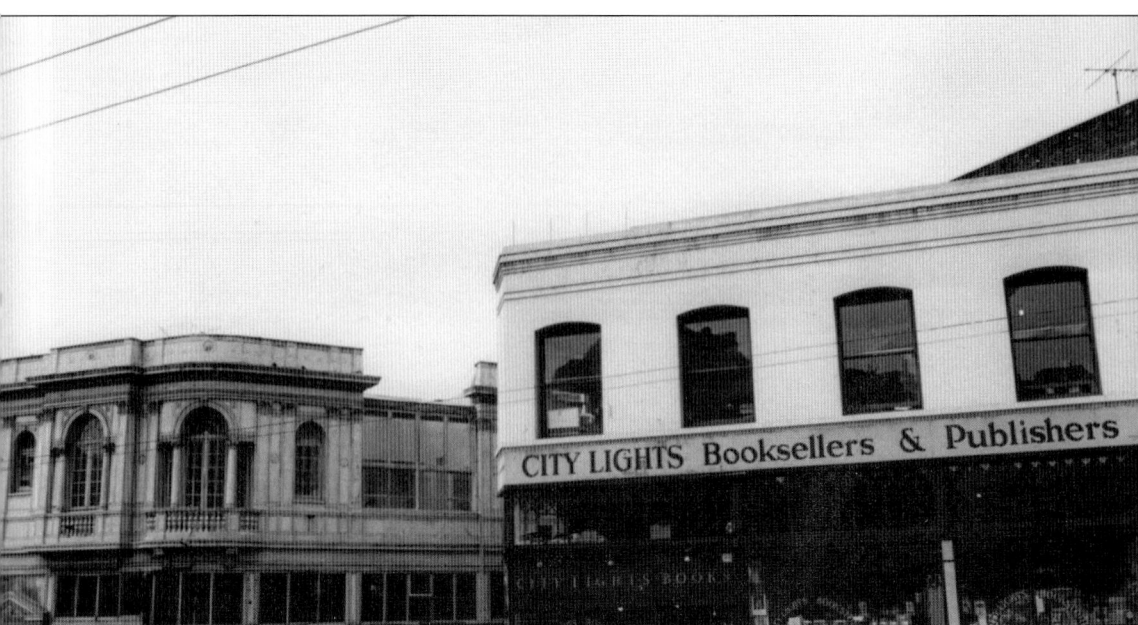

There are so many landmark establishments in North Beach, and here are two of the best, standing side by side: Vesuvio Café and City Lights Bookstore, separated only by Jack Kerouac Alley (formerly Adler Place). A historical account reads, "The site was a tiny storefront in the triangular Artigues Building located at 261 Columbus Avenue, near the intersection of Broadway in North Beach. Built on the ruins of a previous building destroyed in the fire following the 1906 earthquake, the building was designed by Oliver Everett in 1907." Next door, Vesuvio Café is a world-renowned San Francisco saloon that was established in 1948. Originally it attracted bay area bohemians but soon intrigued bon vivants from all walks of life. Jack Kerouac and other famous beat poets would hang out at the bar to discuss their next literary endeavors. (CAA.)

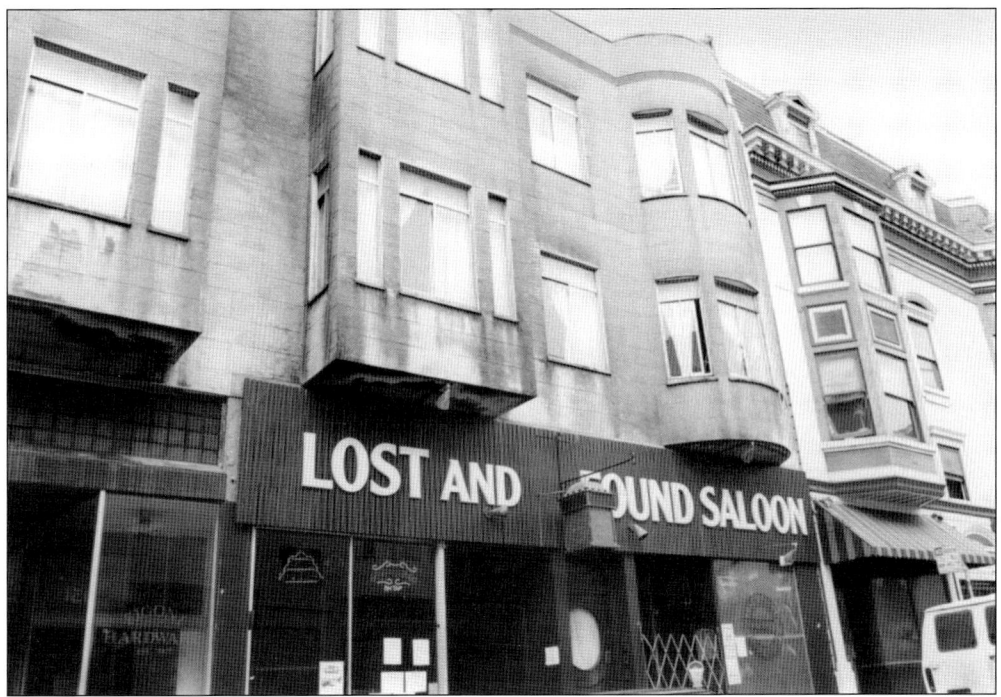

The Lost and Found Saloon was originally called the Coffee Gallery. In the 1960s, it hosted Blabbermouth Night. During the hippie days, the likes of Janis Joplin and Grace Slick with The Great Society rock band (and later with Jefferson Airplane) would rock the house. When the name changed to the Lost and Found Saloon, Robert Plant (of Led Zeppelin fame) surprised customers with a rocking blues jam. (CAA.)

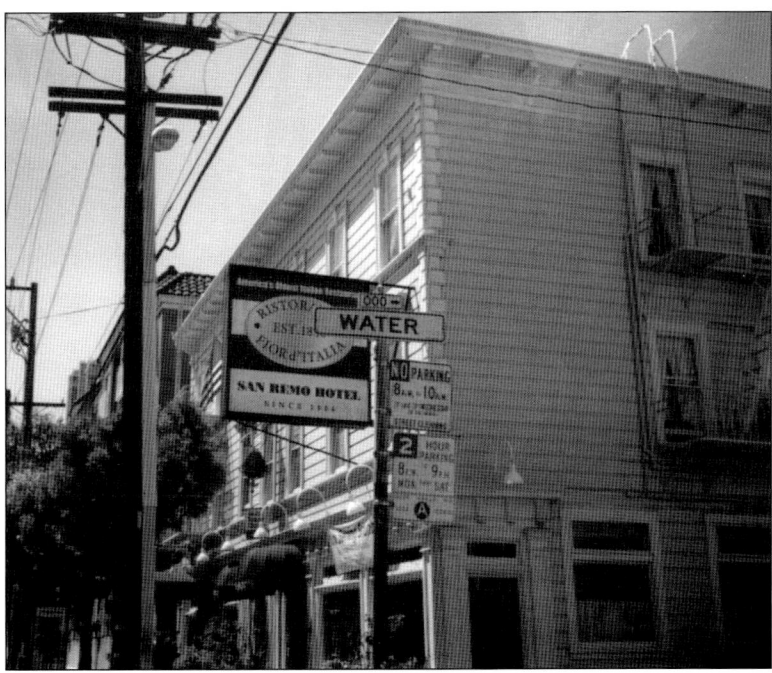

Water Street is a block-long piece of San Francisco history. The water's edge was here in the beginning. The street has a stable dating from 1907 and warehouses dating from 1929, where A. Friscia Seafoods did business from the 1940s to 2004. (CAA.)

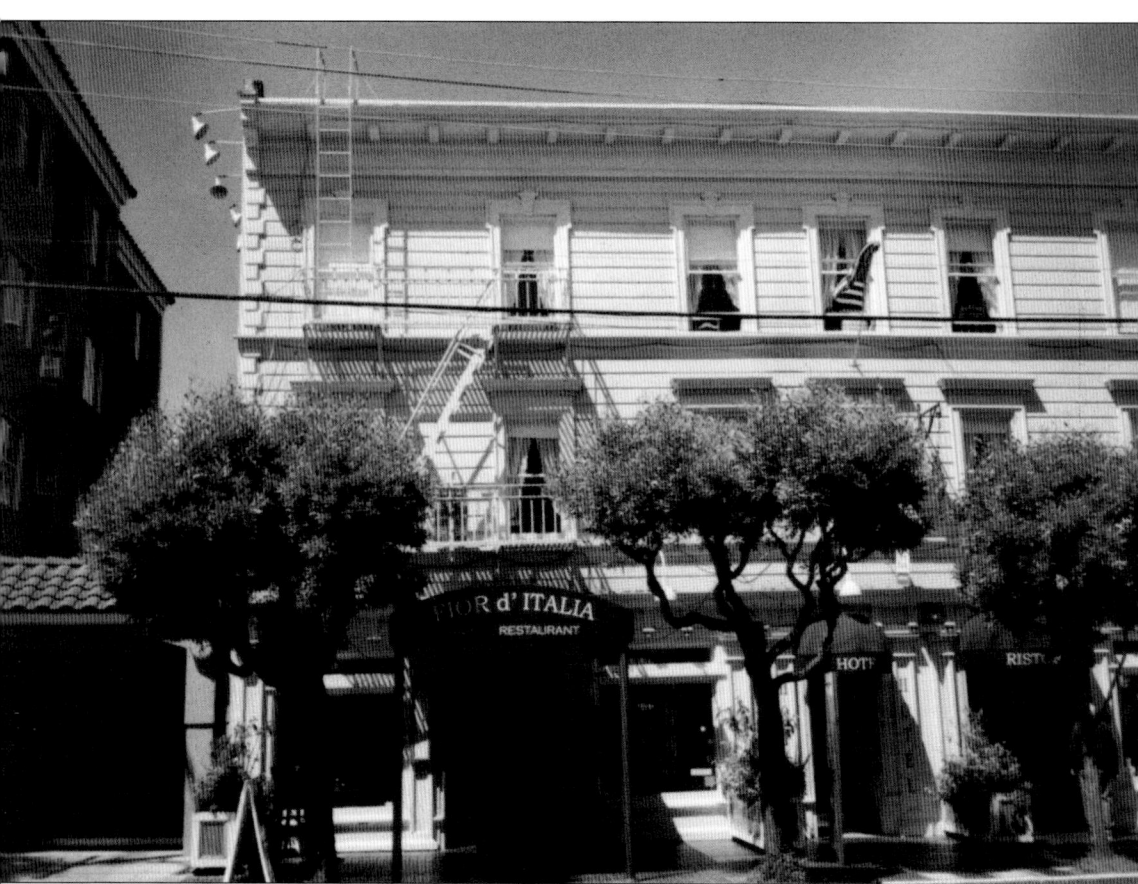

This image is of the Fior d' Italia restaurant in its new location on Mason Street near Bay Street. This famous Italian restaurant was originally located at the corner of Columbus Avenue and Kearny Street. Later it was relocated to the corner of Union and Stockton Streets and is now at Mason Street. Fior d' Italia, "America's Oldest Italian Restaurant," has served San Francisco's citizens and visitors since 1886. It has been said, "If you haven't dined at 'The Fior, you haven't been to San Francisco." In its early days, free meals and rooms were given to many workers who assisted the city's recovery after the 1906 disaster. Other guests were merchant seamen, waterfront workers, poets, journalists, and pensioners. Penniless artists paid with their paintings. In 1922, the hotel was renamed the San Remo, after an Italian town. Full-course dinners were offered for 50¢ during the Depression. (CAA.)

In 1961, Howard Pease wrote the book *Mystery on Telegraph Hill*. The book opens, "You want to know how the while thing began? Very well. Blame it on the fog." These words were uttered by the main character, Tod Moran, in a house on Castle Street. Castle is one several alleyways on Telegraph Hill, and it links Green and Union Streets. Historical accounts indicate Castle Street had at least three other names in the past, including Garibaldi, Vincent, and St. Vincent. These streets of San Francisco take one off the beaten track into the mysterious past of North Beach. (Both, CAA.)

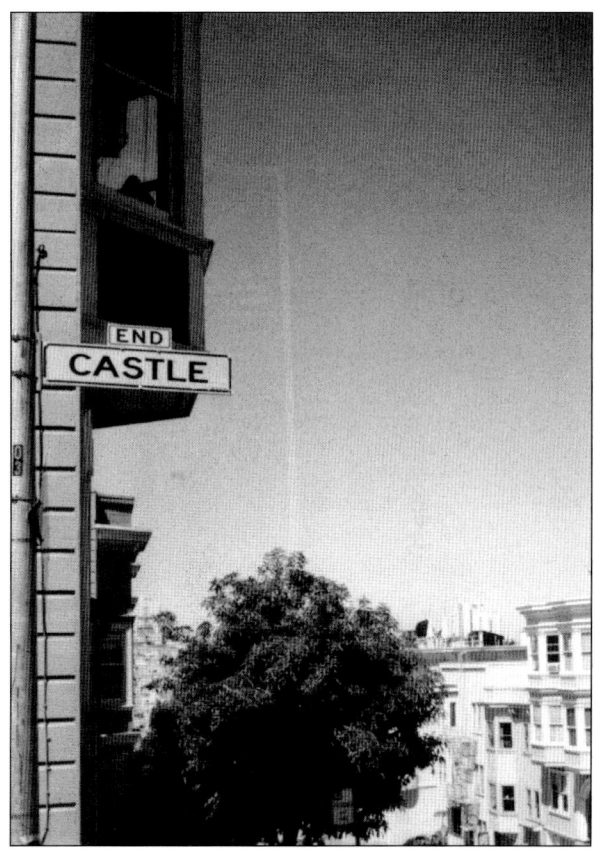

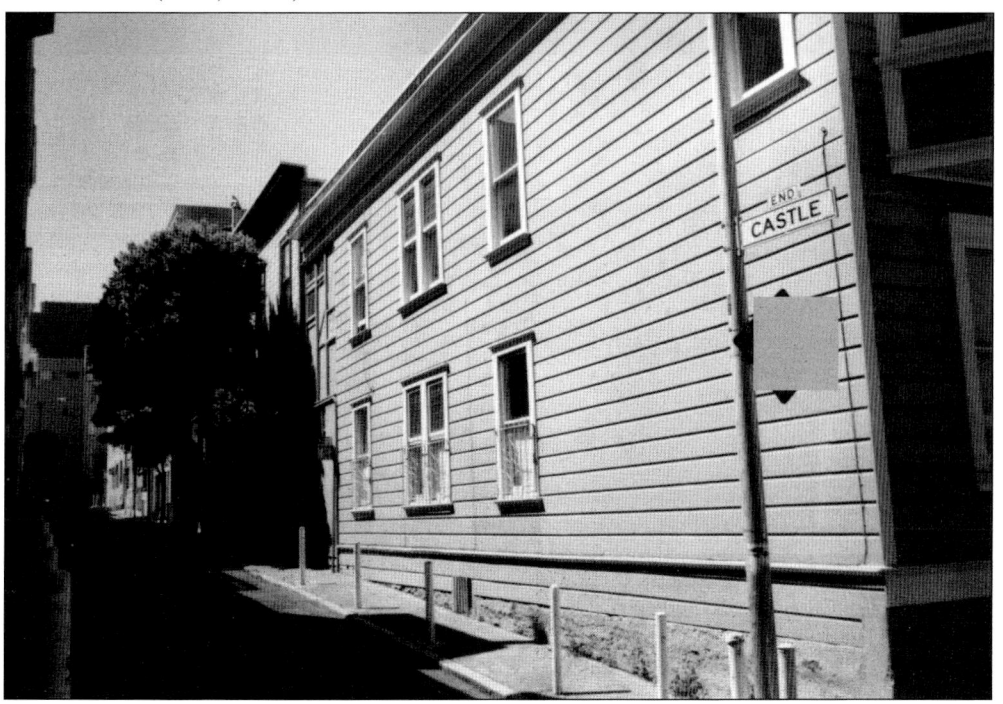

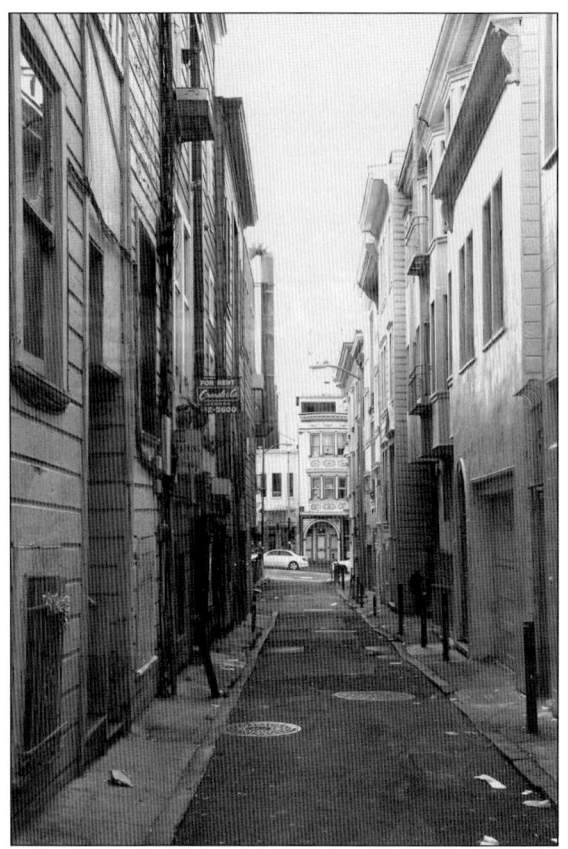

Here is Bannam Place, one of the alleys of North Beach. Writers, poets, and filmmakers are inspired by locations like this. In fact, quite a number of books were set in locations just like this. These books include *Mystery on Telegraph Hill* by Howard Pease (1961), *North Beach Girl* by John Trinian (1960), and *Bohemian Heart* by James Dalessandro (1993). (CAA.)

This aerial view of North Beach was taken on September 6, 1927. Washington Square is clearly visible in the center left. Across the street is SS. Peter and Paul Church, and diagonally across the center is Columbus Avenue. At the center top is Telegraph Hill, just six years before the construction of Coit Tower in 1933. (SFHC.)

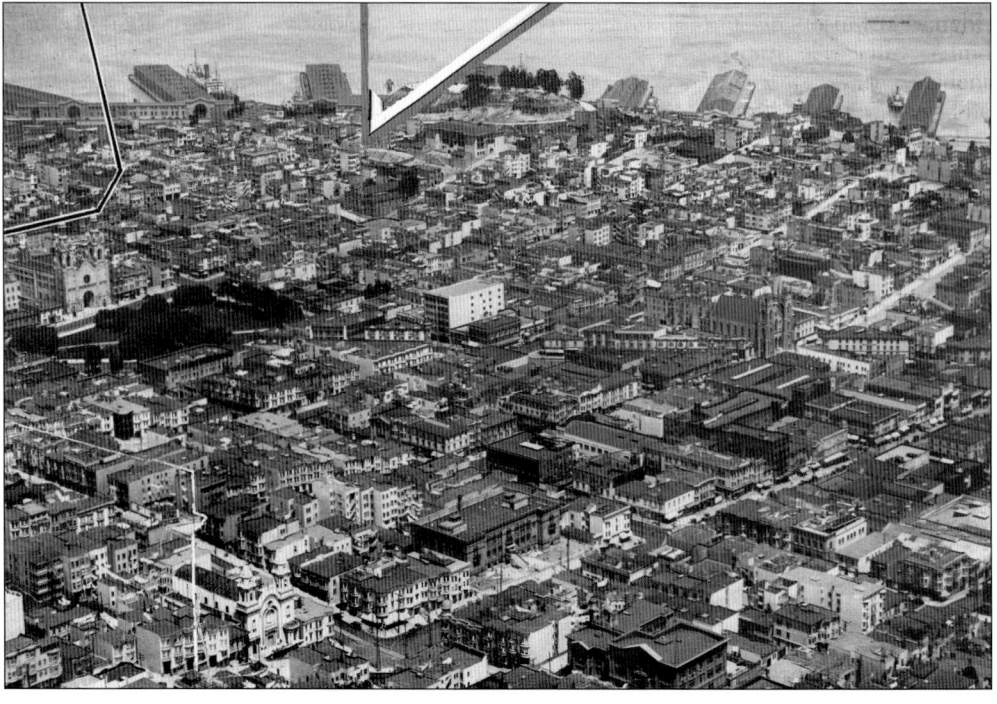

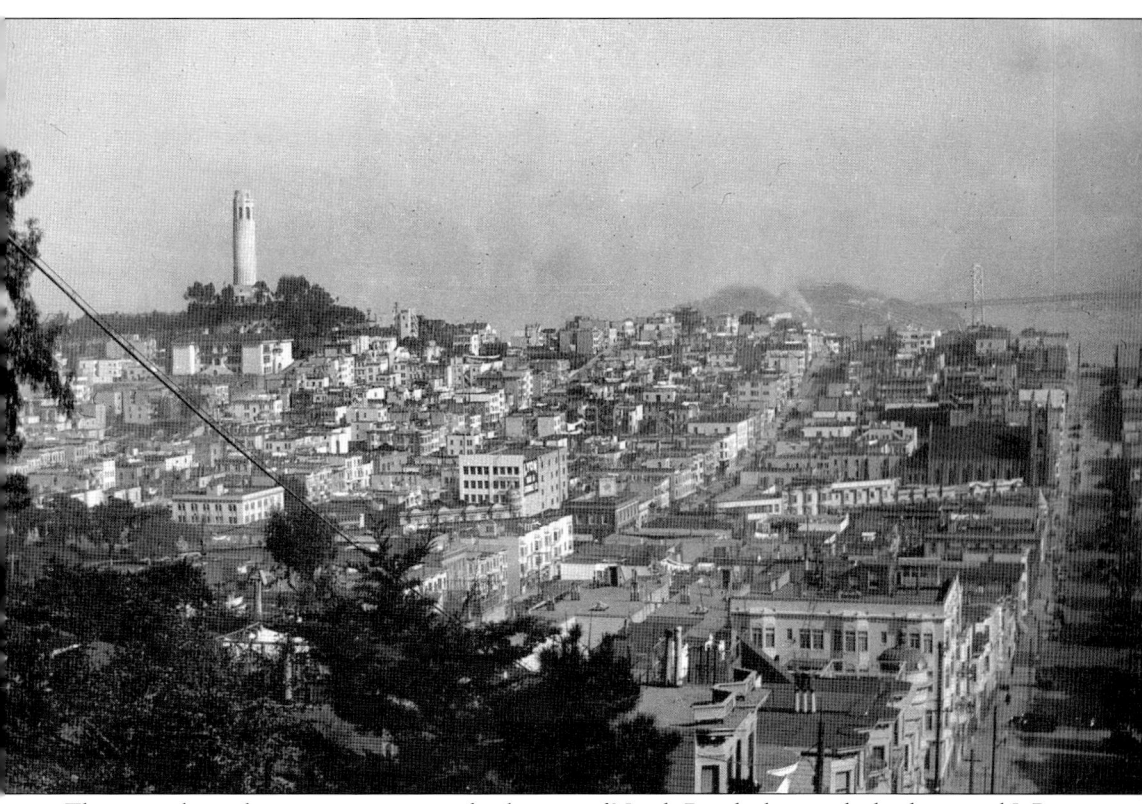

There may be no better way to enjoy a final image of North Beach than with this historical J. B. Monaco photograph taken in 1938. Seventy-two years later, all the wonderment and charm is still there, delighting both resident and visitor. On June 19–20, 2010, the 56th annual North Beach Festival took place in the heart of North Beach. It featured over 125 arts and crafts booths, 20 gourmet food booths, 3 stages of live entertainment, Italian street painting, beverage gardens, a large children's activity area, and the blessing of the animals. In 2007, the American Planning Association announced the North Beach neighborhood as one of the "10 Great Neighborhoods" in their Great Places in America program. (JBM.)

www.arcadiapublishing.com

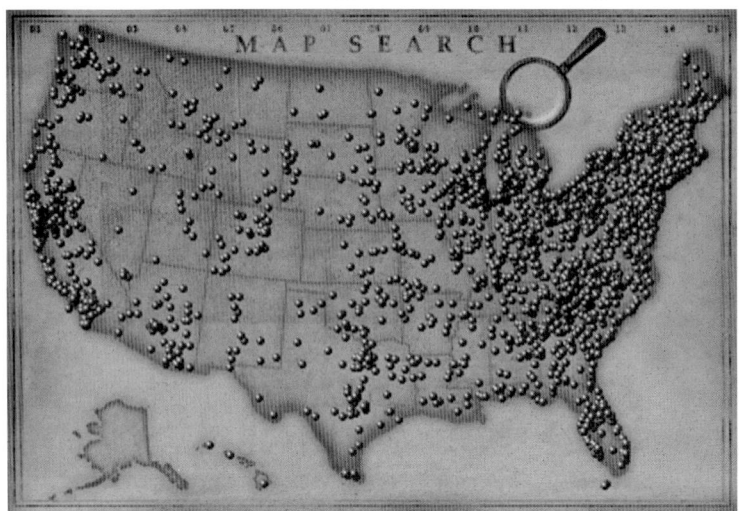

Discover books about the town where you grew up, the cities where your friends and families live, the town where your parents met, or even that retirement spot you've been dreaming about. Our Web site provides history lovers with exclusive deals, advanced notification about new titles, e-mail alerts of author events, and much more.

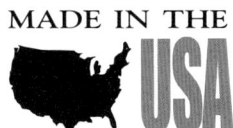

MADE IN THE USA

Arcadia Publishing, the leading local history publisher in the United States, is committed to making history accessible and meaningful through publishing books that celebrate and preserve the heritage of America's people and places. Consistent with our mission to preserve history on a local level, this book was printed in South Carolina on American-made paper and manufactured entirely in the United States.

This book carries the accredited Forest Stewardship Council (FSC) label and is printed on 100 percent FSC-certified paper. Products carrying the FSC label are independently certified to assure consumers that they come from forests that are managed to meet the social, economic, and ecological needs of present and future generations.

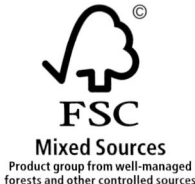

FSC
Mixed Sources
Product group from well-managed forests and other controlled sources
Cert no. SW-COC-001530
www.fsc.org
© 1996 Forest Stewardship Council

Find Your Place in History.